영어 회화 패턴 훈련

1차 임계점

신원섭 · Diana Salazar

국제 부부인 두 사람은 영어 전문 채널 '잉글리시 몬스터'를 함께 운영하며,
10년 넘게 영어 교육 현장과 소셜 미디어를 오가며 활발히 활동하고 있다.
영어를 배우는 한국 학습자의 어려움을 누구보다 잘 아는 신원섭과 원어민으로서
기민한 영어 감각을 가진 Diana는 실생활에 밀착된 자연스러운 영어 회화를 연구하고,
모든 연령대의 학습자가 '영어의 기초 뼈대'를 세우며 꾸준히 말하고 익히는 힘을
기를 수 있도록 돕고 있다. TESOL 자격을 갖춘 영어 교육자이자 콘텐츠 크리에이터로서
그들은 '배우는 영어'보다 '말이 되는 영어'를 전하고 있다.

유튜브/인스타그램 잉글리시 몬스터 English Monster

영어 회화 패턴 훈련 - 1차 임계점

초판 1쇄 인쇄 | 2025년 10월 23일
초판 1쇄 발행 | 2025년 11월 3일

지은이 | 신원섭 · Diana Salazar

발행인 | 박효상
편집장 | 김현
기획·편집 | 오혜순

교정·교열 | 이수정
디자인 | 고희선

마케팅 | 이태호, 이전희
관리 | 김태옥

종이 | 월드페이퍼   인쇄·제본 | 예림인쇄·바인딩   녹음 | YR 미디어

발행처 | 사람in   출판등록 | 제10-1835호

주소 | 04034 서울시 마포구 양화로 11길 14-10 (서교동) 3F
전화 | 02) 338-3555(代)   팩스 | 02) 338-3545
E-mail | saramin@netsgo.com   Website | www.saramin.com
인스타그램 | www.instagram.com/saramin_books   블로그 | blog.naver.com/saramcom

ⓒ 신원섭 2025
ISBN | 979-11-7101-195-7 14740   979-11-7101-194-0 (세트)

책값은 뒤표지에 있습니다.
파본은 바꾸어 드립니다.

영어 회화 패턴 훈련

1차 임계점

신현섭·Diana Salazar 지음

사람in

들어가는 글

영어 말하기는 운동과 아주 닮았습니다. 수영을 잘하는 사람에게 설명을 백 번 듣고, 교육 영상을 백 번 본다고 해서 우리가 곧바로 헤엄칠 수 있는 건 아니잖아요? 실제로 물속에 들어가 몸으로 부딪혀 훈련하고, 물도 먹고, 여러 번 실패하면서 감을 익혀야 비로소 헤엄쳐 앞으로 나아갈 수 있습니다. 영어도 마찬가지입니다. 영어 문법책을 백 번 읽고 영어 관련 영상을 아무리 봐도, 내 입으로 내뱉어 보고 꾸준히 연습하지 않으면 영어는 절대 늘지 않습니다.

꾸준한 연습 없이 머릿속에만 있던 영어를 꺼내 소리 내어 말하다 보면, 상황에 맞지 않는 어색한 표현 때문만이 아니라, 스스로 듣기 거북한 낯선 발음과 조음 때문에 혀가 더 꼬이고 얼굴이 뜨거워질 때도 있습니다. 저희는 이 과정을 입에 땀이 나는 시간이라고 부릅니다. 어색함을 참고 꾸준히 입 밖으로 내뱉는 연습을 하는 이런 순간들이 반복되고 쌓이면, 어느새 영어 패턴이 입에 새겨지고 입 근육으로 기억되는 진짜 성장의 단계가 옵니다.

익숙하지 않은 패턴들을 반복적으로 연습하다 보면, 어느 순간 그 문장이 생각보다 먼저 입 밖으로 나오는 순간이 찾아옵니다. 마치 "사과가 영어로 뭐예요?"라고 물어 오면 망설임 없이 "apple이요."라고 대답할 수 있는 것처럼요. 이 책에 담긴 패턴들도 그렇게 여러분의 입에서 자연스럽게 튀어나오길 바랍니다.

요즘에는 유튜브와 인스타그램을 비롯해 영어를 배울 수 있는 자료들이 많습니다. 그런데 영상을 보면서는 알아듣는 것 같아도 막상 말해야 할 순간에 "이걸 내가 실제로 써먹을 수 있을까?" 하면 대답은, 글쎄요. 그래서 저희는 지식으로 쌓는 영어가 아니라, 입으로 익히는 영어를 위해 고민했습니다.

다이애나와 함께 우리 일상에서 자주 사용하는 영어 패턴들을 모으고, 그 중에서도 원어민들이 정말 자연스럽게 사용하는 패턴 100개를 선별했습니다. 이 패턴들은 "영어로 어떻게 말하지?" 하는 순간에, 속 시원하게 막힘없이 말하도록 돕는 패턴들입니다. 이 패턴들을 통해, 머리가 아니라 입이 먼저 반응하는 진짜 영어 훈련을 경험하실 수 있을 겁니다.

알고 있는 영어 패턴을 쓸 순간이 실제로 왔을 때 머뭇거림 없이, 자신감 있게, 자연스럽게 말할 수 있도록 실생활 대화에 힘을 기울였습니다. 또, 패턴을 활용해서 우리가 흔히 말할 수 있는 문장들을 패턴 활용에 담았습니다. 5개 패턴을 배우고 나면 내 이야기를 할 수 있는 패턴 강화와 다시 한 번 대화 맥락을 복기하는 맥락 적용으로 끊임없이 연습하고 되새김할 수 있도록 책을 구성했습니다.

영어 회화 패턴은 결국 입 근육을 만드는 훈련이라고 생각합니다. 이 책의 구성이 효과를 내기 위해서는 반드시 반복해서 소리 내어 말하는 연습이 필요합니다. 머리로만 이해하는 영어는 금방 머릿속에서 사라집니다. 입과 귀가 기억해야 오래 남습니다. 여러분에게 저희가 그 반복 훈련의 가장 든든한 파트너가 되길 바랍니다.

언어를 배우는 여러분의 노력을 진심으로 응원합니다.
You've got this! We believe in you!

이 책의 구성과 활용법

〈영어 회화 패턴 훈련 1차 임계점〉은 일상에서 자주 사용하는 영어 패턴 100개를 선별해,
1) 실생활 대화를 통해 실제로 써먹는 패턴 맥락을 제대로 알고
2) 손과 입과 귀가 기억하는 말하기 강화 훈련 루틴을 마련했습니다.

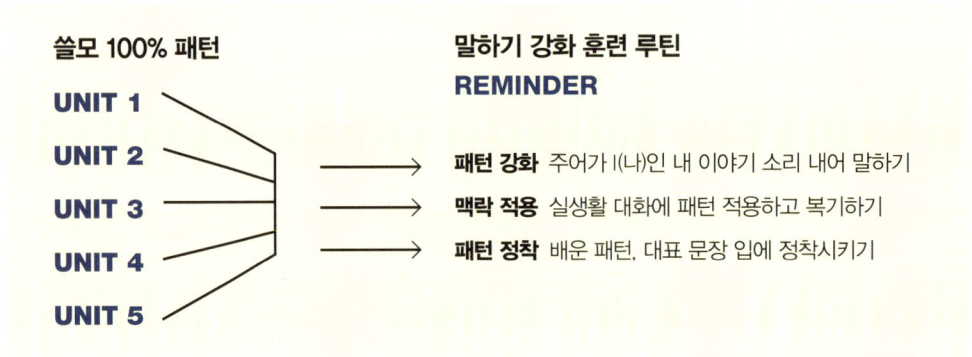

패턴 활용의 핵심은 맥락 파악입니다.

일상적인 소재를 다룬 실생활 대화에서 맥락 속에 녹아든 패턴을 확인하세요.

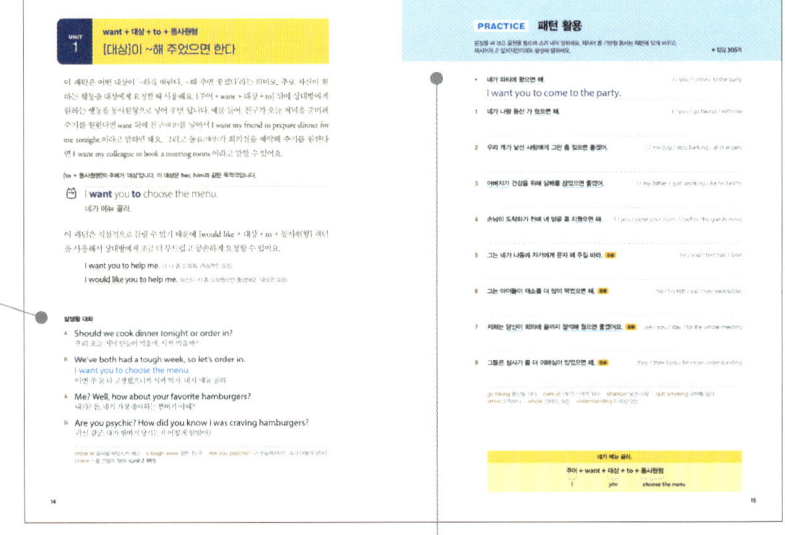

맞고 틀리고 보다 중요한 건 꾸준한 말하기 연습입니다.

패턴을 실제 써먹을 수 있는 문장들을 연습하는 패턴 활용에는 패턴을 제외한 모든 표현을 제시해, 중간에 포기하는 일이 없도록 도와드립니다.
1) 동사는 기본형으로 제시해서 중요한 문법은 항상 염두에 두도록 돕습니다.
2) 의미 단위를 끊어주는 슬래시(/)는 패턴이 들어갈 자리를 알려주는 힌트가 됩니다.
3) 더블슬래시(//)는 절이나 긴 부사구가 이어질 때, 단계적으로 끊어서 연습하도록 돕습니다.

내 이야기를 할 수 있어야 쓸모 있는 패턴입니다.

Reminder는 5개 유닛마다 반복되는 기억 강화 훈련으로, 첫 번째 패턴 강화에서는 1인칭 주어로 말할 법한 문장을 패턴으로 말해 보는 훈련을 합니다.

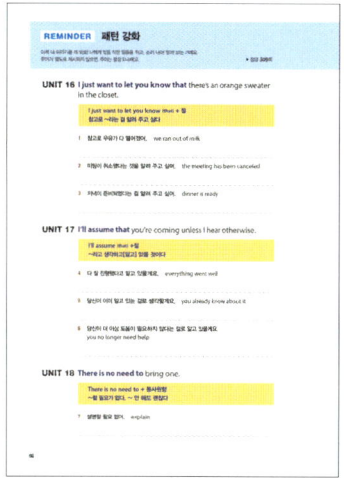

연필 잡고, 직접 쓰고, 말해 봐야, 써먹습니다.

5개 유닛마다 반복되는 기억 강화 훈련 두 번째, 맥락 적용에서는 실생활 대화문으로 패턴들의 맥락을 다시 한 번 복기할 수 있습니다.

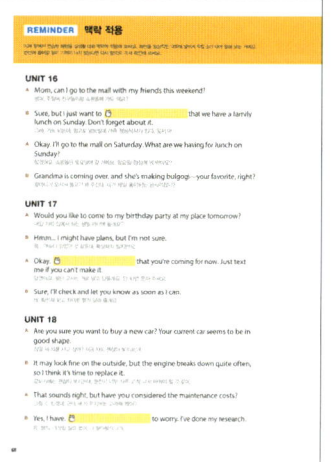

시간 차 기억 강화 훈련으로 패턴을 입에 정착시키세요.

20개 유닛마다 반복되는 기억 강화 훈련 세 번째, 패턴 정착으로 앞에서 배운 패턴 문장을 소리 내어 말할 수 있는지 확인하세요.

7

차례

	들어가는 글	4
	이 책의 구성과 활용법	6
UNIT 1	…이 ~해 주었으면 한다	14
UNIT 2	~를 간절히 원한다	16
UNIT 3	~를 어느 정도 한다[잘한다/못한다]	18
UNIT 4	~할 시간이다	20
UNIT 5	어서 ~를 하고 싶다	22
REMINDER	패턴 강화	24
REMINDER	맥락 적용	26
UNIT 6	~할 것이 있다	28
UNIT 7	~와 상관없다	30
UNIT 8	~해서 나쁠 건 없다	32
UNIT 9	~하곤 했다	34
UNIT 10	~하는 데 익숙하다	36
REMINDER	패턴 강화	38
REMINDER	맥락 적용	40
UNIT 11	막 ~하려는 참이다	42
UNIT 12	혹시 ~하세요?	44
UNIT 13	~ 중 하나[한 명]는	46
UNIT 14	~라는 것은 없다	48
UNIT 15	혹시 아는지 모르겠지만,	50
REMINDER	패턴 강화	52
REMINDER	맥락 적용	54
UNIT 16	참고로 ~라는 걸 알려 주고 싶다	56
UNIT 17	~라고 생각하고 있을 것이다	58
UNIT 18	~할 필요가 없다	60
UNIT 19	기분 나쁘게 할 의도는 아니지만,	62
UNIT 20	~하는 건 너답지 않다	64
REMINDER	패턴 강화	66
REMINDER	맥락 적용	68
REMINDER	패턴 정착	70

UNIT 21	~해서 미안하다	72	
UNIT 22	꼭 ~하겠다	74	
UNIT 23	~할 방법이 없다	76	
UNIT 24	그래서 ~한 거다	78	
UNIT 25	…가 가장 먼저 할 일은 ~이다	80	
REMINDER	패턴 강화	82	
REMINDER	맥락 적용	84	
UNIT 26	~하지 않을 수 없다	86	
UNIT 27	…가 ~할 거라고는 상상도 못 했다	88	
UNIT 28	설마 ~는 아니겠지?	90	
UNIT 29	편하게 ~하세요	92	
UNIT 30	~할 의도는 아니었다	94	
REMINDER	패턴 강화	96	
REMINDER	맥락 적용	98	
UNIT 31	~할 것 같다	100	
UNIT 32	~에 매우 만족하다	102	
UNIT 33	~할 때 너무 좋다[싫다]	104	
UNIT 34	~하기로 되어 있다	106	
UNIT 35	…가 하려는 말은 ~라는 것이다	108	
REMINDER	패턴 강화	110	
REMINDER	맥락 적용	112	
UNIT 36	지금이 ~하기 가장 좋은 때다	114	
UNIT 37	~라고 치자	116	
UNIT 38	그건 ~할 수 있는 정말 좋은 방법이다	118	
UNIT 39	~하는 게 당연하다	120	
UNIT 40	~만큼 좋은 게 없다	122	
REMINDER	패턴 강화	124	
REMINDER	맥락 적용	126	
REMINDER	패턴 정착	128	

UNIT 41	~가 장난이 아니다	130	
UNIT 42	도저히 ~할 수 없다	132	
UNIT 43	~하고 나니까 기분이 나아지다	134	
UNIT 44	오해하지 마, ~	136	
UNIT 45	…가 우연히 ~를 발견하면	138	
REMINDER	패턴 강화	140	
REMINDER	맥락 적용	142	
UNIT 46	~라는 예감이 들다	144	
UNIT 47	결론적으로[핵심은] ~이다	146	
UNIT 48	…의 말은 ~라는 것이다	148	
UNIT 49	항상 ~하고 싶었다	150	
UNIT 50	…는 ~하기만 하면 된다	152	
REMINDER	패턴 강화	154	
REMINDER	맥락 적용	156	
UNIT 51	이왕 이렇게 된 거 ~할까 보다	158	
UNIT 52	너무 ~에게 엄격하지 마	160	
UNIT 53	~해도 괜찮다	162	
UNIT 54	~가 핵심이다	164	
UNIT 55	~할 확률이 얼마나 될까?	166	
REMINDER	패턴 강화	168	
REMINDER	맥락 적용	170	
UNIT 56	~할 생각은 꿈도 꾸지 마	172	
UNIT 57	~하는 편이다	174	
UNIT 58	속으로 ~라고 생각했다	176	
UNIT 59	~해도 소용없다	178	
UNIT 60	~를 하기 위해 노력[최선]을 다하다	180	
REMINDER	패턴 강화	182	
REMINDER	맥락 적용	184	
REMINDER	패턴 정착	186	

UNIT 61	~를 하러 오다	188
UNIT 62	~인지 알아보려고	190
UNIT 63	시간 날 때	192
UNIT 64	~했어야 했다	194
UNIT 65	~할 수 있었는데	196
REMINDER	패턴 강화	198
REMINDER	맥락 적용	200
UNIT 66	~했을 텐데	202
UNIT 67	~하자마자	204
UNIT 68	~할 때쯤	206
UNIT 69	~라니 아쉽다	208
UNIT 70	~여서 다행[안심]이다	210
REMINDER	패턴 강화	212
REMINDER	맥락 적용	214
UNIT 71	~할수록 더 ~하다	216
UNIT 72	~에 푹 빠져 있다	218
UNIT 73	~할 기분이 아니다	220
UNIT 74	~(하)겠다	222
UNIT 75	~에 소질[재능]이 있다	224
REMINDER	패턴 강화	226
REMINDER	맥락 적용	228
UNIT 76	~하느라 시간 가는 줄 모른다	230
UNIT 77	…라서가 아니라, ~라서 그런 것이다	232
UNIT 78	~할 정도로 …하다	234
UNIT 79	~의 비결이 뭐야?	236
UNIT 80	하는 김에, ~해 줄래요?	238
REMINDER	패턴 강화	240
REMINDER	맥락 적용	242
REMINDER	패턴 정착	244

UNIT 81	~에 너무 얽매이지 마	246
UNIT 82	~가 신경 쓰이다	248
UNIT 83	~가 생각이 날 듯 말 듯하다	250
UNIT 84	…에 ~하러 갈 것이다	252
UNIT 85	자유롭게 ~해도 된다	254
REMINDER	패턴 강화	256
REMINDER	맥락 적용	258
UNIT 86	~하지 않을 수 없다	260
UNIT 87	~에 전혀 관심 없다	262
UNIT 88	~하는 게 어렵다	264
UNIT 89	~가 갑자기 생각났다	266
UNIT 90	~하기에 유용하다	268
REMINDER	패턴 강화	270
REMINDER	맥락 적용	272
UNIT 91	~하고 싶어 죽겠다	274
UNIT 92	~일 리가 없다	276
UNIT 93	~하는 것을 깜빡했다	278
UNIT 94	~는 상상할 수 없다	280
UNIT 95	~를 고민하고 있다	282
REMINDER	패턴 강화	284
REMINDER	맥락 적용	286
UNIT 96	결국 ~하게 되다	288
UNIT 97	~가 도무지 이해가 안 가다	290
UNIT 98	(~를) 네게 알려 줄 것이다	292
UNIT 99	~인지 알기 어렵다	294
UNIT 100	~인 줄 알았는데, 알고 보니 …는 ~였다	296
REMINDER	패턴 강화	298
REMINDER	맥락 적용	300
REMINDER	패턴 정착	302

패턴 활용 & 패턴 강화 정답   304

손으로 쓰고
귀로 들으면서
입으로는 말하는 훈련

위의 QR코드를 스캔하시고 '바로듣기'를 탭하세요.
해당 도서의 음원을 바로 들으실 수 있습니다.
반복 재생과 속도 조절도 가능합니다.

UNIT 1

want + 대상 + to + 동사원형

[대상]이 ~해 주었으면 한다

이 패턴은 어떤 대상이 '~하길 바란다, ~해 주면 좋겠다'라는 의미로, 주로 자신이 원하는 행동을 대상에게 요청할 때 사용해요. [주어 + want + 대상 + to] 뒤에 상대방에게 원하는 행동을 동사원형으로 넣어 주면 됩니다. 예를 들어, 친구가 오늘 저녁을 준비해 주기를 원한다면 want 뒤에 친구(대상)를 넣어서 I want my friend to prepare dinner for me tonight.이라고 말하면 돼요. 그리고 동료(대상)가 회의실을 예약해 주기를 원한다면 I want my colleague to book a meeting room.이라고 말할 수 있어요.

[to + 동사원형]의 주체가 '대상'입니다. 이 대상은 her, him과 같은 목적격입니다.

 I **want** you **to** choose the menu.
네가 메뉴 골라.

이 패턴은 직설적으로 들릴 수 있기 때문에 [would like + 대상 + to + 동사원형] 패턴을 사용해서 상대방에게 조금 더 부드럽고 공손하게 요청할 수 있어요.

I <u>want</u> you <u>to</u> help me. 너 나 좀 도와줘. (직설적인 요청)
I <u>would like</u> you <u>to</u> help me. 당신이 저 좀 도와줬으면 좋겠어요. (공손한 요청)

실생활 대화

A Should we cook dinner tonight or order in?
우리 오늘 저녁 만들어 먹을까, 시켜 먹을까?

B We've both had a tough week, so let's order in.
I want you to choose the menu.
이번 주 둘 다 고생했으니까 시켜 먹자. 네가 메뉴 골라.

A Me? Well, how about your favorite hamburgers?
내가? 음, 네가 가장 좋아하는 햄버거 어때?

B Are you psychic? How did you know I was craving hamburgers?
귀신 같군. 내가 햄버거 당기는지 어떻게 알았어?

order in 음식을 배달시켜 먹다   a tough week 힘든 한 주   Are you psychic? 너 초능력자야?, 네가 어떻게 알아?
crave ~를 간절히 원하다(unit 2 패턴)

PRACTICE 패턴 활용

문장을 써 보고 음원을 들으며 소리 내어 말하세요. 제시어 중 기본형 동사는 패턴에 맞게 바꾸고, 제시어의 // 앞까지만이라도 완성해 말하세요. ▶ 정답 305쪽

- 네가 파티에 왔으면 해. I / you / come / to the party
  I want you to come to the party.

1. 네가 나랑 등산 가 줬으면 해. I / you / go hiking / with me

2. 우리 개가 낯선 사람에게 그만 좀 짖으면 좋겠어. I / my dog / stop barking / at strangers

3. 아버지가 건강을 위해 담배를 끊었으면 좋겠어. I / my father / quit smoking / for his health

4. 손님이 도착하기 전에 네 방을 좀 치웠으면 해. I / you / clean your room // before the guests arrive

5. 그는 네가 나중에 자기에게 문자 해 주길 바라. [응용] he / you / text him / later

6. 그는 아이들이 채소를 더 많이 먹었으면 해. [응용] he / his kids / eat more vegetables

7. 저희는 당신이 회의에 끝까지 참석해 줬으면 좋겠어요. [응용] we / you / stay / for the whole meeting

8. 그들은 상사가 좀 더 이해심이 있었으면 해. [응용] they / their boss / be more understanding

go hiking 등산을 가다   bark at (개가) ~에게 짖다   stranger 낯선 사람   quit smoking 담배를 끊다
arrive 도착하다   whole 전체의, 모든   understanding 이해심 있는

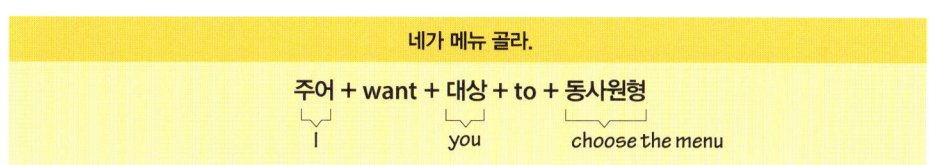

UNIT 2

be craving + 명사

~를 간절히 원한다

이 패턴은 어떤 음식을 너무 먹고 싶거나 혹은 어떤 활동을 너무 하고 싶을 때 사용해요. 배가 약간 출출할 때는 peckish, 배가 고플 때는 hungry, 너무 배고파서 미칠 것 같을 때는 starving이라고 하는데, 가끔 정말 뭔가 먹고 싶을 때가 있지 않나요? 이렇게 뭔가를 간절히 원할 때는 동사 crave를 써요. crave는 want보다 더 강한 욕구나 갈망을 표현할 수 있어서 감정을 더 생생하게 전달해요. 예를 들어, 피자가 정말 먹고 싶을 때는 I'm craving pizza, 너무 피곤해서 푹 자고 싶을 때는 I'm craving a good night's sleep. 이라고 말할 수 있어요.

be craving 진행시제 뒤에는 **crave**의 목적어인 명사가 옵니다.

 I'm seriously **craving** pizza right now.
난 지금 피자가 너무 당겨.

달달하거나 매운 '뭔가'가 당긴다고 말하고 싶을 때도 있죠? 이런 경우에는 be craving 뒤에 [something/anything + 형용사] 형태를 쓰면 돼요. I'm craving something sweet, I'm craving anything spicy. 같이요.

실생활 대화

A What do you want for dinner tonight?
오늘 저녁 뭐 먹고 싶어?

B I'm seriously craving pizza right now.
난 지금 피자가 너무 당겨.

A Really? I'm actually in the mood for Chinese food.
그래? 나는 사실 중국 음식이 먹고 싶은데.

B How about we order what each of us is craving?
그럼 각자 먹고 싶은 걸 시켜 먹는 건 어때?

seriously 진지하게, 정말로   actually 실제로(는), 사실은   be in the mood for (구어) ~하고 싶은 기분이다
How about ~는 어때?

PRACTICE 패턴 활용

문장을 써 보고 음원을 들으며 소리 내어 말하세요. 제시어 중 기본형 동사는 패턴에 맞게 바꾸고,
제시어의 // 앞까지만이라도 완성해 말하세요.

▶ 정답 305쪽

- 난 점심으로 초밥이 너무 먹고 싶어.　　　　　　　　　　　　　　　　I / sushi / for lunch

  I'm craving sushi for lunch.

1 난 커피가 너무 당기는데 카페인을 줄이려고 노력 중이야.
  I / coffee // but I'm trying to cut down on caffeine

2 난 멀리 어디론가 떠나는 휴가가 간절해.　　　　　　　　I / a vacation / somewhere far away

3 난 지금 초콜릿이 미친 듯이 먹고 싶어.　　　　　　　　　I / seriously / chocolate / right now

4 난 이런 쌀쌀한 날엔 따끈한 국물이 너무 당겨.　　　　I / a hot bowl of soup / on this chilly day

5 그들은 또 버블티를 먹고 싶어 해. 응용　　　　　　　　　　　　they / bubble tea / again

6 그녀는 지금 매운 게 당겨. 응용　　　　　　　　　　　　she / anything spicy / right now

7 그는 아이스크림이나 스무디처럼 차가운 게 당긴대. 응용
  he / something cold // like ice cream or a smoothie

8 그는 일주일 내내 야근해서 푹 자고 싶어 해. 응용
  he / a good night's sleep // after working late all week

---

for lunch 점심으로 　cut down on ~를 줄이다 　chilly 쌀쌀한, 추운 　a good night's sleep 숙면
work late 늦게까지 일하다

난 지금 피자가 너무 당겨.

주어 + be craving + 명사
　I'm　　seriously　　pizza right now

UNIT 3

be okay[good/bad] at + 명사[동명사]

~를 어느 정도 한다[잘한다/못한다]

이 패턴은 특정 활동에서 자신의 능력이나 실력 수준을 표현할 때 사용해요. 자신이 잘하는 것(good), 보통 수준으로 하는 것(okay), 또는 못하는 것(bad)을 말할 때 모두 적용해서 쓸 수 있어요. 예를 들어, 요리를 잘한다면 I'm good at cooking, 축구를 보통 수준으로 한다면 I'm okay at playing soccer.라고 말할 수 있어요. 이 패턴으로 여러분이 잘하거나 못하는 것, 또는 잘하진 않지만 못하지도 않는 것을 표현해 보세요.

전치사 at 뒤에는 명사 또는 동명사(-ing)를 써야 합니다.

 I'm good at English, but just **okay at** other languages.
영어는 잘하는데, 다른 말은 그냥 그럭저럭해.

실생활 대화

A How are you with foreign languages?
너 외국어 잘하니?

B I'm good at English, but just okay at other languages.
영어는 잘하는데, 다른 말은 그냥 그럭저럭해.

A I'm learning Spanish, but I'm still not very good at it.
난 요즘 스페인어 배우고 있는데, 아직 잘 못해.

B Learning a language takes time, so take it slow. You've got this!
언어를 배우는 건 시간이 걸리니까 천천히 해. 넌 할 수 있어!

How are you with ~은 잘해?, ~에 익숙해?　foreign language 외국어　learn 배우다　still 여전히　take time 시간이 걸리다　take it slow 천천히 하다　You've got this. (구어) 넌 할 수 있어.

PRACTICE 패턴 활용

문장을 써 보고 음원을 들으며 소리 내어 말하세요. 제시어 중 기본형 동사는 패턴에 맞게 바꾸고,
제시어의 // 앞까지만이라도 완성해 말하세요.

▶ 정답 305쪽

• 난 요리를 꽤 잘해. I / pretty / cook
  I'm pretty good at cooking.

1 난 요리는 그럭저럭해. I / cook

2 난 그림을 못 그려. I / draw

3 난 노래를 잘해. I / sing

4 난 기타를 잘 쳐. I / play the guitar

5 그녀는 이름을 잘 기억해. 응용 she / remember names

6 그녀는 비밀을 잘 못 지켜. 응용 she / keep secrets

7 그는 이탈리아 요리를 정말 잘해. 응용 he / really / cook Italian food

8 제인은 영어 말하기는 그럭저럭하는데 여전히 실수해. 응용
  Jane / speak English // but still makes mistakes

pretty 어느 정도, 꽤   remember 기억하다   keep secrets 비밀을 지키다   make mistakes 실수하다

영어는 잘하는데, 다른 말은 그냥 그럭저럭해.

주어 + be good at + 명사, but just okay at + 명사
   I'm   English   other languages

UNIT 4

It's time to + 동사원형

~할 시간이다, ~할 때다

이 패턴은 어떤 행동을 시작해야 할 시간이나 때가 되었을 때 사용해요. 예를 들어, 일어날 시간이 되었다면 It's time to get up, 저녁 먹을 시간이 되었다면 It's time to have dinner, 결정을 내려야 할 때가 되었다면 It's time to make a decision.이라고 말하면 돼요.

It's time to 뒤에는 동사원형이 옵니다.

 It's time to go to bed.
이제 자야 할 시간이야.

아이에게 "이제 양치할 시간이야."라고 말하고 싶다면 It's time to brush your teeth.라고 할 수 있어요. 하지만 더 직접적으로 대상(사람)을 강조하고 싶을 때는 [for + 대상 + to + 동사원형] 형태를 사용해서 It's time for you to brush your teeth.라고 말할 수도 있어요. 이렇게 누구에게 무엇을 하라고 말하고 싶을 때는 for 뒤에 그 대상(사람)을 넣으면 돼요.

실생활 대화

A Is it already this late? I always lose track of time when I binge-watch dramas on Netflix.
벌써 시간이 이렇게 됐어? 넷플릭스 정주행할 때마다 시간 가는 줄 몰라.

B Yeah, it's already 1 AM. It's time to go to bed.
응, 벌써 새벽 1시야. 이제 자야 할 시간이야.

A But I want to finish this episode.
그래도 이번 화는 보고 싶은데.

B Alright, but just this one episode!
알겠어, 하지만 이번 한 편만이야!

---

lose track of time 시간 가는 줄 모르다(unit 76 패턴)   binge-watch (TV 프로그램을) 정주행하다, 연달아 보다
episode 시리즈물의 한 편

PRACTICE 패턴 활용

문장을 써 보고 음원을 들으며 소리 내어 말하세요. 제시어 중 기본형 동사는 패턴에 맞게 바꾸고, 제시어의 // 앞까지만이라도 완성해 말하세요.

▶ 정답 305쪽

- 이제 공부할 시간이야. study
  It's time to study.

1 집 청소할 시간이야. clean the house

2 이제 샤워할 시간이야. take a shower

3 아침 먹을 시간이야. eat breakfast

4 이제 미루는 거 그만할 때야. stop procrastinating

5 네 운전면허증을 갱신할 때가 됐어. renew your driver's license

6 이제 출발할 시간이야. 안 그러면 가는 길에 막힐지도 몰라.
   leave // or we might get stuck in traffic on the way

7 모두 앉을 시간이야. 응용 everyone / sit down

8 우리 아들이 학교에 다닐 때가 됐어. 응용 my son / start school

take a shower 샤워하다   procrastinate 미루다, 질질 끌다   renew 갱신하다, 연장하다   might ~일지도 모른다
get stuck in traffic 교통 체증 때문에 꼼짝 못 하다   on the way 가는 중에

이제 자야 할 시간이야.

It's time to + 동사원형
              go to bed

21

UNIT 5

can't wait to + 동사원형

어서 ~를 하고 싶다, ~가 너무 기대된다

어린 시절 소풍 가기 전날 너무 기대되고 설레어 잠도 잘 안 올 때가 있었죠? 그때 그 마음처럼 이 패턴은 어떤 일을 빨리 하고 싶은 기대감이나 설렘을 표현할 때 사용해요. 예를 들어, 휴가를 빨리 가고 싶은 마음을 표현하고 싶다면 I can't wait to go on vacation, 친구를 빨리 만나고 싶을 때는 I can't wait to see my friend.라고 말할 수 있어요.

can't wait to 뒤에는 동사원형을 써서 하고 싶은 행동을 나타냅니다.

 I **can't wait to** see him again.
얼른 그 사람 다시 보고 싶다.

실생활 대화

A How was the party last night?
어젯밤 파티 어땠어?

B Amazing! I totally hit it off with someone.
I think he would be a great fit for me.
정말 좋았어! 어떤 사람이랑 완전 잘 통했어. 그 사람 나랑 잘 맞을 것 같아.

A Wow! Do you have any plans to meet again?
와! 다시 보기로 했어?

B Yes, this weekend! I can't wait to see him again.
응, 이번 주말에! 얼른 그 사람 다시 보고 싶다.

---

hit it off (처음 만난 사람과) 잘 통하다, 죽이 잘 맞다   be a great fit 아주 잘 어울리다, 딱 맞다

PRACTICE 패턴 활용

문장을 써 보고 음원을 들으며 소리 내어 말하세요. 제시어 중 기본형 동사는 패턴에 맞게 바꾸고, 제시어의 // 앞까지만이라도 완성해 말하세요.　　▶ 정답 305쪽

• 너랑 가는 캠핑 진짜 기대돼.　　　　　　　　　　　　　　　　　I / go camping / with you
  I can't wait to go camping with you.

1 오늘 밤 불꽃놀이 보는 거 너무 기대돼.　　　　　　　　　　　I / see the fireworks / tonight

2 이번 가을에 캐나다 가는 거 너무 기대돼.　　　　　　　　　　I / travel to Canada / this fall

3 새로 생긴 이탈리아 식당을 간다니 너무 기대돼.　　　　　　I / try the new Italian restaurant

4 다음 주에 새 아파트로 이사 가는 게 정말 설레.　　　　I / move into my new apartment / next week

5 그는 어서 운전면허를 따고 싶어 해.　　　　　　　　　　　　he / get his driver's license

6 그는 이번 겨울에 스키 타러 가는 걸 기대하고 있어.　　　　he / go skiing / this winter

7 우린 새로 오픈한 카페에 어서 가 보고 싶어.　　　　we / try out the new café // that just opened

8 우리는 집들이 손님맞이를 정말 기대하고 있어. **응용**
  we / welcome our guests / to the housewarming party

travel to ~로 여행 가다　　move into ~로 이사하다　　get one's driver's license 운전면허를 따다
go skiing 스키 타러 가다　　try out 시도해 보다　　welcome 환영하다　　housewarming party 집들이 파티

얼른 그 사람 다시 보고 싶다.

주어 + can't wait to + 동사원형
　I　　　　　　　　　see him again

REMINDER 패턴 강화

이제 내 이야기를 해 봐요! 나에게 있음 직한 일들을 적고, 소리 내어 말해 보는 거예요.
주어가 별도로 제시되지 않으면, 주어는 항상 I(나)예요.

▶ 정답 305쪽

UNIT 1 I **want** you **to** choose the menu.

> want + 대상 + to + 동사원형
> [대상]이 ~해 주었으면 한다

1 네가 나한테 솔직했으면 해.   you / be honest with me

2 네가 이 케이크를 먹어 봤으면 해.   you / try this cake

3 그가 그녀에게 사과했으면 해.   him / apologize to her

UNIT 2 I'm seriously **craving** pizza right now.

> be craving + 명사
> ~를 간절히 원한다

4 아이스크림처럼 뭔가 달달한 게 당겨.   something sweet like ice cream

5 혼자만의 시간을 간절히 원해.   some alone time

6 저녁으로 매운 거 아무거나 원해.   anything spicy for dinner

UNIT 3 I'm **good at** English, but just **okay at** other languages.

> be okay[good/bad] at + 명사[동명사]
> ~를 어느 정도 한다[잘한다/못한다]

7 사람들 앞에서 말을 그럭저럭해.   speaking in front of others

8   돈 모으는 걸 못해.   saving money

9   레시피 없이 요리를 잘해.   cooking without a recipe

UNIT 4   It's time to go to bed.

> **It's time to + 동사원형**
> ~할 시간이다, ~할 때다

10   이메일을 보낼 시간이야.   send the email

11   하루를 시작할 때야.   start the day

12   아이들이 간식을 먹을 시간이야. 응용   the kids / have some snacks

UNIT 5   I can't wait to see him again.

> **can't wait to + 동사원형**
> 어서 ~를 하고 싶다, ~가 너무 기대된다

13   그에게 어서 좋은 소식을 전하고 싶어.   tell him the good news

14   고등학교 졸업이 기대돼.   graduate from high school

15   제주도로 여름휴가라니 너무 기대돼.   go on summer vacation to Jeju

REMINDER 맥락 적용

이제 앞에서 연습한 패턴을 실생활 대화 맥락에 적용해 보세요. 패턴을 일상적인 대화에 넣어서 직접 소리 내어 말해 보는 거예요. 빈칸에 들어갈 말이 기억이 나지 않는다면 다시 앞으로 가서 확인해 보세요.

UNIT 1

A What should we do this weekend?
이번 주말에 뭐 할까?

B I _____ you to go hiking with me.
네가 나랑 등산 가줬으면 좋겠어.

A Hiking? I've never done that before. Won't it be difficult?
등산? 한번도 해 본 적 없는데. 어렵지 않을까?

B It won't be hard with me. It's great exercise and the views are amazing. Let's do it together!
나랑 가면 어렵지 않을 거야. 운동도 되고 경치도 좋아. 같이 가자!

UNIT 2

A Why are you sighing so much?
왜 그렇게 한숨을 쉬고 있어?

B I'm _____ coffee, but I'm trying to cut down on caffeine.
커피가 너무 당기는데 카페인을 줄이려고 하는 중이거든.

A Oh, I see. How about some decaf?
그렇구나. 디카페인은 어때?

B That's a good idea. I should try that.
좋은 생각이네. 그걸 마셔 봐야겠다.

UNIT 3

A How are your cooking skills?
네 요리 실력은 어때?

B I'm pretty _____ cooking. How about you?
나 요리 꽤 잘해. 넌?

A I'm just _____ cooking. What is your signature dish?
난 뭐 그냥 그럭저럭 해. 네 시그니처 요리가 뭔데?

B I'm especially _____ making pasta.
난 파스타가 특히 자신 있어.

UNIT 4

A The kids are still playing at the playground.
애들이 아직 놀이터에서 놀고 있어.

B Yeah. It's almost 🐱 _____ give the kids a bath.
그러게. 이제 곧 목욕시킬 시간인데.

A Do you want to call them, or should I go?
당신이 애들 불러 올래, 아니면 내가 갈까?

B I'll go. Could you please fill the bathtub with water so we can bathe them right away when they come home?
내가 갈게. 당신은 아이들 집에 오면 바로 씻길 수 있게 욕조에 물 좀 받아 줄래?

UNIT 5

A It's not long until graduation.
졸업까지 얼마 안 남았네.

B Yeah, 🐱 _____ graduate.
그러게. 빨리 졸업하고 싶다.

A What are you planning to do after graduation?
졸업하고 뭐 할 거야?

B I'm planning to go on a trip first.
일단 여행부터 다녀올 계획이야.

어휘 sigh 한숨을 내쉬다 | cut down on ~를 줄이다 | signature 서명, 특징 | bathe 씻다
         go on a trip 여행을 가다

정답 want | craving | good at, okay at, good at | time to | I can't wait to

UNIT 6

have something to + 동사원형
~할 것이 있다

이 패턴은 누군가에게 말할 게 있거나 뭔가 할 일이 있을 때 사용하는 표현이에요. 예를 들어, 누군가에게 말할 것이 있다면 I have something to tell you, 이번 주 토요일까지 끝내야 할 일이 있다면 I have something to finish by this Saturday. 등으로 표현할 수 있어요.

have something to 뒤에는 동사원형을 써서 해야 할 행동을 나타냅니다.

 I **have something to** confess.
고백할 게 있어.

"중요하게 드릴 말씀이 있어요."의 '중요하게'처럼 something을 좀 더 구체적으로 전달하고 싶다면 something 바로 뒤에 important(중요한), interesting(흥미로운), funny(웃긴)와 같은 형용사를 넣어 말할 수 있어요. 그러니까, 중요한 용건이 있을 때는 I have something important to tell you.라고 말할 수 있어요.

실생활 대화

A I have something to confess.
고백할 게 있어.

B What is it? You look serious.
뭔데? 심각해 보이네.

A I accidentally broke your favorite mug.
실수로 네가 제일 좋아하는 머그컵을 깼어.

B Oh, that's okay. Are you alright? Did you get hurt? The mug isn't a big deal.
아, 괜찮아. 넌 괜찮아? 다치진 않았어? 머그컵은 별거 아니야.

confess 고백[자백]하다 **accidentally** 실수로 **get hurt** 다치다 **a big deal** 중요한 일, 큰 문제, 대단한 일

PRACTICE 패턴 활용

문장을 써 보고 음원을 들으며 소리 내어 말하세요. 제시어 중 기본형 동사는 패턴에 맞게 바꾸고, 제시어의 // 앞까지만이라도 완성해 말하세요.

▶ 정답 306쪽

- 오늘 밤에 할 일이 있어.   I / do / tonight
  I have something to do tonight.

1 말할 게 있어.   I / tell you

2 물어볼 게 있어.   I / ask you

3 이번 주말에 할 일이 있어.   I / do / this weekend

4 이번 주에 읽어 볼 게 있어.   I / read / this week

5 그들은 너에게 보여 줄 재미있는 게 있어. 응용   they / interesting / show you

6 그녀는 이번 주까지 제출해야 할 중요한 게 있어. 응용   she / important / submit / by this week

7 그는 정오 전에 끝내야 할 급한 일이 있어. 응용   he / urgent / finish / before noon

8 우리는 다음 주말에 아이들이랑 재미있게 할 일이 있어. 응용   we / fun / do / with the kids / next weekend

submit 제출하다   urgent 긴급한   before noon 정오 전에, 오전 중에

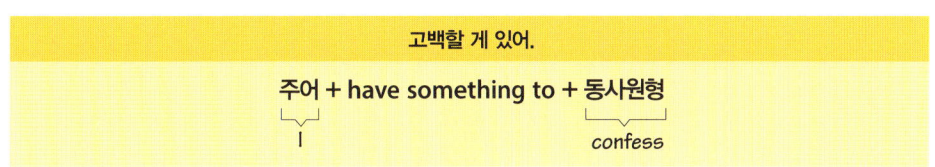

UNIT 7

have nothing to do with + 명사(절)

~와 상관없다, ~와 관련 없다

이 패턴은 특정한 일이나 상황과 관련이 없다는 것을 말할 때 사용해요. "난 아무 상관없어." 또는 "난 관련 없어."라는 의미예요. 예를 들어, 누군가가 창문을 깼는데 나는 그 일과 무관하다는 것을 표현하고 싶다면 I have nothing to do with that.이라고 말할 수 있어요. 또한, 반대되는 의미로 I have something to do with~를 사용하여 관련이 있다는 것을 표현할 수 있어요. 예를 들어, "사라가 그 깨진 창문과 관련이 있어."라고 말하고 싶다면 Sarah has something to do with the broken window.라고 하면 돼요.

전치사 with 다음에는 명사(절)가 와야 합니다.

 I **have nothing to do with** that.
　　난 관련 없는데.

참고로, have 앞에 don't나 doesn't를 쓸 경우에는 nothing이 아닌 anything을 써야 해요. nothing은 not anything을 뜻하니까요.

　　I <u>don't</u> have <u>nothing</u> to do with that. (X)
　　I <u>don't</u> have <u>anything</u> to do with that. (O)

실생활 대화

A　Hey, James, did you eat the last slice of pizza in the fridge?
　　제임스, 네가 냉장고에 피자 남은 거 먹었어?

B　Nope, I have nothing to do with that. I've been on a diet, remember?
　　아니, 난 관련 없는데(안 먹었는데). 난 다이어트 중이잖아. 기억 안 나?

A　Oh, right. I forgot about your diet.
　　Do you have any idea who might have eaten it?
　　아, 맞네. 다이어트 하는 거 깜빡했어. 그거 누가 먹었을 거 같아?

B　Maybe check with Sarah?
　　She was complaining about being hungry earlier.
　　사라한테 물어보는 게 어때? 아까 배고프다고 툴툴거렸거든.

---

on a diet 다이어트 중인　forget about ~를 잊다, ~은 신경 쓰지 않다
Do you have any idea ~? 혹시 ~에 대해 알아?, ~할 생각 있어?　complain 불평하다, 투덜거리다

PRACTICE 패턴 활용

문장을 써 보고 음원을 들으며 소리 내어 말하세요. 제시어 중 기본형 동사는 패턴에 맞게 바꾸고, 제시어의 // 앞까지만이라도 완성해 말하세요.

▶ 정답 306쪽

• 난 그 결정과 아무 관련 없어.   I / that decision
  I have nothing to do with that decision.

1 그 소문은 나랑 전혀 관련 없어.   I / that gossip

2 엉망이 된 부엌이랑 난 전혀 관련 없어.   I / the mess / in the kitchen

3 엄마가 지갑 잃어버린 거랑 나는 전혀 상관없어.   I / mom's missing wallet

4 너는 이 문제랑 아무 상관없으니까 걱정하지 마.   you / this problem // so don't worry

5 우리는 그 싸움이랑 아무 상관없어. 우린 다 끝나고 도착했어.
we / the fight // we just got there after it happened

6 그들은 이 문제랑 아무 상관없어! 그들이 일으킨 게 아니야.   they / this issue // they didn't cause it

7 그녀가 화가 난 이유는 나랑 아무 상관없어. `응용`   I / why she's mad

8 그녀는 그 결정이랑 아무 상관없어! 그녀는 회의에도 참석하지 않았어. `응용`
she / the decision // she wasn't even in the meeting

gossip 험담, 소문; 험담하다, 소문을 퍼뜨리다   mess 엉망진창, 지저분한 상태   missing 잃어버린
mad 화난, 열광적인   cause ~을 유발하다; 원인

난 관련 없는데.

주어 + have nothing to do with + 명사
    I   that

UNIT 8

It doesn't hurt to + 동사원형
~해서 나쁠 건 없다, ~해서 손해 볼 건 없다

지금은 비가 오지 않지만 곧 비가 올 것 같은 느낌이 들 때, 상대방에게 혹시 모르니까 우산을 챙겨가라고 말할 수 있겠죠? 이럴 때 이 패턴을 사용하여 It doesn't hurt to bring an umbrella.라고 말할 수 있어요. 우산을 챙겨가도 나쁠 건 없다는 말이죠. 이 패턴은 손해 볼 게 없고, 해 볼 만한 가치가 있으니 시도해도 괜찮다는 의미가 담겨 있어요. 예를 들어, 친구의 조언을 들어 보는 것이 나쁠 건 없다고 말하고 싶다면 It doesn't hurt to listen to advice from your friend.라고 하면 돼요.

It doesn't hurt to 뒤에는 동사원형을 써서 해도 나쁘지 않은 행동을 나타냅니다.

 It doesn't hurt to give it a shot.
한번 시도해 봐서 나쁠 건 없지.

doesn't 앞에 부사 probably(아마도), definitely(확실히)를 추가하거나 문장 끝에 just in case (혹시 모르니) 같은 표현을 덧붙일 수도 있어요. "혹시 모르니까 우산 챙겨."는 It doesn't hurt to bring an umbrella, just in case.라고 하면 되겠지요.

실생활 대화

A Should I start my own YouTube channel?
I'm not sure if I'm interesting enough.
유튜브를 시작할까? 내가 충분히 재미있을지 모르겠지만.

B **It doesn't hurt to give it a shot.** You might discover a hidden talent.
한번 시도해 봐서 나쁠 건 없지. 숨겨진 재능을 발견할 수도 있어.

A That's true. What kind of content do you think I should make?
맞아. 어떤 종류의 콘텐츠를 만들어야 할까?

B Start with something you're passionate about.
Authenticity is key on YouTube.
네가 열정을 가지고 있는 것부터 시작해 봐. 유튜브에서는 진정성이 핵심이야.

---

give it a shot (구어) 한번 시도해 보다   a hidden talent 숨겨진 재능   passionate 열정적인
authenticity 진정성   be key ~가 가장 중요하다, ~가 핵심이다(unit 54 패턴)

PRACTICE 패턴 활용

문장을 써 보고 음원을 들으며 소리 내어 말하세요. 제시어 중 기본형 동사는 패턴에 맞게 바꾸고, 제시어의 // 앞까지만이라도 완성해 말하세요.

▶ 정답 306쪽

- 먼저 사과하는 것도 나쁘지 않아.   say sorry / first

  It doesn't hurt to say sorry first.

1. 매달 조금씩 저축해도 손해 볼 건 없어.   save a little money / each month

2. 다른 의사 소견도 받아 봐서 나쁠 건 없어.   get a second opinion / from another doctor

3. 중요한 서류는 제출하기 전에 한 번 더 확인해도 나쁠 건 없어.
   double-check important documents / before submitting

4. 시야를 넓히고 싶다면, 새로운 언어를 배우는 것도 나쁠 건 없어.
   learn a new language // if you want to expand your horizons

5. 추워질 수도 있으니까 재킷 하나 챙겨도 나쁘지 않지.   bring a jacket // in case it gets cold

6. 네 감정에 솔직한 것도 아마 괜찮을 거야. `응용`   probably / be honest / about how you feel

7. 교통 체증이 있을지도 모르니까 일찍 출발해도 나쁘지 않아. `응용`   leave early // just in case there's traffic

8. 카드가 안 될 수도 있으니까 현금을 좀 가져가는 것도 나쁠 건 없어. `응용`
   bring some cash // just in case your card doesn't work

---

get a second opinion 다른 사람의 의견을 들어 보다. (특히 의료 관련해서) 다른 의사의 소견을 듣다
double-check 다시 확인하다   **expand one's horizons** 시야를 넓히다, 견문을 넓히다
in case ~할 경우를 대비해서   **get cold** 추워지다, 감기에 걸리다   **work** 작동하다, 효과가 있다

한번 시도해 봐서 나쁠 건 없지.

It doesn't hurt to + 동사원형

give it a shot

UNIT 9

used to + 동사원형

(예전에는) ~하곤 했다, ~였다

예전에 했던 어떤 행동을 현재는 더 이상 하지 않을 때, 과거의 어떤 상태가 현재는 지속되지 않을 때 이 패턴을 사용해요. 어렸을 때 귀신을 정말 무서워했는데 지금은 무서워하지 않는다면 I used to be so scared of ghosts when I was a kid, 어렸을 때는 자전거를 타곤 했지만 이제는 더 이상 타지 않는다면 I used to ride a bike.라고 말할 수 있어요.

used to 뒤에는 동사원형을 사용해서 예전에 하곤 했던 행동을 표현합니다.

 I used to watch a lot of movies in English.
예전엔 영어로 된 영화 많이 봤어요.

실생활 대화

A Your English is really good! Did you study abroad?
영어 정말 잘하시네요! 유학 다녀오셨어요?

B No, but I used to watch a lot of movies and TV shows in English.
아니요, 예전엔 영어로 된 영화랑 TV 프로그램을 많이 봤어요.

A That's impressive. How often did you watch them?
정말 대단하네요. 얼마나 자주 보셨어요?

B Pretty much every day!
It really helped improve my overall English skills.
거의 매일 봤어요! 영어 실력을 전반적으로 늘리는 데 정말 도움이 됐어요.

study abroad 해외에서 공부하다   impressive 인상적인, 감명을 주는   overall 전반적인

PRACTICE 패턴 활용

문장을 써 보고 음원을 들으며 소리 내어 말하세요. 제시어 중 기본형 동사는 패턴에 맞게 바꾸고, 제시어의 // 앞까지만이라도 완성해 말하세요.

▶ 정답 306쪽

• 예전엔 뉴욕에 살았어요.   I / live in New York
  I used to live in New York.

1 예전엔 매일 밤 책을 읽곤 했어요.   I / read books / every night

2 예전엔 인스턴트 음식을 정말 많이 먹었어요.   I / eat a lot of junk food

3 예전엔 줄넘기를 했는데, 지금은 안 해요.   I / jump rope / but not anymore

4 예전엔 채소를 정말 싫어했는데, 지금은 정말 좋아해요.   I / hate vegetables // but now I love them

5 저 식당은 예전에 서점이었어요.   that restaurant / be a bookstore

6 그 버스는 예전엔 10분마다 왔는데, 지금은 덜 자주 와요.
the bus / come every 10 minutes // but now it's less frequent

7 그녀는 예전에 매우 수줍음이 많고 내성적이었는데, 지금은 외향적이에요.
she / be very shy / and introverted // but now she is extroverted

8 우리가 자랄 때 그녀는 아는 척을 많이 했는데, 이제는 다른 사람들 얘기를 더 잘 들어요. 〔응용〕
she / be a know-it-all // when we were growing up // but now she's more open to listening to others

---

jump rope 줄넘기를 하다   **frequent** 잦은, 빈번한   **introverted** 내성적인   **extroverted** 외향적인
a know-it-all 아는 척하는 사람, 뭐든지 다 안다고 생각하는 사람   **open to** ~에 열려 있는, ~를 받아들일 준비가 된
listen to ~를 듣다, ~의 말을 듣다

예전엔 영어로 된 영화 많이 봤어요.

주어 + used to + 동사원형

I   watch a lot of movies in English

UNIT 10

be used to + 동명사[명사]
~하는 데 익숙하다

어떤 행동을 반복적으로 하다 보면, 그 행동에 익숙해지죠? 이럴 때 사용할 수 있는 패턴이 바로 be used to예요. 이 패턴은 어떤 것에 익숙해져서 그것을 자연스럽게 할 수 있을 때 사용해요. 예를 들어, 1년 내내 추운 곳에서 사는 사람이 추운 날씨에 익숙하다면 People who live in cold places are used to cold weather, 또는 아침 일찍 일어나는 것에 익숙하다면 I'm used to waking up early, 긴 시간 동안 일하는 것에 익숙하다면 I'm used to working long hours.라고 말할 수 있어요.

be used to 뒤에 동명사(-ing) 또는 명사를 써야 합니다.

 I'm used to waking up early.
일찍 일어나는 데 익숙해요.

이 패턴 뒤에 익숙한 이유를 추가할 수 있어요. 접속사 because를 써서 패턴 뒤에 절을 이어주는 거예요. 추운 겨울 날씨에 익숙한 이유가 러시아에서 왔기 때문이라면 She's used to the cold weather because she is from Russia.라고 말하면 돼요.

실생활 대화

A How do you manage to wake up so early every day?
   어떻게 매일 그렇게 일찍 일어날 수 있어요?

B I'm used to waking up early. I've been doing it for years.
   일찍 일어나는 데 익숙해요. 몇 년째 이렇게 하고 있어요.

A That's impressive. Don't you ever feel tired in the morning?
   대단하네요. 아침에 피곤하지 않으세요?

B Not really. Once you get into the habit, it becomes second nature. Plus, I go to bed early, too.
   그렇지 않아요. 습관이 되면 익숙해져요. 게다가 저는 일찍 자기도 해요.

---

manage (힘든 일을) 용케 해내다   for years 수년 동안, 오랫동안   get into the habit 습관이 붙다
become second nature 몸에 배다, 습관처럼 되다   plus (구어) 게다가   go to bed early 일찍 자다

PRACTICE 패턴 활용

문장을 써 보고 음원을 들으며 소리 내어 말하세요. 제시어 중 기본형 동사는 패턴에 맞게 바꾸고, 제시어의 // 앞까지만이라도 완성해 말하세요.

▶ 정답 306쪽

- 저는 영어로 말하는 게 익숙해요. I / speak in English
  I'm used to speaking in English.

1. 사람들 앞에서 말하는 데 익숙해요. I / speak in front of people

2. 매일 1시간 넘게 출퇴근하는 데 익숙해요. I / commute / for over an hour / every day

3. 지하철 타는 게 익숙해요. I / take the subway

4. 마스크 쓰는 게 익숙해요. I / wear a mask

5. 그는 소방관이라 위급한 상황에서도 침착한 데 익숙해요. 응용
   he / stay calm / in emergencies // because he's a firefighter

6. 그녀는 차가 없어서 먼 거리를 걷는 게 익숙해요. 응용
   she / walk long distances // because she doesn't have a car

7. 우리는 가족 사업을 해서 주말에도 일하는 게 익숙해요. 응용
   we / work / on weekends // because we run a family business

8. 그는 매일 아침 수업이 있어서 일찍 일어나는 게 익숙해요. 응용
   he / wake up early // because he has morning classes every day

---

stay calm 침착함을 유지하다, 진정하다   in emergency 유사시   walk long distances 먼 거리를 걷다
run a family business 가업을 운영하다

일찍 일어나는 데 익숙해요.

주어 + be used to + 동명사
  I'm   waking up early

REMINDER 패턴 강화

이제 내 이야기를 해 봐요! 나에게 있음 직한 일들을 적고, 소리 내어 말해 보는 거예요.
주어가 별도로 제시되지 않으면, 주어는 항상 I(나)예요.

▶ 정답 307쪽

UNIT 6   I **have something to** confess.

> **have something to + 동사원형**
> ~할 것이 있다

1. 사과할 게 있어. apologize for

2. 우린 중대 발표가 있어. 응용 we / important / announce

3. 그녀는 처리해야 할 어려운 일이 있어. 응용 she / difficult / deal with

UNIT 7   I **have nothing to do with** that.

> **have nothting to do with + 명사(절)**
> ~와 상관없다, ~와 관련 없다

4. 휴대폰 망가진 거랑 나랑 아무 상관없어. the broken phone

5. 커피 쏟은 거랑 나랑 아무 상관없어. the spilled coffee

6. 그 말다툼은 나랑 아무 상관없어. the argument

UNIT 8   **It doesn't hurt to** give it a shot.

> **It doesn't hurt to + 동사원형**
> ~해서 나쁠 건 없다, ~해서 손해 볼 건 없다

7. 설명서를 읽어서 손해 볼 건 없어. read the instructions

38

8 매일 연습해서 나쁠 건 없어.   practice every day

9 다시 물어봐서 나쁠 건 없어.   ask again

UNIT 9 I **used to** watch a lot of movies in English.

> **used to + 동사원형**
> (예전에는) ~하곤 했다, ~였다

10 예전에는 담배를 피웠어.   smoke

11 예전에는 늦게 일어났어.   wake up late

12 그는 예전엔 축구를 했어.   he / play soccer

UNIT 10 I'**m used to** waking up early.

> **be used to + 동명사[명사]**
> ~하는 데 익숙하다

13 매운 음식에 익숙해.   spicy food

14 그녀는 더운 날씨에 익숙해.   she / hot weather

15 혼자 먹는 것에 익숙해.   eating alone

REMINDER 맥락 적용

이제 앞에서 연습한 패턴을 실생활 대화 맥락에 적용해 보세요. 패턴을 일상적인 대화에 넣어서 직접 소리 내어 말해 보는 거예요. 빈칸에 들어갈 말이 기억이 나지 않는다면 다시 앞으로 가서 확인해 보세요.

UNIT 6

A   Do you _____ in mind to watch tonight?
오늘 밤 뭐 볼 만한 거 있어?

B   Yeah, I found a new series we can binge-watch together.
응. 같이 정주행할 수 있는 시리즈를 찾았어.

A   Sounds perfect! I can't wait to see it.
완벽해! 빨리 보고 싶다.

B   Awesome! Let's grab some snacks and settle in.
좋아! 간식 좀 챙겨서 편히 앉아서 보자.

UNIT 7

A   You didn't eat much at dinner. Isn't it to your taste?
저녁 별로 안 먹었네. 입맛에 안 맞아?

B   No, the reason I'm not eating has _____ the taste of the food.
아니. 내가 많이 안 먹는 건 음식 맛이랑은 상관없어.

A   Well, that's a relief. Just let me know if you want something else.
그럼 다행이고. 다른 거 먹고 싶은 거 있으면 말해.

B   Thanks, it's just that I had a late lunch, so I'm not really hungry.
고마워. 그냥 점심을 늦게 먹어서 배가 별로 안 고파서 그래.

UNIT 8

A   I'm thinking of surprising my girlfriend with flowers. Is that too cheesy?
여자친구에게 깜짝 선물로 꽃을 주려고 해. 너무 오글거릴까?

B   _____ be romantic sometimes. I'm sure she'll appreciate it.
가끔은 로맨틱한 것도 나쁘지 않아. 분명 좋아할 거야.

A   You think so? I hope she doesn't think it's too cliché.
그래? 너무 뻔하다고 생각하지 않았으면 좋겠는데.

B   Follow your gut! You know your girlfriend better than anyone.
네 느낌을 믿어 봐! 네 여자친구는 누구보다 네가 잘 알잖니.

UNIT 9

A Did you always like vegetables?
원래 채소를 좋아했어요?

B No, I ⬚_____ hate vegetables when I was a kid.
아뇨. 어렸을 때는 채소를 정말 싫어했어요.

A Really? What changed your mind?
정말이요? 어떻게 바뀐 거예요?

B As I grew older, I learned about their health benefits and started trying different recipes. Now I love them!
나이가 들면서 채소가 건강에 좋다는 점을 알게 됐고, 다양하게 요리해 먹기 시작했어요. 이제는 정말 좋아해요!

UNIT 10

A Aren't you nervous about the presentation?
발표가 긴장되지 않으세요?

B No, I'm ⬚_____ speaking in public. I do it often.
아뇨. 사람들 앞에서 말하는 것에 익숙해요. 자주 하거든요.

A That's great. How did you become so comfortable with public speaking?
대단해요. 남들 앞에서 말하는 게 어떻게 그렇게 편안해진 거예요?

B Practice, mostly. I started with small groups and gradually worked my way up to larger audiences.
주로 연습이죠. 적은 사람들로 시작해서 점점 더 많은 사람들 앞에서도 하게 됐어요.

어휘 settle in 자리잡다   suit one's taste 취향에 맞다   That's a relief. 다행이네.   Cheesy 느끼한
cliché 진부한   Follow your gut. 네 직감을 따라.   benefit 이익, 이로움
work one's way 노력하며 나아가다

정답 have something | nothing to do with | It doesn't hurt to | used to | used to

UNIT 11

be about to + 동사원형

막 ~하려는 참이다, ~할 예정이다

이 패턴은 곧 일어날 일을 표현할 때 사용해요. 예를 들어, 곧 집을 나가려고 한다면 I'm about to leave the house, 이제 막 버스를 타려고 한다면 I'm about to get on the bus, 영화가 곧 시작하려고 한다면 The movie is about to start.라고 말하면 돼요. 또한 이 패턴은 상대적으로 곧 일어날 예정인 미래의 상황을 나타낼 때도 사용돼요. 예를 들어서, 이제 대학 졸업까지 한 학기만 남은 상황에서는 "곧 졸업해."라고 말할 수 있겠죠? 이럴 땐 I'm about to graduate from college.라고 말하면 돼요.

be about to 뒤에는 동사원형을 씁니다.

 The movie **is about to** start.
영화가 곧 시작할 거야.

실생활 대화

A We'd better hurry. The movie is about to start. How much time do we have left?
서두르는 게 좋겠어. 영화가 곧 시작할 거야. 시간 얼마나 남았어?

B It's about to begin. We've only got 5 minutes left. Let's grab some popcorn real quick and head in!
곧 시작할 거야. 5분밖에 안 남았어. 빨리 팝콘 사서 들어가자!

A Oh no, the line for popcorn is so long. Should we skip it?
어휴, 팝콘 줄 너무 길어. 그냥 생략할까?

B You're right. We're about to miss the opening scene. Let's just go in and enjoy the movie.
그래. 시작 장면 놓치겠어. 그냥 들어가서 영화 보자.

---

had better ~하는 게 좋겠다(강한 충고나 경고의 뉘앙스)   **real quick** (구어) 아주 잠깐만, 금방   **head in** 들어가다
skip 건너뛰다, 생략하다, (학교나 수업을) 빼먹다

PRACTICE 패턴 활용

문장을 써 보고 음원을 들으며 소리 내어 말하세요. 제시어 중 기본형 동사는 패턴에 맞게 바꾸고, 제시어의 // 앞까지만이라도 완성해 말하세요.

▶ 정답 307쪽

- **공항으로 막 떠나려던 참이야.** I / leave / for the airport
  I'm about to leave for the airport.

1 **막 아침 먹으려던 참이야.** I / eat breakfast

2 **이제 설거지를 하려던 참이야.** I / do the dishes

3 **막 나가려는 참인데, 뭐 필요한 거 있어?** I / leave // do you need anything

4 **그녀에게 곧 프로포즈를 할 거야. 심장이 터질 것 같아.**
   I / propose to her // my heart feels like it's going to explode

5 **버스가 곧 출발해. 서둘러!** the bus / leave / hurry up

6 **공연이 곧 시작됩니다. 자리에 앉아 주세요.** the show / begin // please take your seats

7 **비행기가 곧 착륙합니다. 안전벨트를 매 주세요.** the plane / land // please fasten your seatbelt

8 **우리 지금 저녁 먹으러 나가려던 참이야. 같이 갈래?** `응용`
   we / head out / for dinner // do you want to come

do the dishes 설거지를 하다   explode 폭발하다, 터지다   land 착륙하다
fasten one's seatbelt 안전벨트를 매다   head out 나가다, 출발하다

영화가 곧 시작할 거야.

주어 + be about to + 동사원형
  └─ The movie is ─┘   └─ start ─┘

UNIT 12

Do you happen to + 동사원형?
혹시 ~하세요?

일상에서 대화하다 보면 상대방에게 '혹시 ~하세요?'라고 조심스럽게 묻고 싶을 때가 많죠? 예를 들어, "혹시 오늘 시간 있으세요?"처럼 말이죠. 이럴 때 유용하게 쓸 수 있는 패턴이 [Do you happen to + 동사원형?]이에요. 이 패턴은 '우연히 일어난 일'을 강조하면서, 동시에 정중하게 물어볼 때 자주 사용돼요. 예를 들어, 누군가에게 도서관이 어디 있는지 묻고 싶을 때 Do you know where the library is?라고 할 수도 있지만, 여기에 '혹시'라는 뉘앙스를 더해 Do you happen to know where the library is?라고 정중하게 말할 수 있어요.

happen to 뒤에는 동사원형을 씁니다.

 Do you happen to remember where we parked the car?
혹시 우리 차 어디에 주차했는지 기억나요?

[happen to + 동사원형]은 정중하게 물어볼 때뿐만 아니라, 우연히 무언가를 하게 되었을 때도 사용해요. 예를 들어, "우연히 고등학교 때 친구를 카페에서 만났어."는 I happened to meet my friend from high school at a café.라고 하면 돼요. 이처럼 happen to는 '우연히 ~하다, 마침 ~하다'의 뜻으로도 많이 쓰는 표현이에요.

실생활 대화

A **Do you happen to remember where we parked the car?**
혹시 우리 차 어디에 주차했는지 기억나요?

B **I'm drawing a blank. What color was the section we parked in?**
전혀 생각이 안 나요. 우리가 주차한 구역 색깔이 뭐였죠?

A **I think it was red... or maybe green? I'm not sure now.**
빨간색이었던 것 같은데... 아니면 초록색? 잘 모르겠어요.

B **Let's try the red section first. I have a feeling it might be there.**
빨간 구역부터 찾아봐요. 거기일 것 같은 느낌이 들어요.

park the car 차를 주차하다　draw a blank 아무 생각이 나지 않다, 기억이 나지 않다
have a feeling ~한 느낌이 들다, ~할 것 같은 예감이 들다

PRACTICE 패턴 활용

문장을 써 보고 음원을 들으며 소리 내어 말하세요. 제시어 중 기본형 동사는 패턴에 맞게 바꾸고, 제시어의 // 앞까지만이라도 완성해 말하세요.

▶ 정답 307쪽

- 혹시 이번 주말에 시간 되세요? be free / this weekend
  Do you happen to be free this weekend?

1. 혹시 회의 몇 시에 시작하는지 아세요? know what time the meeting starts

2. 혹시 스페인어를 하시나요? 통역이 필요해서요. speak Spanish // we need an interpreter

3. 혹시 제가 잠깐 빌릴 수 있는 충전기 있으세요? have a charger // I could borrow

4. 혹시 우산 가져오셨나요? 비가 올 수도 있을 것 같아요. 응용 bring an umbrella // it looks like it might rain

5. 그는 마침 오늘 저녁 시간 돼요. 응용 he / be free / this evening

6. 마침 티켓이 여분으로 있어요. 하나 드릴까요? 응용 I / have some extra tickets // do you want one

7. 그녀는 마침 거기서 일하는 친구가 있어요. 응용 she / have a friend / who works there

8. 그가 길에서 우연히 이걸 주웠는데, 당신 거예요? 응용 he / find this / on the street // is it yours

interpreter 통역   charger 충전기   look like ~처럼 보이다, ~인 것 같다   extra 여분의

혹시 우리 차 어디에 주차했는지 기억나요?

Do you happen to + 동사원형?

remember where we parked the car

UNIT 13

One of the + 복수명사 + 단수동사

~ 중 하나[한 명]는

이 패턴은 여러 대상 중 하나를 특정할 때 사용해요. 예를 들어, one of the books는 여러 책 중 하나를 의미하고, one of the students는 여러 학생 중 한 명을 의미해요. 이때 one of the 뒤에는 항상 복수명사가 오고, 이 패턴이 주어로 사용될 때는 동사로 단수형을 써요. 예를 들어, One of the students is missing.은 여러 학생 중 한 명이 사라졌다는 뜻이에요.

One of the 뒤에는 항상 복수명사가 오고, 동사는 단수형을 사용합니다.

 One of the dishes is really spicy.
요리 중 하나는 진짜 맵더라.

one of the는 특정 그룹을 나타낼 때 사용되며, one of 뒤에는 the 외에도 my, our, these 같은 소유격이나 한정사를 쓰기도 해요.

실생활 대화

A This place is nice. I like the food.
여기 괜찮다. 음식도 마음에 들어.

B Yeah, but **one of the dishes is really spicy.**
응, 근데 요리 중 하나는 진짜 맵더라.

A Really? I thought everything was mild.
정말? 다 순한 줄 알았는데.

B Try the one with the red sauce. It's really spicy.
빨간 소스 있는 거 먹어 봐. 진짜 매워.

place 장소   spicy 매운   mild 순한

PRACTICE 패턴 활용

문장을 써 보고 음원을 들으며 소리 내어 말하세요. 제시어 중 기본형 동사는 패턴에 맞게 바꾸고,
제시어의 // 앞까지만이라도 완성해 말하세요.

▶ 정답 307쪽

• 학생 중 한 명이 오늘 결석했어요.   students / be absent / today

  One of the students is absent today.

1 케이크 중 하나가 정말 맛있어 보여요.   cakes / look delicious

2 휴대폰 중 하나가 울리고 있어요.   phones / be ringing

3 그 멤버 중 한 명이 한국 사람이에요.   members / be from Korea

4 손님 중 한 명이 땅콩 알레르기가 있어요.   guests / be allergic to peanuts

5 이 동네 개 중에 한 마리가 밤마다 짖어요.   dogs / in this neighborhood / be always barking / at night

6 제가 도서관에서 빌린 책 중 하나가 없어졌는데, 아무리 찾아도 못 찾겠어요. `응용`
books that I borrowed from the library / be missing // and I can't seem to find it anywhere

7 발코니에 있는 식물 중 하나가 상태가 안 좋아서, 물을 더 자주 줘야 할 것 같아요.
plants / on the balcony / be not doing well // so I need to water it more often

8 어제 산 셔츠 중 하나가 안 맞아서 환불받으려고 해요. `응용`
shirts I bought yesterday / doesn't fit me // so I'm going to ask for a refund

---

absent 결석한, 부재중인   **be allergic to** ~에 알레르기가 있다   **I can't seem to** 아무리 해도 ~가 잘 안 되다
water (식물 등에) 물을 주다   **fit** (사이즈가) 꼭 맞다   **ask for a refund** 환불을 요청하다

요리 중 하나는 진짜 맵더라.

One of the + 복수명사 + 단수동사
                     dishes   is really spicy

UNIT 14

There is no such thing as + 명사
~라는 것은 없다, ~는 존재하지 않는다

이 패턴은 어떤 것이 존재하지 않는다는 것을 확실히 말하고 싶을 때 사용해요. 예를 들어, "세상에 귀신이란 건 없어."라고 말하고 싶다면 There is no such thing as ghosts in this world, "완벽한 사람은 없어."라고 말하고 싶다면 There is no such thing as a perfect person, "노력 없이 성공할 수 있는 것은 없어."는 There is no such thing as success without hard work.라고 말하면 돼요.

There is no such thing as 뒤에는 명사를 씁니다.

 There is no such thing as success without failure.
실패 없는 성공이란 건 없어.

실생활 대화

A I want to succeed without failing. Is that possible?
실패 없이 성공하고 싶어. 그게 가능할까?

B I'm sorry, but there is no such thing as success without failure.
미안하지만, 실패 없는 성공이란 건 없어.

A So, failure is inevitable?
그럼 실패는 피할 수 없는 거야?

B Yes. Failure is part of the journey to success.
You learn and grow through failures.
맞아. 실패는 성공으로 가는 길의 일부야. 실패를 통해 배우고 성장하는 거지.

succeed 성공하다   inevitable 피할 수 없는   journey 여정, 여행   grow through failures 실패를 통해 성장하다

PRACTICE 패턴 활용

문장을 써 보고 음원을 들으며 소리 내어 말하세요. 제시어 중 기본형 동사는 패턴에 맞게 바꾸고,
제시어의 // 앞까지만이라도 완성해 말하세요.

▶ 정답 307쪽

- 공짜 점심 같은 건 없어.   a free lunch
  There is no such thing as a free lunch.

1 쉬운 일 같은 건 없어.   an easy job

2 노력 없는 행운 같은 건 없어.   luck without effort

3 살이 빠지는 마법의 약 같은 건 없어.   a magic pill / for weight loss

4 갑작스러운 성공 같은 건 없어   overnight success

5 실수하지 않는 그런 사람은 없어.   someone who never makes mistakes

6 도전이 없는 인생이란 건 없어. 그게 우리가 성장하고 배우는 과정이야.
  a life without challenges // it's how we grow and learn

7 완벽한 타이밍 같은 건 없어. 그냥 행동해야 해.   perfect timing // you just have to take action

8 바보 같은 질문이라는 것은 없어. 모든 질문은 새로운 것을 배울 수 있는 기회야. `응용`
  a stupid question // every question is a chance to learn something new

---

effort 노력   pill 약   weight loss 체중 감량   overnight 하룻밤 사이의, 갑작스러운   challenge 도전, 어려움
take action 조치를 취하다, 행동에 옮기다   stupid 멍청한

실패 없는 성공이란 건 없어.

There is no such thing as + 명사
                        success without failure

UNIT 15

I don't know if you know, but + 절
혹시 아는지(들었는지) 모르겠지만,

이 패턴은 상대방이 어떤 주제에 대해 알지 못할 수도 있다고 가정할 때 사용해요. '아는지 모르겠지만'으로 시작하는 표현이에요. 문장이 길어 보일 수 있지만, 하나의 덩어리로 외워 두고 but 뒤에 말하고 싶은 내용을 절(주어+동사)로 말하면 돼요.

I don't know if you know, but 뒤에는 절(주어+동사)이 옵니다.

 I don't know if you know, but Jihun just got a job at a big company.
혹시 들었는지 모르겠는데, 지훈이가 이번에 대기업에 들어갔대.

I don't know 대신 I'm not sure를 써도 돼요. I don't know는 더 직설적인 느낌이라 회화에서는 좀 더 편한 관계나 캐주얼한 상황에서 사용되죠. 직장에서 상사와 이야기하거나 격식 있는 자리라면 I'm not sure을 써서 더 공손하고 조심스러운 말투를 완성할 수 있어요.

실생활 대화

A How's Jihun doing these days?
지훈이 요즘 어떻게 지내?

B I don't know if you know, but Jihun just got a job at a big company.
혹시 들었는지 모르겠는데, 지훈이가 이번에 대기업에 들어갔대.

A Wow, really? Which company? I should congratulate him.
와, 정말? 어느 회사인데? 지훈이한테 축하 인사 해야겠어.

B It's Google. He's throwing a party next week to celebrate. Do you want to go together?
구글이래. 다음 주에 축하 파티도 한다고 하던데, 같이 갈래?

---
get a job 취직하다 a big company 대기업 congratulate 축하하다 throw a party 파티를 열다
celebrate 축하하다

PRACTICE 패턴 활용

문장을 써 보고 음원을 들으며 소리 내어 말하세요. 제시어 중 기본형 동사는 패턴에 맞게 바꾸고, 제시어의 // 앞까지만이라도 완성해 말하세요. ▶ 정답 307쪽

• 혹시 아는지 모르겠지만, 그 가게는 현금만 받아. that store only takes cash
  I don't know if you know, but that store only takes cash.

1. 너도 아는지 모르겠는데, 우리 학교 근처에 새 카페 생겼어. there's a new café / near our school

2. 혹시 알고 있을지 모르겠는데, 오늘 제이콥 생일이야. it's Jacob's birthday / today

3. 혹시 들었는지 모르겠는데, 에밀리가 지난 주말에 약혼했대. Emily got engaged / last weekend

4. 혹시 아는지 모르겠지만, 사라가 다음 달에 뉴욕으로 이사 간대.
   Sarah is moving to New York / next month

5. 아는지 모르겠지만, 커피 머신이 또 고장 났어. the coffee machine broke down / again

6. 혹시 알고 계신지 모르겠지만, 금요일까지 서류를 제출하셔야 해요. 응용
   you need to submit the form / by Friday

7. 알고 있는지 모르겠지만, 최근에 시내에 새 미술관이 문을 열었어.
   a new art gallery recently opened / downtown

8. 혹시 아시는지 모르겠지만, 여기는 학생 할인을 받으실 수 있어요. 응용
   you can get a student discount / here

---

cash 현금   get engaged 약혼하다   break down 고장 나다, 감정이 무너지다
submit the form 서류를 제출하다   get a discount 할인받다

혹시 들었는지 모르겠는데, 지훈이가 이번에 대기업에 들어갔대.

I don't know if you know, but + 절

Jihun just got a job at a big company

REMINDER 패턴 강화

이제 내 이야기를 해 봐요! 나에게 있음 직한 일들을 적고, 소리 내어 말해 보는 거예요.
주어가 별도로 제시되지 않으면, 주어는 항상 I(나)예요.

▶ 정답 308쪽

UNIT 11 The movie **is about to** start.

> be about to + 동사원형
> 막 ~하려던 참이다, ~할 예정이다

1 막 자려던 참이야.   go to bed

2 막 유튜브를 보려던 참이야.   watch YouTube

3 막 나가려던 참이야.   go out

UNIT 12 **Do you happen to** remember where we parked the car?

> Do you happen to + 동사원형?
> 혹시 ~하세요?

4 혹시 정답 알아요?   know the answer

5 마침 이번 주말에 시간 돼요. 응용   be free this weekend

6 제가 우연히 모든 걸 봤어요. 응용   see everything

UNIT 13 **One of the** dishes is really spicy.

> One of the + 복수명사 + 단수동사
> ~중 하나[한 명]는

7 자동차 중 한 대가 타이어에 펑크가 났어요.   cars / has a flat tire

8   멤버 중 한 명이 늦었어요.   members / is late

9   친구 중 한 명이 해외에 살아요. 응용   my friends / lives abroad

UNIT 14 There is no such thing as success without failure.

> There is no such thing as + 명사
> ~라는 것은 없다, ~는 존재하지 않는다

10   말하는 고양이는 없어.   a talking cat

11   완벽한 자동차는 없어.   a perfect car

12   숙제 없는 학교란 없어.   a homework-free school

UNIT 15 I don't know if you know, but Jihun just got a job at a big company.

> I don't know if you know, but + 절
> 혹시 아는지(들었는지) 모르겠지만,

13   혹시 알고 있는지 모르겠는데, 온라인으로 예약을 취소할 수 있어.
    you can cancel the reservation online

14   혹시 알고 있는지 모르겠는데, 이곳 주차는 무료가 아니야.
    parking here is not free

15   혹시 알고 계신지 모르겠는데, 미리 회의실을 예약하실 수 있어요. 응용
    you can book the meeting room in advance

REMINDER 맥락 적용

이제 앞에서 연습한 패턴을 실생활 대화 맥락에 적용해 보세요. 패턴을 일상적인 대화에 넣어서 직접 소리 내어 말해 보는 거예요. 빈칸에 들어갈 말이 기억이 나지 않는다면 다시 앞으로 가서 확인해 보세요.

UNIT 11

A Something smells amazing! What are you cooking?
냄새 정말 좋다! 뭐 만들어?

B I've made your favorite pasta. I'm _____ serve dinner, so hurry up and take a seat at the table.
네가 제일 좋아하는 파스타. 이제 막 저녁 차리려던 참이니까 얼른 식탁에 앉아.

A Wow, that's so sweet of you! Thank you! Can I help with anything?
와, 정말 감동이야! 고마워! 내가 뭐 도울까?

B Thanks, but I'm _____ finish up. Just sit down and relax. Dinner will be ready in a minute.
고맙지만 거의 다 됐어. 그냥 앉아서 쉬어. 곧 저녁 준비 끝나.

UNIT 12

A Did you _____ clean your room before the guests arrived?
혹시 손님들 도착 전에 네 방 청소했니?

B Yes, mom, I did! It's spotless now.
네, 엄마, 했어요! 이제 완전 깨끗해요.

A Thank you for your help! Let's try to keep our place neat and tidy.
도와줘서 고마워! 우리 집 계속 깔끔하게 유지하자.

B Okay! Look, it makes a big difference, doesn't it?
알겠어요! 이거 보세요, 차이가 확실히 나죠?

UNIT 13

A Where are you planning to go for your next vacation?
다음 휴가 때 어디로 갈 생각이에요?

B I want to go to _____ countries I've never visited.
한 번도 가본 적 없는 나라 중에서 하나 가고 싶어요.

A That sounds really interesting! Which country are you thinking of?
정말 재밌네요! 어느 나라를 생각하는데요?

B I'm considering Japan or Italy.
일본이나 이탈리아를 고려 중이에요.

UNIT 14

A Your marriage looks so perfect. How do you make it work?
너희 결혼생활은 정말 완벽해 보여. 어떻게 그렇게 유지할 수 있어?

B Actually, ███████████████████████████ a perfect relationship. We put in a lot of effort.
사실, 완벽한 관계라는 건 없어. 우리도 많이 노력해.

A But you two seem to get along so well.
그래도 너희 부부는 정말 잘 지내는 것처럼 보여.

B True. We try to understand each other and work together to solve problems when they arise.
맞아. 서로를 이해하려고 노력하고, 문제가 생기면 같이 해결하려고 해.

UNIT 15

A Do you want to work out this evening?
오늘 저녁에 운동하러 갈까?

B ███████████████████████████, but your favorite trainer is on vacation starting this week.
혹시 아는지 모르겠지만, 네가 좋아하는 트레이너가 이번 주부터 휴가래.

A Oh, really? Should we try working out with another trainer? Or just go by ourselves?
아, 그래? 그럼 다른 트레이너랑 운동해 볼까? 아니면 그냥 우리끼리 할까?

B Working out by ourselves sounds good too. We can also look for new workout routines.
우리끼리 하는 것도 좋겠다. 새로운 운동 루틴도 찾아보고.

어휘   spotless 티끌 하나 없는   neat and tidy 깔끔하고 정돈된   arise (일이) 발생하다

정답   about to, about to | happen to | one of the | there is no such thing as |
       I don't know if you know

UNIT 16

I just want to let you know (that) + 절

참고로 ~라는 걸 알려 주고 싶다

이 패턴은 상대방에게 부담 없이 정보를 전달할 때 사용해요. 예를 들어, 친구에게 가볍게 "내일이 내 생일이야."라고 말하고 싶다면, I just want to let you know that tomorrow is my birthday.라고 할 수 있어요. 정보를 좀 더 진지하게 전달하고 싶을 때는 just를 생략하고 I want to let you know로 시작할 수 있어요. 예를 들어, "당신이 열심히 공부하는 것이 너무 자랑스럽다고 말하고 싶어요."는 I want to let you know that I'm really proud of how hard you're studying.이라고 말할 수 있어요.

I just want to let you know (that) 뒤에는 주어와 동사로 이루어진 절을 씁니다.

 I just want to let you know that there's an orange sweater in the closet.
참고로 옷장에 주황색 스웨터가 있어.

실생활 대화

A Have you seen my blue sweater? I can't find it anywhere.
내 파란색 스웨터 봤어? 아무리 찾아도 없네.

B I put it in the laundry basket. It had a stain.
내가 빨래 바구니에 넣어 뒀어. 얼룩이 있더라고.

A Oh, really? I didn't know, thanks.
Do you think the stain will come out?
정말? 몰랐네, 고마워. 그 얼룩 지워질까?

B Don't worry. I pre-treated it with a stain remover. It should come out in the wash. Also, I just want to let you know that there's an orange sweater you can wear instead in the closet.
걱정 마. 얼룩 제거제를 미리 발라 놨어. 세탁하면 깨끗해질 거야.
참고로 옷장에 대신 입을 수 있는 주황색 스웨터가 있어.

---

laundry basket 빨래 바구니   stain 얼룩   come out (얼룩이) 빠지다, 나오다   pre-treat (얼룩 등을) 미리 처리하다
stain remover 얼룩 제거제   instead 대신에

PRACTICE 패턴 활용

문장을 써 보고 음원을 들으며 소리 내어 말하세요. 제시어 중 기본형 동사는 패턴에 맞게 바꾸고, 제시어의 // 앞까지만이라도 완성해 말하세요.

▶ 정답 308쪽

• 우리는 네가 자랑스럽다는 거 말해 주고 싶어.   we're proud of you

  I just want to let you know that we're proud of you.

1. 네가 오늘 정말 잘했다는 말 하고 싶어.   you did a great job / today

2. 네 택배가 도착했다고 알려 주려고.   your package arrived

3. 7시에 예약해 뒀다는 거 알려 주려고.   I made a reservation / for 7 PM

4. 참고로 오늘 조금 늦을 것 같아.   I'll be a little late / today

5. 네 발표가 정말 인상적이었다는 걸 알려 주고 싶어.   your presentation was impressive

6. 참고로 휴게실에 커피가 떨어졌어.   we're out of coffee / in the break room

7. 참고로 네가 음악에 대한 감각이 뛰어나다는 걸 말해 주고 싶어.   you have an ear for music

8. 그건 그렇고, 아이들이 당신을 많이 보고 싶어 한다는 걸 알려 주고 싶어요. 〔응용〕
   by the way / the kids miss you / a lot

---

do a great job 잘 해내다   package 소포, 꾸러미; 포장하다   make a reservation for (+ 시간) ~시로 예약하다
presentation 발표   be out of ~이 떨어지다, ~이 없다
have an ear for (음악, 언어 감각 등)에 대해 듣는 귀가 있다, ~을 잘 알아듣다   by the way 그건 그렇고
miss 그리워하다; 놓치다

참고로 옷장에 주황색 스웨터가 있어.

I just want to let you know that + 절

there's an orange sweater in the closet

UNIT 17

I'll assume (that) + 절
~라고 생각하고 [알고] 있을 것이다

이 패턴은 대화가 모호하게 끝나거나, 상대방의 대답이 불확실한 상황에서 '그럼 ~로 알고 있을게요'라며 다시 상기시켜 줄 때 사용하는 표현이에요. 동사 assume은 '~라고 추정하다, ~라고 생각하다'라는 의미로, 상대방의 의도를 확신할 수 없을 때 사용해요. 예를 들어, 상대방이 약속 장소를 정하지 않고 대화를 끝낸 상황이라면 I'll assume that we're meeting at the usual place. (우리가 늘 만나던 곳에서 만나는 걸로 알고 있을게요.)라고 말할 수 있어요. 또 다른 예로는 어떤 계획에 대해 의견을 나누다가 상대방에게 I'll assume that you're okay with the plan. (그 계획이 괜찮으신 걸로 알고 있을게요.)라고 말할 수 있어요.

I'll assume (that) 뒤에는 주어와 동사가 포함된 절이 옵니다.

 I'll assume that you're coming unless I hear otherwise.
따로 연락이 없으면 오시는 걸로 알고 있을게요.

실생활 대화

A Are you coming to the meeting tomorrow?
내일 회의에 오실 거예요?

B I'm not sure yet. I'll have to check my schedule.
아직 확실하지 않네요. 일정을 확인해 봐야 해요.

A Okay, I'll assume that you're coming unless I hear otherwise.
알겠습니다. 따로 연락이 없으면 오시는 걸로 알고 있을게요.

B Thanks, I'll be sure to let you know if I can't make it.
네, 고마워요. 못 가게 되면 꼭 알려 드릴게요.

check one's schedule 일정을 확인하다   hear otherwise 다르게 듣다, 다르게 전해 듣다

PRACTICE 패턴 활용

문장을 써 보고 음원을 들으며 소리 내어 말하세요. 제시어 중 기본형 동사는 패턴에 맞게 바꾸고, 제시어의 // 앞까지만이라도 완성해 말하세요. ▶ 정답 308쪽

• 관심이 없는 걸로 이해할게요. you're not interested
  I'll assume that you're not interested.

1 오후 3시에 시간 되시는 걸로 할게요. you're available / at 3 PM

2 제 메시지 받으신 걸로 알고 있을게요. you received my message

3 바쁘신 걸로 생각하고 나중에 다시 연락할게요. you're busy / and check back later

4 이번 주말에 가족 여행 가는 걸로 알고 있을게요. we're going on a family trip / this weekend

5 당신이 매운 음식을 잘 먹는 걸로 알고 있을게요. you can handle spicy food

6 제 계획에 동의하시는 걸로 알고 있을게요. you agree with my plan

7 무언가 변경되면 알려 주시는 걸로 알고 있을게요. you'll let me know // if anything changes

8 별말 없으셨으니 이번 주말에 당신이 시간이 있는 걸로 알고 있을게요. 응용
  you're free / this weekend // since you haven't said otherwise

---

interested 관심이 있는   available (사람들을 만날) 시간이 있는   check back 다시 연락하다
go on a family trip 가족 여행을 가다   agree with ~에 동의하다   otherwise 다르게; 그렇지 않으면

오시는 걸로 알고 있을게요.

I'll assume that + 절
            └ you're coming

UNIT 18

There is no need to + 동사원형

~할 필요가 없다, ~ 안 해도 괜찮다

이 패턴은 어떤 일이 필요 없다는 것을 표현할 때 사용해요. 예를 들어, 걱정할 필요가 없을 때는 There is no need to worry, 서두를 필요가 없을 때는 There is no need to hurry.라고 말할 수 있어요.

There is no need to 뒤에는 동사원형을 사용하여 필요하지 않은 행동을 나타냅니다.

 There is no need to bring one.
가져갈 필요 없어.

일상생활에서 말하는 내용에 더 확실성을 부여하고 싶을 때는 [there is no need to + 동사원형] 앞에 I'm telling you를 붙여서 말해요. I'm telling you, there is no need to worry.라고 하면 "걱정할 거 진짜 하나도 없어."라는 뜻의 강한 어조가 돼요.

실생활 대화

A Should we bring a gift to the housewarming party?
집들이에 선물 가져가야 할까?

B There's no need to bring one.
Logan specifically said not to bring anything.
가져갈 필요 없어. 로건이 분명히 아무것도 가져오지 말라고 했어.

A Are you sure? I feel a bit awkward going empty-handed.
정말? 빈손으로 가는 게 좀 어색할 것 같은데.

B Come to think of it, you're right.
Let's buy the bottle of wine that Logan likes.
생각해 보니 네 말이 맞는 것 같아. 로건이 좋아하는 와인 한 병 사 가자.

---

housewarming party 집들이 파티   specifically 구체적으로, 명확히   awkward 어색한, 불편한
go empty-handed 빈손으로 가다   come to think of it 그러고 보니, 생각해 보니

PRACTICE 패턴 활용

문장을 써 보고 음원을 들으며 소리 내어 말하세요. 제시어 중 기본형 동사는 패턴에 맞게 바꾸고, 제시어의 // 앞까지만이라도 완성해 말하세요.

▶ 정답 308쪽

- 아무것도 가져올 필요 없어. 다 준비돼 있어.　　　bring anything // everything's ready

  There is no need to bring anything. Everything's ready.

1 서두를 필요 없어. 가는 데 시간이 충분하니까.　　　hurry // we have plenty of time to get there

2 택시를 부를 필요 없어. 내가 집까지 데려다 줄게.　　　call a taxi // I can give you a ride home

3 꾸미지 않아도 괜찮아. 그냥 친구들과의 편한 모임이니까.
   get dolled up // it's just a casual get-together with friends

4 선물에 많은 돈을 쓸 필요 없어. 중요한 건 마음이야.
   spend so much on a gift // it's the thought that counts

5 그렇게 돈을 많이 쓸 필요 없어. 〔응용〕　　　spend that much money

6 그거 가지고 스트레스 받을 필요 없어, 진짜. 〔응용〕　　　stress over it

7 정말 사과할 필요 없어. 네 잘못 아니야. 〔응용〕　　　apologize // it wasn't your fault

8 정말 남이랑 비교할 필요 없어. 〔응용〕　　　compare yourself to others

---

have plenty of time 시간이 넉넉하다　　give ~ a ride ~를 태워주다　　get dolled up 예쁘게 꾸미다, 멋 부리다
get-together 모임, 친목회　　count 중요하다　　stress over ~ 때문에 스트레스를 받다　　apologize 사과하다
compare A to B A를 B에 비교[비유]하다

가져갈 필요 없어.

There is no need to + 동사원형
　　　　　　　　　　　bring one

UNIT 19

No offense, but + 절

기분 나쁘게 할 의도는 아니지만,

이 패턴은 상대방의 기분이 상할 수 있는 말을 해야 하는 상황에서 '기분 나쁘게 할 의도는 아닌데…'라는 뉘앙스를 주면서 말을 하고 싶을 때 사용해요. 주로 솔직한 의견을 전달하거나 상대방이 불편할 수도 있는 말을 덧붙일 때 쓰죠. 예를 들어, 소셜 미디어에 시간을 낭비하는 친구에게 "기분 나쁘게 할 의도는 아닌데, 너 소셜 미디어에 너무 많은 시간을 쓰는 것 같아."라고 말하고 싶을 때 No offense, but I think you're spending too much time on social media.라고 할 수 있어요.

No offense, but 뒤에는 주어와 동사를 포함한 절이 옵니다.

 No offense, but I don't think it looks great on you.
기분 나쁘게 듣진 마. 그거 너한테 안 어울리는 것 같아.

좀 더 부드럽게 표현하고 싶다면 I don't mean to offend you, but... 혹은 I hope this doesn't come off the wrong way, but...과 같은 표현을 사용할 수 있어요.

실생활 대화

A Do you like my new shirt?
내 새 셔츠 어때?

B No offense, but I don't think it looks great on you.
기분 나쁘게 듣진 마. 그거 너한테 안 어울리는 것 같아.

A Really? I thought it looked pretty stylish.
정말? 나는 꽤 멋지다고 생각했는데.

B The color just doesn't go well with your skin tone.
Maybe try a different shade?
그 색이 네 피부 톤이랑은 잘 안 어울려. 다른 색 계열 한번 입어보는 건 어때?

stylish 세련된, 멋진　go well with ~와 조화롭다　skin tone 피부색　shade 색조, 그늘

PRACTICE 패턴 활용

문장을 써 보고 음원을 들으며 소리 내어 말하세요. 제시어 중 기본형 동사는 패턴에 맞게 바꾸고,
제시어의 // 앞까지만이라도 완성해 말하세요.

▶ 정답 308쪽

- **미안한데, 이 케이크는 내 스타일이 아니야.**　　　　　　　this cake is not my cup of tea

  No offense, but this cake is not my cup of tea.

1. **기분 나쁘게 하려는 건 아닌데, 내 생각은 조금 달라.**　　　I see it a bit differently

2. **기분 나빠하지 말고 들어. 네가 과잉 반응하는 것 같아.**　　I think you're overreacting

3. **기분 나쁘게 듣지 말고, 솔직히 이 수프는 별로야.**　　　I honestly don't like this soup

4. **기분 나쁘게 듣지 마. 난 피자에 파인애플은 진짜 별로야.**　I really don't like pineapple / on pizza

5. **기분 나쁘게 듣지 마. 너 글씨 정말 읽기 힘들어.**　　　your handwriting is really hard to read

6. **기분 나쁘게 듣진 말고, 그 옷은 좀 과한 것 같아.**　　　I just think that outfit is a bit too much

7. **기분 나쁘게 들릴 수도 있지만, 네 발표는 좀 지루했어.**　your presentation was a bit boring

8. **제 말 오해하지 말았으면 좋겠어요. 이 점에 대해서는 동의하기 어려워요.** 응용
   I find it hard to agree with you / on this

---

cup of tea 기호에 맞는 것, 취향　　a bit (구어) 다소, 약간　　differently 다르게　　overreact 과잉 반응하다
handwriting 손글씨, 필체　　boring 지루한　　find it hard to ~하는 것이 어렵다고 느끼다

기분 나쁘게 듣진 마. 그거 너한테 안 어울리는 것 같아.

No offense, but + 절

I don't think it looks great on you

UNIT 20

It's not like you to + 동사원형
~하는 건 너답지 않다

이 패턴은 상대방이 평소 행동이나 성격과 다른 행동을 할 때 사용해요. 예를 들어, 지각을 하지 않았던 친구가 갑자기 지각을 한다면 "네가 늦다니 평소답지 않아."라고 말을 할 수 있겠죠? 그때 이 패턴을 사용해 It's not like you to be late.라고 말하면 돼요. 또는 매일 아침을 먹던 친구가 갑자기 아침을 먹지 않을 때도 이 패턴을 활용하여 You usually don't skip breakfast. It's not like you to skip breakfast. Is everything okay? (평소에 아침을 거르지 않잖아. 너답지 않은데, 무슨 일 있어?)"라고 물어볼 수 있어요.

It's not like you to 뒤에는 상대방의 평소 행동과 다른 행동을 나타내는 동사원형을 씁니다.

 It's not like you to skip lunch.
점심을 거르다니 너답지 않네.

실생활 대화

A I noticed you didn't eat lunch today.
오늘 점심 안 먹은 거 같던데.

B Yeah, I skipped lunch. I've been busy.
응, 건너뛰었어. 오늘 진짜 바빴어.

A It's not like you to skip lunch. That's not good for your health though. How about I get you a sandwich?
점심을 거르다니 평소 너답지 않네. 건강에 안 좋은데. 내가 샌드위치라도 사다 줄까?

B Wow, that would be great.
I don't normally need help, but today I really do.
와, 그럼 진짜 고맙지. 내가 보통은 그러지 않지만, 오늘은 도움이 필요해.

---

skip (일을) 거르다, 빼먹다   normally 평소에, 보통은

PRACTICE 패턴 활용

문장을 써 보고 음원을 들으며 소리 내어 말하세요. 제시어 중 기본형 동사는 패턴에 맞게 바꾸고, 제시어의 // 앞까지만이라도 완성해 말하세요.

▶ 정답 309쪽

- 늦는 건 평소 너답지 않아.   be late

  It's not like you to be late.

1. 수업 빠지는 건 너답지 않아.   miss class

2. 이렇게 조용한 건 너답지 않아.   be this quiet

3. 중요한 걸 잊는 건 너답지 않아.   forget something important

4. 사소한 일로 화내는 건 너답지 않아.   get angry over something small

5. 회의 중에 말을 많이 안 하더군요. 평소답지 않게 조용하던데, 무슨 걱정 있어요? 〔응용〕
   you haven't said much during the meeting / be quiet // do you have any concerns

6. 저희 곧 결정을 내려야 해요. 당신이 우유부단한 건 평소답지 않은데, 무엇 때문에 망설이나요? 〔응용〕
   we need to make a decision soon / be indecisive // what's holding you back

7. 최근에 운동을 안 하는 것 같아요. 당신이 운동을 거르는 건 평소답지 않은데, 무슨 일 있어요? 〔응용〕
   it seems like you haven't been exercising lately / skip workouts // is everything okay

8. 몇 시간 동안 메시지를 안 보는 건 평소 너답지 않은데, 괜찮아?
   ignore messages / for hours // are you okay

---

get angry over ~에 화를 내다   concern 걱정, 우려   make a decision 결정을 내리다   indecisive 우유부단한
hold back (행동을) 망설이다, (감정 등을) 억누르다, 참다   lately 요즘, 최근에   ignore 무시하다

점심을 거르다니 너답지 않네.

It's not like you to + 동사원형
                 skip lunch

65

REMINDER 패턴 강화

이제 내 이야기를 해 봐요! 나에게 있음 직한 일들을 적고, 소리 내어 말해 보는 거예요. 주어가 별도로 제시되지 않으면, 주어는 항상 I(나)예요.

▶ 정답 309쪽

UNIT 16 **I just want to let you know that** there's an orange sweater in the closet.

> I just want to let you know (that) + 절
> 참고로 ~라는 걸 알려 주고 싶다

1 참고로 우유가 다 떨어졌어.   we ran out of milk

2 미팅이 취소됐다는 것을 알려 주고 싶어.   the meeting has been canceled

3 저녁이 준비되었다는 걸 알려 주고 싶어.   dinner is ready

UNIT 17 **I'll assume that** you're coming unless I hear otherwise.

> I'll assume (that) +절
> ~라고 생각하고[알고] 있을 것이다

4 다 잘 진행됐다고 알고 있을게요.   everything went well

5 당신이 이미 알고 있는 걸로 생각할게요.   you already know about it

6 당신이 더 이상 도움이 필요하지 않다는 걸로 알고 있을게요.
   you no longer need help

UNIT 18 **There is no need to** bring one.

> There is no need to + 동사원형
> ~할 필요가 없다, ~ 안 해도 괜찮다

7 설명할 필요 없어.   explain

8 속상해할 필요 없어.   get upset

9 긴장할 필요 없어.   be nervous

UNIT 19 **No offense, but** I don't think it looks great on you.

> No offense, but + 절
> 기분 나쁘게 할 의도는 아니지만,

10 기분 나쁘게 들릴 수도 있지만, 오늘 좀 정신 없어 보여.
   you seem a bit distracted today

11 기분 나쁘게 듣지 말고, 그건 좀 더 좋은 말투로 말할 수 있어.
   there is a better way to say that

12 기분 나빠하지 말고 들어. 이 영화 좀 지루해.   this movie is kind of boring

UNIT 20 **It's not like you to** skip lunch.

> It's not like you to + 동사원형
> ~하는 건 너답지 않다

13 답장하지 않는 건 너답지 않아.   not reply

14 차갑게 구는 건 너답지 않아.   act distant

15 늦게 온 건 너답지 않아.   show up late

REMINDER 맥락 적용

이제 앞에서 연습한 패턴을 실생활 대화 맥락에 적용해 보세요. 패턴을 일상적인 대화에 넣어서 직접 소리 내어 말해 보는 거예요. 빈칸에 들어갈 말이 기억이 나지 않는다면 다시 앞으로 가서 확인해 보세요.

UNIT 16

A Mom, can I go to the mall with my friends this weekend?
   엄마, 주말에 친구들이랑 쇼핑몰에 가도 돼요?

B Sure, but I just want to _____ that we have a family lunch on Sunday. Don't forget about it.
   그래, 가도 되는데, 참고로 일요일에 가족 점심식사가 있다. 잊지 마.

A Okay. I'll go to the mall on Saturday. What are we having for lunch on Sunday?
   알겠어요. 쇼핑몰은 토요일에 갈 거예요. 일요일 점심에 뭐 먹어요?

B Grandma is coming over, and she's making bulgogi—your favorite, right?
   할머니가 오셔서 불고기 해 주신대. 네가 제일 좋아하는 음식이잖니?

UNIT 17

A Would you like to come to my birthday party at my place tomorrow?
   내일 저희 집에서 하는 생일 파티에 올래요?

B Hmm... I might have plans, but I'm not sure.
   음... 약속이 있었던 것 같은데, 확실하지 않지만요.

A Okay. _____ that you're coming for now. Just text me if you can't make it.
   알겠어요. 일단 오시는 거로 알고 있을게요. 안 되면 문자 주세요.

B Sure, I'll check and let you know as soon as I can.
   네, 확인해 보고 최대한 빨리 알려 줄게요.

UNIT 18

A Are you sure you want to buy a new car? Your current car seems to be in good shape.
   정말 새 차를 사고 싶어? 지금 차도 괜찮아 보이는데.

B It may look fine on the outside, but the engine breaks down quite often, so I think it's time to replace it.
   겉보기에는 괜찮아 보이는데, 엔진이 너무 자주 고장 나서 바꿔야 할 것 같아.

A That sounds right, but have you considered the maintenance costs?
   그럴 수 있겠네. 근데 새 차 유지비는 고려해 봤어?

B Yes, I have. _____ to worry. I've done my research.
   응, 했지. 걱정할 필요 없어. 다 알아봤으니까.

UNIT 19

A How was the movie I recommended?
내가 추천한 영화 어땠어?

B _____, but I found it a bit predictable.
기분 나빠 하지 말고 들어. 영화가 좀 뻔했어.

A Oh, really? I thought the plot twists by the end were quite surprising.
그래? 나는 결말에서 반전이 꽤 놀라웠다고 생각했는데.

B I guess we have different tastes.
우린 취향이 다른가 봐.

UNIT 20

A Did you forget about the meeting?
회의 깜빡한 거야?

B I'm sorry. _____ me to forget things.
미안해. 나 원래 이런 거 안 잊어버리는데.

A It's okay, everyone makes mistakes. But is everything alright? You seem a bit overwhelmed lately.
괜찮아, 누구나 실수할 수 있지. 근데 무슨 일 있어? 요즘 좀 정신없어 보이는데.

B Actually, I've been swamped with work recently. Normally I'd manage it better, but this time I think I could use some help.
사실 요즘 일이 너무 많아. 평소 같으면 잘해 냈을 텐데, 이번엔 도움을 좀 받았으면 해.

어휘 current 현재의   be in good shape 때깔이 좋다   maintenance cost 유지비   do research 조사를 하다
predictable 뻔한   plot twist 반전   have different tastes 취향이 다르다   overwhelmed 압도된
be swamped with work 일에 치이다

정답 let you know | I'll assume | There's no need | No offense | It's not like

REMINDER 패턴 정착

앞에서 배운 20개 패턴을 머릿속에 새기는 시간이에요.
문장을 보고 패턴을 이용해 영어로 소리 내어 말해 보세요.

1　　네가 메뉴 골라.

2　　난 지금 피자가 너무 당겨.

3　　영어는 잘하는데, 다른 말은 그냥 그럭저럭해.

4　　이제 자야 할 시간이야.

5　　얼른 그 사람 다시 보고 싶다.

6　　고백할 게 있어.

7　　난 관련 없는데.

8　　한번 시도해 봐서 나쁠 건 없지.

9　　예전엔 영어로 된 영화 많이 봤어요.

10　　일찍 일어나는 데 익숙해요.

11　　영화가 곧 시작할 거야.

12　　혹시 우리 차 어디에 주차했는지 기억나요?

13　　요리 중 하나는 진짜 맵더라.

14　　실패 없는 성공이란 건 없어.

15　　혹시 들었는지 모르겠는데, 지훈이가 이번에 대기업에 들어갔대.

16　　참고로 옷장에 주황색 스웨터가 있어.

17　　따로 연락이 없으면 오시는 걸로 알고 있을게요.

18　　가져갈 필요 없어.

19　　기분 나쁘게 듣진 마. 그거 너한테 안 어울리는 것 같아.

20　　점심을 거르다니 평소 너답지 않네.

UNIT 21

be sorry for + 동명사[명사]

~해서 미안하다

이 패턴은 사과할 때 사용하는데, for 뒤에는 보통 사과에 대한 이유가 들어가요. 예를 들어, "늦어서 미안해."라고 말하고 싶다면 I'm sorry for being late, "불편을 끼쳐서 미안해."라고 말하고 싶다면 I'm sorry for the inconvenience, "실수해서 미안해."라고 말하고 싶다면 I'm sorry for the mistake.라고 하면 돼요.

be sorry for 뒤에는 사과의 이유를 나타내는 동명사(-ing)나 명사를 씁니다.

 I'm sorry for not calling you.
전화 안 해서 미안해요.

조금 더 공식적인 상황에서 격식을 갖춰 사과를 한다면 동사 apologize를 써서 [apologize for + 동명사/명사] 패턴을 사용해요. 우리말로 '~해서 죄송합니다' 정도로 해석할 수 있겠지요.

실생활 대화

A Why didn't you call me last night?
왜 어젯밤에 전화 안 했어요?

B **I'm sorry for not calling you.** I was really busy.
전화 안 해서 미안해요. 너무 바빴어요.

A I was worried sick. You could have at least sent a text.
정말 걱정했잖아요. 적어도 문자라도 보냈으면 좋았을 텐데.

B You're right, I should have. **I'm really sorry for making you worry.**
당신 말이 맞아요. 그렇게 했어야 했는데, 걱정시켜서 정말 미안해요.

---

be worried sick (구어) 걱정돼 죽을 지경이다　**at least** 적어도

PRACTICE 패턴 활용

문장을 써 보고 음원을 들으며 소리 내어 말하세요. 제시어 중 기본형 동사는 패턴에 맞게 바꾸고, 제시어의 // 앞까지만이라도 완성해 말하세요.

▶ 정답 309쪽

- **어제 전화를 못 받아서 미안해요.**　　　　　　　　　　　　　　I / not answer your call / yesterday
  I'm sorry for not answering your call yesterday.

1. **우유 사오는 걸 깜빡해서 미안해요. 지금 당장 가게에 다녀올게요.**
   I / forget to buy milk // I'll go to the store right now

2. **회의에 늦어서 죄송해요. 다시는 이런 일이 없을 거예요.**
   I / be late / to the meeting // it won't happen again

3. **전화를 못 받아서 미안해요. 회의 중이라 받을 수 없었어요.**
   I / miss your call // I was in a meeting and couldn't answer

4. **스웨터를 물어보지도 않고 빌려 입어서 미안해요. 내일 세탁해서 돌려 줄게요.**
   I / borrow your sweater without asking // I'll wash it and return it tomorrow

5. **기다리게 해서 죄송합니다.** 응용　　　　　　　　　　　　　　　　　　　we / make you wait

6. **그들은 갑자기 취소한 걸 미안해하고 있어요.** 응용　　　　　　　they / cancel / at the last minute

7. **그는 당신에게 전화 못 해서 미안해하고 있어요.** 응용　　　　　　　　　　he / not call you back

8. **그녀가 어젯밤 당신 파티에 못 간 거 미안해하고 있어요. 몸이 안 좋아서 분위기 망치고 싶지 않았대요.** 응용
   she / miss your party / last night // she wasn't feeling well // and didn't want to ruin the mood

without asking 물어보지 않고　　at the last minute 막판에　　make someone wait 누군가를 기다리게 하다
ruin the mood 분위기를 망치다

전화 안 해서 미안해요.

주어 + be sorry for + 동명사
　I'm　　　　　　not calling you

UNIT 22

promise to + 동사원형

꼭 ~하겠다, ~할 것을 약속하다

이 패턴은 어떤 일을 약속할 때 사용해요. 예를 들어, 직전에 나온 패턴 I'm sorry for 와 연결해서 "이번에 못 도와줘서 미안해. 다음번에는 꼭 도와줄게."라고 말하고 싶다면 I'm sorry for not helping you this time. I promise to help you next time. "다음번에는 늦지 않겠다고 약속해."라고 말하고 싶다면 I promise to be on time next time. 또는 I promise not to be late next time.으로 표현할 수 있어요.

promise to 뒤에 동사원형을 써서 약속하는 행동을 나타냅니다.

 I **promise to** be there on time.
꼭 제시간에 갈게.

실생활 대화

A I'm planning to do some deep cleaning this weekend. Can you help me?
이번 주말에 대청소할 건데, 좀 도와줄 수 있을까?

B Of course. What time should I come?
당연하지. 몇 시쯤 가면 돼?

A How about Saturday at 10 AM?
토요일 오전 10시 괜찮아?

B Sounds good. I promise to be there on time.
좋아. 꼭 제시간에 갈게.

---

deep cleaning 대청소   Sounds good. (구어) 좋아, 괜찮아.(동의할 때)   on time 제시간에

PRACTICE 패턴 활용

문장을 써 보고 음원을 들으며 소리 내어 말하세요. 제시어 중 기본형 동사는 패턴에 맞게 바꾸고,
제시어의 // 앞까지만이라도 완성해 말하세요.

▶ 정답 309쪽

- 집에 도착하자마자 바로 꼭 전화할게.   I / call you back // as soon as I get home
  I promise to call you back as soon as I get home.

1. 매일 피아노 연습하겠다고 약속할게.   I / practice the piano / every day

2. 빌린 책 다음 주까지 꼭 돌려줄게.   I / return the book I borrowed / by next week

3. 이번 학기엔 공부를 더 열심히 하겠다고 약속할게.   I / try harder / in my studies / this semester

4. 앞으로는 건강 관리 더 잘하겠다고 약속할게.   I / take better care of my health / from now on

5. 그는 다음에는 더 조심하겠다고 약속했어. `응용`   he / be more careful / next time

6. 그들은 다음번엔 제시간에 도착하겠다고 약속했어. `응용`   they / arrive on time / next time

7. 그녀는 이번 학기에 더 열심히 공부하겠다고 약속했어. `응용`   she / study harder / this semester

8. 회사가 3일 이내에 환불해 주겠다고 약속했어. `응용`   the company / send a refund / within 3 days

practice 연습하다   return 돌려주다   try harder 더 열심히 노력하다   take care of ~를 돌보다
from now on 지금부터   arrive on time 제시간에 도착하다   within ~ 이내에

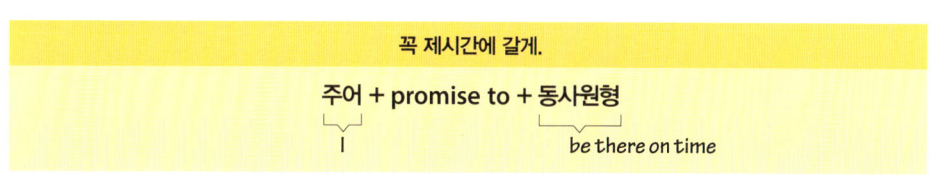

꼭 제시간에 갈게.
주어 + promise to + 동사원형
 I   be there on time

UNIT 23

have no way of + 동명사

~할 방법이 없다

이 패턴은 어떤 해결책이나 다른 방안을 아무리 생각해 봐도 떠오르지 않거나 방법이 없을 때 사용할 수 있는 표현이에요. 예를 들어, 핸드폰이 꺼져서 전화할 방법이 없을 때 I'm sorry that I couldn't call you. I had no way of calling you because my phone died. (전화 못해서 미안해요. 휴대폰이 꺼져서 전화할 방법이 없었어요.)라고 말할 수 있어요.

have no way of 뒤에는 동명사(-ing)를 사용하여 자신이 할 수 없는 행동을 나타냅니다.

 I'm afraid I **have no way of** reaching him.
미안하지만 그에게 연락할 방법이 없어요.

have no way 뒤에 [to + 동사원형]이 올 수도 있어요. 마찬가지로 '~할 방법이 없다'라는 의미예요. 추가로, '~할 방법이 있다'고 할 때는 no를 빼고, [have a way to + 동사원형]의 형태를 사용하면 돼요. 예를 들어, 친구에게 연락할 방법이 있다면 I have a way to reach him.이라고 말할 수 있어요.

실생활 대화

A **Could you contact John for me?**
존에게 연락해 줄 수 있나요?

B **I'm afraid I have no way of reaching him. He changed his number recently.**
미안하지만 그에게 연락할 방법이 없어요. 최근에 번호를 바꿨거든요.

A **I see. Do you know anyone else who might have his new number?**
그렇군요. 혹시 그의 새 번호를 알고 있을 만한 다른 사람은 없나요?

B **I could try asking Sarah. She might have a way to contact him.**
사라에게 물어볼 수 있을 것 같아요. 존에게 연락할 방법을 알고 있을지도요.

reach 연락하다, ~에 이르다, 도달하다   recently 최근에   I could try -ing 내가 ~해 볼 수도 있다

PRACTICE 패턴 활용

문장을 써 보고 음원을 들으며 소리 내어 말하세요. 제시어 중 기본형 동사는 패턴에 맞게 바꾸고, 제시어의 // 앞까지만이라도 완성해 말하세요.

▶ 정답 309쪽

- 지금은 인터넷에 접속할 수 있는 방법이 없어요. I / access the Internet / right now
  I have no way of accessing the Internet right now.

1. 영수증 없이는 환불받을 방법이 없어요. I / get a refund / without the receipt

2. 그가 번호를 바꿔서 연락할 방법이 없어요. I / contact him // since he changed his number

3. 차 없이는 그곳에 갈 방법이 없어요. 진퇴양난에 빠졌어요.
   I / make it to that place / without a car // I'm between a rock and a hard place

4. 창문을 깨지 않는 한 열쇠 없이는 집에 들어갈 방법이 없어요.
   I / enter the house / without my keys // unless I break a window

5. 그는 이번 달에 대출금을 갚을 방법이 없어요. 응용 he / pay back the loan / this month

6. 우리는 그가 어디 갔는지 알 방법이 있어요. 응용 we / know where he went

7. 우리는 누가 선거에서 이길지 알 방법이 없어요. we / know who will win the election

8. 그들은 고객들이 새 제품에 어떻게 반응할지 예측할 방법이 없어요.
   they / predict how customers will react to the new product

---

access the Internet 인터넷에 접속하다   receipt 영수증   contact 연락하다
make it to ~에 도착하다, ~에 참석하다   between a rock and a hard place 진퇴양난에 빠진
enter ~에 들어가다   unless ~하지 않는 한   pay back the loan 대출금을 갚다
win the election 선거에서 이기다   predict 예측하다   react to ~에 반응하다

그에게 연락할 방법이 없어요.

주어 + have no way of + 동명사
  I   reaching him

UNIT 24

That explains why + 절

그래서 ~한 거다

여러분도 이해가 안 되는 부분이 있었는데 어떤 설명을 듣고, "아~ 그래서 그런 거였구나."라고 말할 때가 있죠? 이 패턴은 어떤 상황에 대한 이유를 듣고, 납득이 되었을 때 사용해요. 예를 들어, 친구가 지하철 파업 때문에 지각했다는 것을 알게 되었어요. 그때 "그래서 늦었구나."라고 말할 수 있는데, 이때 That explains why 패턴을 사용해서 That explains why you were late.이라고 말하면 돼요.

That explains why 뒤에는 이유를 주어와 동사가 포함된 절로 나타냅니다.

 That explains why there are so many cars on the road.
그래서 도로에 차가 이렇게 많은 거구나.

실생활 대화

A Why is the traffic so bad today?
오늘 왜 이렇게 교통 체증이 심해?

B There's a big concert downtown.
도심에서 큰 콘서트가 열리고 있어.

A Oh, that explains why there are so many cars on the road.
아, 그래서 도로에 차가 이렇게 많은 거구나.

B Yeah, it's going to be like this all evening.
응, 저녁 내내 이럴 거야.

downtown 시내에   all evening 저녁 내내

PRACTICE 패턴 활용

문장을 써 보고 음원을 들으며 소리 내어 말하세요. 제시어 중 기본형 동사는 패턴에 맞게 바꾸고, 제시어의 // 앞까지만이라도 완성해 말하세요.

▶ 정답 310쪽

• 그래서 그가 메시지에 전혀 답장을 안 했던 거구나.   he hasn't been responding to any messages

  That explains why he hasn't been responding to any messages.

1 A Did you notice that the book is out of print? 그 책이 절판된 거 알았어?
   B 그래서 그렇게 찾기가 어려웠구나.   it's so hard to find

2 A I saw her running again this morning. 오늘 아침에도 그녀가 달리는 걸 봤어.
   B She's training for a marathon. 그녀가 마라톤 준비 중이래.
   A Ah, 그래서 항상 달리기 연습을 하는 거구나.   she's always running

3 A The store is super crowded today! 오늘 그 가게에 사람이 너무 많아!
   B I heard they're having a huge sale. 대규모 세일을 하고 있대.
   A 그래서 오늘 이렇게 사람이 많았던 거야.   it's so crowded / today

4 A John looks really happy today. 존이 오늘 정말 행복해 보여.
   B Yeah, he patched things up with his girlfriend. 응. 여자친구와 화해했나 봐.
   A 그래서 하루 종일 입이 귀에 걸려 있었군.   he's been smiling / ear to ear / all day

5 A Chris hasn't been eating much these days. 크리스는 요즘 거의 안 먹더라.
   B He just got his wisdom teeth removed. 사랑니를 막 뺐대.
   A 그래서 딱딱한 음식은 피했던 거구나.   he's been avoiding solid food

6 A My dad keeps forgetting little things these days. 우리 아빠가 요즘 사소한 걸 자꾸 잊어버리세요.
   B He's been under a lot of stress at work. 요즘 회사에서 스트레스를 엄청 받으신대.
   A 그래서 요즘 그렇게 자꾸 깜빡깜빡 하셨던 거구나.   he's been so forgetful / lately

---

out of print (책이) 절판된   super crowded 매우 붐비는   have a huge sale 대규모 세일을 하다
patch up with ~와 화해하다   smile ear to ear 입이 귀에 걸리다   get ~ removed ~를 제거하다
wisdom tooth 사랑니   be under stress 스트레스를 받다   forgetful 잘 잊는, 건망증이 있는

그래서 도로에 차가 이렇게 많은 거구나.

That explains why + 절
                    ↓
         there are so many cars on the road

79

UNIT 25

The first thing + 주어 + be going to do is + 동사원형

[주어]가 가장 먼저 할 일은 ~이다

이 패턴은 우선 순위를 세울 때, 가장 첫 번째로 할 일을 강조하거나 어떤 행동이 매우 중요하다는 점을 강조하고 싶을 때 사용해요. 예를 들어서, 대학 졸업을 앞두고 친구가 "졸업하면 가장 먼저 뭐 할 거야?" (What is the first thing you are going to do when you graduate?)라고 물으면, "가장 먼저 부모님과 전 세계를 여행할 거야."라고 대답할 수 있겠죠? 그러면 이 패턴을 써서 The first thing I'm going to do is travel around the world with my parents.라고 말할 수 있는 거예요.

is 뒤에는 보통 동사원형이 오고, 그 외에 명사구나 형용사구, 부사구도 올 수 있습니다.

 The first thing I'm going to do is cut out sugar.
내가 제일 먼저 할 일은 설탕을 끊는 거야.

is 뒤에 to부정사를 쓰는 것도 가능하지만, 앞의 do가 동작을 나타내기 때문에 그 뒤에는 자연스럽게 to 없이 동사원형을 써요.

All I did was **ask** a question. 난 그냥 질문만 했을 뿐이야.

What I want to do is **sleep** all day. 내가 하고 싶은 건 하루 종일 자는 거야.

실생활 대화

A Didn't you say you're starting a diet?
다이어트 시작한다고 하지 않았어?

B That's right. **The first thing I'm going to do is cut out sugar.**
맞아. 내가 제일 먼저 할 일은 설탕을 끊는 거야.

A Wow, that won't be easy.
와, 그거 쉽지 않을 텐데.

B I think it's worth trying though.
그래도 해볼 만한 일인 것 같아.

---

cut out sugar 설탕을 끊다   worth trying 시도해 볼 만한

PRACTICE 패턴 활용

문장을 써 보고 음원을 들으며 소리 내어 말하세요. 제시어 중 기본형 동사는 패턴에 맞게 바꾸고, 제시어의 // 앞까지만이라도 완성해 말하세요.

▶ 정답 310쪽

- 제일 먼저 장 보러 갈 거야.   I / go grocery shopping

  The first thing I'm going to do is go grocery shopping.

1. 내가 가장 먼저 할 일은 이메일을 확인하는 거야.   I / check my emails

2. 내가 가장 먼저 할 일은 거실을 페인트칠하는 거야.   I / paint the living room

3. 퇴근 후에 내가 가장 먼저 할 일은 헬스장에 가서 운동하는 거야.
   I / after work / hit the gym / for a workout

4. 비가 그치면 내가 가장 먼저 할 일은 조깅을 하러 나가는 거야.
   I / after the rain dies down / go for a jog

5. 복권에 당첨되면 내가 가장 먼저 할 일은 직장을 그만두는 거야.
   I / after winning the lottery / quit my job

6. 그녀는 몇 달 동안 머리를 안 잘라서 그녀가 제일 먼저 할 일은 머리를 자르는 거야. `응용`
   she / get a haircut // because she hasn't had one in months

7. 결혼식 후 그들이 가장 먼저 할 일은 하와이로 신혼여행을 떠나는 거야. `응용`
   they / after the wedding / fly to Hawaii / for their honeymoon

8. 돈을 절약하기 위해 우리가 가장 먼저 할 일은 외식을 줄이는 거야. `응용`
   we / to save money / cut down on eating out

---

go grocery shopping 장 보러 가다   hit the gym (구어) 헬스장에 가다   die down 차츰 잦아들다
quit one's job 직장을 그만두다   get a haircut 머리를 자르다
haven't had one in months 몇 달 동안 한 번도 안 했다   fly to ~로 비행기를 타고 가다
cut down on ~을 줄이다   eat out 외식하다

내가 제일 먼저 할 일은 설탕을 끊는 거야.

The first thing + 주어 + be going to do is + 동사원형
                       I'm   cut out sugar

REMINDER 패턴 강화

이제 내 이야기를 해 봐요! 나에게 있음 직한 일들을 적고, 소리 내어 말해 보는 거예요.
주어가 별도로 제시되지 않으면, 주어는 항상 I(나)예요.

▶ 정답 310쪽

UNIT 21 I'm sorry for not calling you.

> **be sorry for + 동명사[명사]**
> ~해서 미안하다

1 말도 없이 찾아와서 미안해요.   dropping by without notice

2 기분을 상하게 해서 미안해요.   hurting your feelings

3 목소리 높여서 미안해요.   raising my voice

UNIT 22 I promise to be there on time.

> **promise to + 동사원형**
> 꼭 ~하겠다, ~할 것을 약속하다

4 약속을 지키겠다고 약속할게.   keep my word

5 진실을 말하겠다고 약속할게.   tell the truth

6 최선을 다하겠다고 약속할게.   do my best

UNIT 23 I'm afraid I have no way of reaching him.

> **have no way of + 동명사**
> ~할 방법이 없다

7 당신에게 연락할 방법이 없어요.   contacting you

8 차 없이 그곳에 갈 방법이 없어요.   getting there without a car

9 이것을 고칠 방법이 없어요.   fixing this

UNIT 24 **That explains why** there are so many cars on the road.

> **That explains why + 절**
> 그래서 ~한 거다

10 그래서 날씨가 그렇게 따뜻했구나.   the weather was so warm

11 그래서 그녀가 오늘 쉬는구나.   she is off today

12 그래서 와이파이가 느린 거구나.   the Wi-Fi is slow

UNIT 25 **The first thing I'm going to do is** cut out sugar.

> **The first thing + 주어 + be going to do is + 동사원형**
> [주어]가 가장 먼저 할 일은 ~이다

13 내가 가장 먼저 할 일은 빚을 갚는 거야.   pay off my debt

14 내가 가장 먼저 할 일은 엄마한테 전화하는 거야.   call my mom

15 내가 가장 먼저 할 일은 일찍 자는 거야.   go to bed early

REMINDER 맥락 적용

이제 앞에서 연습한 패턴을 실생활 대화 맥락에 적용해 보세요. 패턴을 일상적인 대화에 넣어서 직접 소리 내어 말해 보는 거예요. 빈칸에 들어갈 말이 기억이 나지 않는다면 다시 앞으로 가서 확인해 보세요.

UNIT 21

A You're late again. We've been waiting for 30 minutes.
또 늦었네. 우리 30분이나 기다렸어.

B _____ being late. The traffic was terrible.
늦어서 정말 미안. 교통 체증이 심했어.

A This is turning into a habit. You should have left earlier.
이제 습관인 거 같아. 더 일찍 출발했어야지.

B You're right. _____ not thinking about the traffic. It won't happen again.
맞아. 교통 상황을 고려하지 않았어. 미안해. 다음엔 이러지 않을게.

UNIT 22

A I have an important presentation tomorrow and I'm really nervous.
내일 중요한 발표가 있어서 너무 긴장돼.

B Don't worry, you'll do great.
걱정하지 마, 잘해 낼 거야.

A Thanks. But I'm afraid I'll make a mistake.
고마워. 그래도 실수할까 봐 걱정돼.

B You've practiced a lot. I _____ cheer you on.
연습 많이 했잖아. 네가 잘할 수 있도록 꼭 응원할게.

UNIT 23

A Do you think we'll make it to the graduation on time?
졸업식에 제시간에 도착할 수 있을까?

B I _____ knowing because of the traffic.
교통 체증 때문에 알 수가 없어.

A Yeah, it's been really bad today. Cars are moving bumper-to-bumper.
응, 오늘 정말 심하네. 차가 꼬리에 꼬리를 물고 있어.

B Let's check the GPS; maybe there's a quicker route we can take.
내비게이션 한번 확인해 보자. 더 빠른 길이 있을지도 몰라.

UNIT 24

A Why hasn't Tom been answering his phone lately?
톰이 요즘 왜 전화를 안 받을까?

B He lost his phone last week.
걔 지난주에 핸드폰 잃어버렸어.

A _____ he hasn't been responding to any messages.
그래서 메시지에 전혀 답장을 안 했던 거구나.

B Right, he's waiting for his new phone to arrive.
맞아. 새 핸드폰이 오길 기다리고 있어.

UNIT 25

A Wow, I heard you won the lottery! Congratulations!
와, 복권에 당첨됐다고? 축하해!

B Thanks. I still can't believe it.
고마워. 아직도 믿기지가 않아.

A So, what are you going to do first?
그래서 뭐부터 할 거야?

B _____ is pay off my loan and then learn about money management.
우선 대출금 갚고, 돈 관리에 대해 배울 거야.

어휘 cheer on ~를 응원하다   bumper-to-bumper (교통이) 정체된   pay off one's loan 대출금을 갚다

정답 I'm sorry for, I'm sorry for | promise to | have no way of | That explains why |
The first thing I'm going to do

UNIT 26

have no choice but to + 동사원형
~하지 않을 수 없다, ~할 수밖에 없다

이 패턴은 '~할 수밖에 없다, ~하지 않을 수 없다'라는 뜻으로, 특정 행동을 해야만 하는 상황을 설명할 때 사용해요. 그만큼 이걸 할 수밖에 없었다는 걸 강조하고 싶은 거예요. 예를 들어, 여행을 가기 직전에 갑자기 태풍이 불어와서 '어쩔 수 없이' 여행을 취소해야 할 때는 I had no choice but to cancel the trip because of the typhoon.이라고 말하면 되고, 너무 배가 고파서 눈앞에 있었던 케이크를 먹지 않을 수 없었을 때는 I had no choice but to eat the cake because I was starving.이라고 말하면 돼요.

have no choice but to 뒤에는 동사원형을 써서 해야만 하는 행동을 나타냅니다.

 I **have no choice but to** get a roommate.
어쩔 수 없이 룸메이트를 구해야 할 것 같아.

실생활 대화

A I have no choice but to get a roommate.
   The rent in this city is skyrocketing.
   어쩔 수 없이 룸메이트를 구해야 할 것 같아. 이 동네 월세가 너무 오르고 있어.

B I happen to know someone who's looking for a place.
   Do you want me to introduce you?
   마침 내가 아는 사람이 방을 구하는데, 소개해 줄까?

A Really? That would be great! What can you tell me about them?
   진짜? 그거 좋겠다! 그 사람에 대해 알려 줄 수 있어?

B She's a graduate student, quiet, and clean.
   I think you two would get along well.
   대학원생인데, 조용하고 깔끔해. 너희 둘이 잘 맞을 것 같아.

---

skyrocket (가격 등이) 치솟다   **happen to** 우연히 ~하다(unit 12 패턴)   **get along well** 잘 지내다

PRACTICE 패턴 활용

문장을 써 보고 음원을 들으며 소리 내어 말하세요. 제시어 중 기본형 동사는 패턴에 맞게 바꾸고, 제시어의 // 앞까지만이라도 완성해 말하세요.

▶ 정답 310쪽

- 여행을 취소할 수밖에 없어.   I / cancel the trip
  I have no choice but to cancel the trip.

1. 도움을 요청할 수밖에 없어.   I / ask for help

2. 새로운 직장을 구할 수밖에 없어.   I / find a new job

3. 늦게까지 회사에 있을 수밖에 없어.   I / stay late / at work

4. 내일은 어쩔 수 없이 일찍 일어나야 해.   I / wake up / early / tomorrow

5. 팬데믹 때문에 우리 결혼식을 연기할 수밖에 없어.
   we / postpone our wedding / due to the pandemic

6. 그들은 의료비를 내기 위해 차를 팔 수밖에 없어.   they / sell their car // to pay for the medical bills

7. 우리는 일이 산더미처럼 쌓여 있어서 휴가 계획을 취소할 수밖에 없어.
   we / cancel our vacation plans // because we have a pile of work to do

8. 그는 안 좋은 날씨 때문에 여행을 연기할 수밖에 없어. `응용`
   he / postpone his trip // because of the bad weather

---

ask for help 도움을 요청하다   find a new job 새 직장을 구하다   stay late 늦게까지 있다   postpone 연기하다
due to ~ 때문에   medical bill 의료비   vacation 휴가   pile (산)더미

어쩔 수 없이 룸메이트를 구해야 할 것 같아.

주어 + have no choice but to + 동사원형
    | |
    I   *get a roommate*

UNIT 27

never thought + 주어 + would + 동사원형

[주어]가 ~할 거라고는 상상도 못 했다

이 패턴은 어떤 일이 일어날 거라고 전혀 예상하지 못했을 때 사용해요. 예를 들어, "내가 이 일을 할 거라고는 전혀 생각하지 못했어."라고 말하고 싶다면 I never thought I would do this.라고 하면 돼요. 그 생각을 못했던 시점에서 보면 일어나게 될 일이 미래이기 때문에 would를 써서 과거를 회상하며 자신이 놀란 상태를 표현해요.

would 뒤에는 동사원형을 써서 예상하지 못했던 그 동작을 나타냅니다.

 I **never thought** I **would** finish a marathon.
마라톤을 완주할 줄은 상상도 못 했어.

실생활 대화

A I never thought I would finish a marathon.
내가 마라톤을 완주할 줄은 정말 상상도 못 했어.

B That's impressive! How long did you train?
대단한데! 얼마나 연습한 거야?

A About six months. It was tough, but so rewarding.
6개월 정도. 힘들었지만 정말 보람을 느꼈어.

B Congratulations! You must be really proud of yourself.
축하해! 스스로 엄청 자랑스럽겠다.

---

train 훈련하다, 연습하다   tough 힘든   rewarding 보람 있는   be proud of oneself 자신이 자랑스럽다

PRACTICE 패턴 활용

문장을 써 보고 음원을 들으며 소리 내어 말하세요. 제시어 중 기본형 동사는 패턴에 맞게 바꾸고, 제시어의 // 앞까지만이라도 완성해 말하세요.

▶ 정답 310쪽

- 여기서 너를 볼 줄은 전혀 생각하지 못했어.　　　　　　　　　　I / I / see you / here

  I never thought I would see you here.

1 내가 경기를 이길 거라고는 전혀 생각하지 못 했어.　　　　　　I / I / win the game

2 내가 조깅을 이렇게 즐기게 될 줄은 몰랐어.　　　　　　I / I / enjoy jogging / this much

3 내가 아침형 인간이 될 줄은 꿈에도 몰랐어.　　　　　　I / I / become a morning person

4 내가 담배를 끊을 수 있을 줄은 전혀 몰랐어.　　　　　　I / I / be able to quit smoking

5 그녀는 자기가 시험에 붙을 줄은 생각도 못 했어.　　　　　　she / she / pass the exam

6 우리가 콘서트 티켓을 구할 줄은 전혀 몰랐어.　　　　　　we / we / get tickets / to the concert

7 그 회사는 자기네가 이렇게 빨리 성장할 줄은 예상 못 했어.　　the company / it / grow this fast

8 우리는 이 작은 카페가 이렇게 유명해질 줄은 몰랐어.　　we / this small café / become so popular

pass the exam 시험에 합격하다　get tickets 표를 구하다　popular 인기 있는

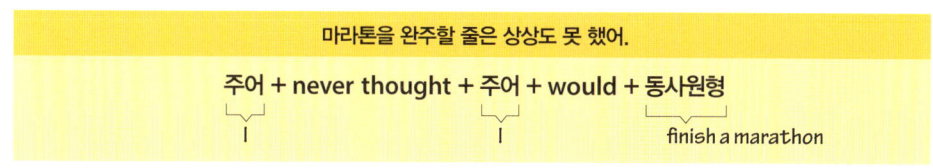

마라톤을 완주할 줄은 상상도 못 했어.

주어 + never thought + 주어 + would + 동사원형

UNIT 28

Don't tell me + 절

설마 ~는 아니겠지?

며칠 계속 야근을 하다가 또 야근을 해야 해서 집에 전화했을 때 상대방이 "설마 또 야근하는 건 아니겠지?"라고 물을 수 있겠죠? 그럴 때 이 패턴을 사용해서 Don't tell me you are working late again.이라고 말하면 돼요. 또는, 밥을 배불리 먹고 식당을 나왔는데 또 먹으러 가자는 상대에게 "설마 또 배고픈 건 아니겠지?"라고 믿기지 않는다는 듯이 말하고 싶다면 Don't tell me you are hungry again.이라고 말할 수 있어요.

Don't tell me 뒤에는 믿기지 않거나 예상하지 못한 일에 대한 내용이 절(주어+동사)로 옵니다.

 Don't tell me you're working overtime again.
설마 또 야근하는 건 아니겠지?

실생활 대화

A I might be late coming home tonight.
오늘 집에 늦을 것 같아.

B Don't tell me you're working overtime again.
That's the third time this week.
설마 또 야근하는 건 아니겠지? 이번 주에 벌써 세 번째야.

A I'm sorry. We have an important project deadline tomorrow...
미안해. 중요한 프로젝트 마감이 내일이라서...

B I understand. But take care of your health, too. Don't overdo it.
알겠어. 하지만 건강도 챙겨야 해. 너무 무리하지 마.

work overtime 야근하다, 초과 근무하다   deadline 마감일   overdo it 무리하다

PRACTICE 패턴 활용

문장을 써 보고 음원을 들으며 소리 내어 말하세요. 제시어 중 기본형 동사는 패턴에 맞게 바꾸고, 제시어의 // 앞까지만이라도 완성해 말하세요.

▶ 정답 311쪽

- 설마 우리 기념일을 잊은 건 아니겠지? 일주일 내내 힌트를 줬잖아.
  you forgot our anniversary // I've been hinting about it all week
  Don't tell me you forgot our anniversary. I've been hinting about it all week.

1 설마 열쇠를 잃어버린 건 아니겠지? 이번 달에만 벌써 세 번째야!
   you lost your keys // that's the third time this month

2 설마 오늘 아침에 고양이 밥 주는 걸 잊은 건 아니겠지?　you forgot to feed the cat / this morning

3 설마 직장을 그만두는 건 아니겠지? 지난달에 승진했잖아.
   you're quitting your job // you just got that promotion last month

4 설마 마지막 남은 케이크 조각을 먹은 건 아니겠지? 다이어트 끝나고 먹으려고 아껴 뒀는데.
   you ate the last piece of cake / I was saving that for after my diet

5 설마 티켓을 안 가져온 건 아니겠지? 우리 지금 입구까지 와 있잖아!
   you didn't bring the tickets // we're already at the entrance

6 설마 주말 내내 비 오는 건 아니겠지? 우리 이 여행 몇 달 전부터 계획했잖아!
   it's going to rain / all weekend // we planned this trip for months

7 설마 또 월세가 오른 건 아니겠지? 지난번 오른 것도 겨우 적응했는데!
   they raised the rent / again // we just got used to the last increase

8 설마 지금까지 30분 동안 줄을 잘못 서 있었던 건 아니겠지?
   we've been waiting in the wrong line / for the past 30 minutes

anniversary 기념일　feed the cat 고양이에게 밥을 주다　promotion 승진
save ~ for later 나중을 위해 아껴 두다　entrance 입구　raise the rent 월세를 올리다
get used to ~에 익숙해지다　increase 증가　wait in line 줄을 서다

설마 또 야근하는 건 아니겠지?

Don't tell me + 절

you're working overtime again

UNIT 29

Feel free to + 동사원형

편하게 ~하세요

이 패턴은 상대방에게 어떤 행동을 자유롭게 해도 된다고 허락하거나 권유할 때 사용해요. 예를 들어, "질문이 있으면 자유롭게 물어보세요."라고 말하고 싶다면 Feel free to ask questions, "원하면 언제든지 나에게 연락하세요."라고 말하고 싶다면 Feel free to contact me anytime.이라고 하면 돼요.

Feel free to 뒤에 동사원형을 써서 권유하는 행동을 나타냅니다.

 Feel free to ask if you need help.
도움이 필요하면 언제든지 말씀하세요.

실생활 대화

A I'm not sure how to use this new coffee machine.
   이 새 커피 머신 어떻게 쓰는지 모르겠어요.

B Feel free to ask if you need help. I've used that machine a lot.
   도움이 필요하면 언제든지 말씀하세요. 그 기계 자주 써 봤거든요.

A Thanks, that would be great.
   Could you show me how to make a latte?
   고마워요. 라떼 만드는 법 좀 알려 주실 수 있나요?

B Sure thing! Let me walk you through it step by step.
   물론이죠! 제가 단계별로 자세히 알려 드릴게요.

walk ~ through ~에게 자세히 알려 주다   step by step 단계적으로

PRACTICE 패턴 활용

문장을 써 보고 음원을 들으며 소리 내어 말하세요. 제시어 중 기본형 동사는 패턴에 맞게 바꾸고, 제시어의 // 앞까지만이라도 완성해 말하세요.

▶ 정답 311쪽

- 음악 편하게 바꾸세요. 저는 아무거나 괜찮아요.   change the music // I'm not picky

  Feel free to change the music. I'm not picky.

1. 강아지도 편하게 데려오세요. 언제나 환영이에요.
   bring your dog // she's always welcome here

2. 이번 주말에 내 차 편하게 써. 다 쓰고 주유만 해 줘.
   use my car / this weekend // just fill up the tank when you're done

3. 늦은 시간이라도 편하게 전화하세요. 저 원래 늦게까지 깨어 있으니까요.
   call me anytime / even if it's late // I'm a night owl anyway

4. 부엌에 있는 거 편하게 드세요. 집처럼 편히 계세요.
   help yourself to anything in the kitchen // make yourself at home

5. 넷플릭스 계정 편하게 쓰세요. 대신 제 시청 목록은 건들지 마세요.
   use my Netflix account // just don't mess up my watchlist

6. 아이들이 지루해하면 놀이방에 있는 장난감 편하게 사용하세요.
   if your kids get bored / use the toys / in the playroom

7. 그녀가 걱정되는 게 있으면 편하게 직접 이메일 보내도 된다고 했어요. 응용
   she said to / email her / directly / with any concerns

8. 선생님이 강의 중에도 질문 있으면 언제든지 하라고 하셨어요. 응용
   the teacher told the students to / ask questions / during the lecture

---

picky 까다로운   **fill up the tank** (차에) 기름을 넣다   **a night owl** 저녁형 인간   **Help yourself to anything.** 마음껏 드세요.   **Make yourself at home.** 집처럼 편하게 계세요.   **Netflix account** 넷플릭스 계정   **mess up** 엉망으로 만들다   **watchlist** 시청 목록   **playroom** 놀이방   **lecture** 강의

도움이 필요하면 언제든지 말씀하세요.

Feel free to + 동사원형

ask if you need help

UNIT 30
didn't mean to + 동사원형
~할 의도는 아니었다

이 패턴은 어떤 행동을 의도하지 않았다는 것을 표현할 때 사용해요. 여기서 mean은 '의미하다'라는 뜻뿐만 아니라 '의도하다'라는 뜻도 있어요. 예를 들어, "나는 너를 화나게 하려고 한 것이 아니었어."는 I didn't mean to upset you, "나는 그렇게 말하려고 한 것이 아니었어."는 I didn't mean to say that.이라고 말할 수 있어요.

didn't mean to 뒤에는 동사원형을 써서 의도하지 않은 행동을 나타냅니다.

 I **didn't mean to** offend you.
기분 상하게 하려던 건 아니었어.

실생활 대화

A That comment you made really upset me.
네가 한 말 때문에 정말 속상했어.

B I didn't mean to offend you. I spoke without thinking.
기분 상하게 하려던 건 아니었는데. 내가 생각 없이 말했어.

A Please be more careful next time.
다음엔 좀 더 조심해 줘.

B I will. I'm really sorry.
그럴게. 정말 미안해.

comment 언급   offend 기분을 상하게 하다

PRACTICE 패턴 활용

문장을 써 보고 음원을 들으며 소리 내어 말하세요. 제시어 중 기본형 동사는 패턴에 맞게 바꾸고, 제시어의 // 앞까지만이라도 완성해 말하세요.

▶ 정답 311쪽

- 그 메시지를 단체 채팅방에 보내려던 건 아니었어.   I / send that message / to the group chat
  I didn't mean to send that message to the group chat.

1. 그 농담으로 네 기분을 상하게 하려던 건 아니었어.   I / hurt your feelings / with that joke

2. 네 머그잔을 깨려던 건 아니었어. 손에서 미끄러졌어.   I / break your mug // it slipped from my hand

3. 기분 상하게 하려던 건 아니야. 그냥 솔직하게 말하고 싶었어.
   I / upset you // I just wanted to be honest

4. 네 메시지를 무시하려던 건 아니야. 회사에서 정말 바빴어.
   I / ignore your message // I was really busy at work

5. 우린 너희 자리에 앉으려던 게 아니었어.   we / sit / at your table

6. 사라는 울려고 한 게 아니라, 그냥 감정이 북받친 거야.   Sarah / cry // she just got emotional

7. 톰은 창문을 깨려던 게 아니었어. 그건 사고였어.   Tom / break the window // it was an accident

8. 그가 네 펜을 가져가려던 건 아니야. 자기 건 줄 알았대.
   he / take your pen // he thought it was his

---

group chat 단체 채팅방   hurt one's feelings ~의 기분을 상하게 하다   mug 머그잔   slip 미끄러지다
upset 속상하게 하다   get emotional 감정이 북받치다   accident 사고

기분 상하게 하려던 건 아니었어.

주어 + didn't mean to + 동사원형
  I   offend you

95

REMINDER 패턴 강화

이제 내 이야기를 해 봐요! 나에게 있음 직한 일들을 적고, 소리 내어 말해 보는 거예요.
주어가 별도로 제시되지 않으면, 주어는 항상 I(나)예요.

▶ 정답 311쪽

UNIT 26 I **have no choice but to** get a roommate.

> have no choice but to + 동사원형
> ~하지 않을 수 없다, ~할 수밖에 없다

1 지하철을 탈 수밖에 없어.   take the subway

2 줄 서서 기다릴 수밖에 없어.   wait in line

3 하고 싶은 말을 참을 수밖에 없어.   bite my tongue

UNIT 27 I **never thought** I **would** finish a marathon.

> never thought + 주어 + would + 동사원형
> [주어]가 ~할 거라고는 상상도 못 했다

4 내가 해외에 살 줄은 몰랐어.   live abroad

5 너 같은 사람과 사랑에 빠질 줄은 몰랐어.   fall in love with someone like you

6 내가 TV에 나올 줄은 몰랐어.   be on TV

UNIT 28 **Don't tell me** you're working overtime again.

> Don't tell me + 절
> 설마 ~는 아니겠지?

7 설마 버스를 놓친 건 아니겠지?   you missed the bus

8   아직도 그를 사랑하는 건 아니겠지?   you still love him

9   밤새 한숨도 못 잔 건 아니겠지?   you didn't sleep at all

UNIT 29 **Feel free to** ask if you need help.

Feel free to + 동사원형
편하게 ~하세요

10   언제든지 편하게 전화하세요.   call anytime

11   편하게 연락하세요.   reach out

12   이 방 편하게 사용하세요.   use this room

UNIT 30 I **didn't mean to** offend you.

didn't mean to + 동사원형
~할 의도는 아니었다

13   무례하게 굴려던 건 아니었어.   be rude

14   너를 제외시키려던 건 아니었어.   leave you out

15   문제를 일으키려던 건 아니었어.   cause trouble

REMINDER 맥락 적용

이제 앞에서 연습한 패턴을 실생활 대화 맥락에 적용해 보세요. 패턴을 일상적인 대화에 넣어서 직접 소리 내어 말해 보는 거예요. 빈칸에 들어갈 말이 기억이 나지 않는다면 다시 앞으로 가서 확인해 보세요.

UNIT 26

A I _____ skip lunch today. I have back-to-back meetings all afternoon.
오늘은 어쩔 수 없이 점심을 걸러야 할 것 같아. 오후 내내 회의가 빽빽하게 잡혀 있어.

B That's not good for your health. Should I bring you a sandwich later?
그러면 건강에 안 좋을 텐데. 나중에 샌드위치라도 가져다줄까?

A That would be amazing, thank you! I'll be in the conference room on the 3rd floor.
그래 주면 너무 고맙지! 난 3층 회의실에 있을 거야.

B No problem, I'll drop it off around 2 PM. Good luck with your meetings!
알겠어. 2시쯤 가져다줄게. 회의 잘하고!

UNIT 27

A I _____ I would start my own business.
내 사업을 시작할 줄은 상상도 못 했어.

B That's exciting! What kind of business is it?
멋지다! 어떤 사업이야?

A It's an online tutoring platform. I've been thinking about it for years.
온라인 과외 플랫폼이야. 몇 년째 구상했던 거야.

B That's brilliant. The pandemic has really changed the education system, hasn't it?
멋진데. 팬데믹으로 교육 방식이 많이 바뀌었잖아?

UNIT 28

A Um... Our anniversary is tomorrow, right?
저기... 내일 우리 기념일이지?

B _____ you forgot. I've been mentioning it for a week.
설마 잊어버렸다는 건 아니겠지? 내가 일주일 전부터 얘기했는데.

A No, of course I remembered. I just wanted to double-check.
아니, 물론 기억하고 있었어. 그냥 다시 확인하고 싶어서.

B That's a relief. Do you remember we have a reservation at 7 PM tomorrow?
다행이네. 내일 저녁 7시 예약 기억하지?

UNIT 29

A   Is it okay if I leave work early today? I have a doctor's appointment.
오늘 일찍 퇴근해도 될까요? 병원 예약이 있어서요.

B   Of course, feel free to go. Your health comes first.
물론이죠. 편하게 가세요. 건강이 먼저죠.

A   Thank you for understanding. I'll make sure to finish my tasks before leaving.
이해해 주셔서 감사합니다. 가기 전에 업무는 꼭 마무리하고 갈게요.

B   Don't worry about it. Feel free to reschedule any meetings if needed.
그건 걱정하지 말아요. 필요하면 회의 일정도 조정해도 돼요.

UNIT 30

A   Wow, this cake you made is amazing!
와, 네가 만든 케이크 진짜 맛있다!

B   Thanks! I didn't mean to make so much, though. Would you like to take some home?
고마워! 근데 이렇게 많이 만들려던 건 아니었어. 집에 좀 가져갈래?

A   Really? That would be great!
정말? 좋지!

B   I'll wrap some up for you, then.
그럼 내가 조금 포장해 줄게.

어휘   back-to-back 꼬리에 꼬리를 문   mention 말하다   wrap up ~를 포장하다, 싸다

정답   have no choice but to | never thought | Don't tell me | feel free to, Feel free to |
I didn't mean to

UNIT 31

be likely to + 동사원형

~할 것 같다, ~할 가능성이 높다

이 패턴은 어떤 일이 일어날 확률이나 가능성이 높을 때 사용해요. 예를 들어, "나는 내일 늦을 가능성이 높아."라고 말하고 싶다면 I'm likely to be late tomorrow, 또는 "내일 비가 올 가능성이 높아."라고 말하고 싶다면 It's likely to rain tomorrow.라고 표현할 수 있어요.

be likely to 뒤에 일어날 가능성이 높은 일을 나타내는 동사원형을 씁니다.

 That new superhero movie **is likely to** sell out fast.
이번에 그 히어로 영화는 금방 매진될 것 같아.

실생활 대화

A Should we book movie tickets for Friday night?
금요일 밤에 영화표 예매할까?

B Definitely. That new superhero movie is likely to sell out fast.
그럼. 이번에 그 히어로 영화는 금방 매진될 것 같아.

A Good point. Do you want to go for the 7 PM show?
일리 있어. 저녁 7시 상영 어때?

B Sounds perfect. I'll grab the tickets before they're gone.
완전 좋아. 표 다 팔리기 전에 내가 예매할게.

---

book movie tickets 영화표를 예매하다   sell out 매진되다   go for ~를 택하다   grab 재빨리 손에 넣다

PRACTICE 패턴 활용

문장을 써 보고 음원을 들으며 소리 내어 말하세요. 제시어 중 기본형 동사는 패턴에 맞게 바꾸고, 제시어의 // 앞까지만이라도 완성해 말하세요.   ▶ 정답 311쪽

• 이번 주말에 눈이 올 것 같아.   it / snow / this weekend
  It's likely to snow this weekend.

1 가격이 다음 달에 오를 것 같아.   the price / go up / next month

2 이 도로는 출퇴근 시간에 붐빌 가능성이 높아.   this road / be busy / during rush hour

3 그 사람 또 늦을 것 같아. 항상 그러거든.   he / be late / again // he always is

4 내일 비가 올 것 같으니까 우산 잊지 마.   it / rain / tomorrow // so don't forget your umbrella

5 그녀의 경험으로 볼 때, 발표는 아마 잘될 거야. 응용
   given her experience / it / be a successful presentation

6 오늘은 공휴일이라 그 가게가 일찍 문 닫을 것 같으니까, 지금 가자.
   that shop / close early today / because of the holiday // so let's go now

7 그녀는 열심히 공부했으니까 시험에 합격할 것 같아. 그녀의 노력이 좋은 결과로 이어지길 바라.
   she / pass the exam / because she studied hard // I hope her efforts lead to good results

8 그 팀은 올해 우승할 가능성이 높아. 지금까지 가장 좋은 경기 실력을 보여 주고 있거든.
   the team / win the championship / this year // because they've been playing better than ever

go up 오르다, 상승하다   rush hour 출퇴근 시간   given ~을 고려할 때   lead to ~로 이어지다   result 결과
win the championship 우승하다   play better than ever 지금까지 가장 잘하다

이번에 그 히어로 영화는 금방 매진될 것 같아.

주어 + be likely to + 동사원형

That new superhero movie is   sell out fast

UNIT 32

be really happy with + 명사[동명사]

~에 매우 만족하다

이 패턴은 어떤 것이 매우 마음에 들 때 사용해요. 뭔가에 정말 만족했을 때 이렇게 형용사 happy를 써서 말하니까 이번 기회에 확실하게 익혀 두고 일상생활 속에서 자주 활용해 보세요. 예를 들어 "나는 새 직장에 매우 만족해."라고 말하고 싶다면 I'm really happy with my new job, 또는 "나는 우리의 진행 상황에 매우 만족해."는 I'm really happy with our progress.라고 말할 수 있어요.

be really happy with 뒤에 만족하는 대상을 나타내는 명사나 동명사(-ing)를 씁니다.

 I'm really happy with my new phone.
새 폰이 정말 마음에 들어.

실생활 대화

A Is that the new phone you were talking about?
그거 네가 말하던 새 폰이야?

B Yeah! I'm really happy with my new phone. I'm a bit of a foodie, so I take a lot of food pics, and the photos come out amazing.
응! 새 폰이 정말 마음에 들어. 내가 먹는 걸 좋아해서 음식 사진 많이 찍는 편인데, 진짜 잘 나와.

A Oh nice! I've seen your Instagram.
Your ramen shots look professional!
와 좋다! 네 인스타 봤는데, 라면 사진 거의 전문가 수준이던데!

B Thanks! The camera picks up all the colors and textures.
It makes everything look delicious.
고마워! 이 카메라는 색감이랑 질감까지 다 잘 잡아 줘. 음식이 더 맛있어 보이게 나와.

foodie 음식 애호가   pick up (색감이나 디테일을) 포착하다   texture 질감   look delicious 맛있어 보이다

PRACTICE 패턴 활용

문장을 써 보고 음원을 들으며 소리 내어 말하세요. 제시어 중 기본형 동사는 패턴에 맞게 바꾸고, 제시어의 // 앞까지만이라도 완성해 말하세요.

▶ 정답 312쪽

- 나는 서비스에 정말 만족해. I / the service
  I'm really happy with the service.

1. 여기로 이사 오길 정말 잘한 것 같아. I / my decision / to move here

2. 새 노트북 정말 마음에 들어. 빠르고 가벼워. I / my new laptop // it's fast and lightweight

3. 오늘 머리 정말 마음에 들어. 미용사가 정말 잘해 줬어.
   I / the haircut I got / today // the stylist did a great job

4. 그 새 식당 음식 정말 맛있어. 우리 또 가야 해.
   I / the food / at that new restaurant // we should go again

5. 우리 부모님은 전원 생활에 정말 만족하셔. 응용 my parents / live in the countryside

6. 톰과 사라는 주말을 함께 보내는 걸 정말 좋아해. 응용 Tom and Sarah / spend weekends / together

7. 우리는 매달 더 많이 저축하게 되어 정말 기뻐. 응용 we / save more money / every month

8. 우리는 행사 결과에 아주 만족해. 모든 게 순조롭게 진행됐어. 응용
   we / how the event turned out // everything went smoothly

---

move 이사하다   lightweight 가벼운   haircut 머리 깎기   stylist 미용사   countryside 시골, 전원
turned out (일이 특정 방식으로) 되다   smoothly 순조롭게

새 폰이 정말 마음에 들어.

주어 + be really happy with + 명사
  I'm   my new phone

UNIT 33

love[hate] it when + 절
~할 때 너무 좋다[싫다]

이 패턴은 '~할 때 정말 좋아!'라고 말을 하고 싶을 때 사용해요. like에서 한 단계 더 좋아하는 마음을 보여 주고 싶을 때 love를 사용하면 돼요. 그럼 I don't like에서 한 단계 더 싫어하는 마음을 강조하고 싶을 때 어떤 단어를 쓸까요? '~할 때 정말 싫어!'라고 말하고 싶다면 hate을 써서 말할 수 있어요.

love[hate] it when 뒤에 절(주어+동사)이 옵니다.

 I love it when you hold my hand while we walk.
걸으면서 네가 내 손 잡아 줄 때 너무 좋아.

실생활 대화

A It's such a nice evening. I'm glad we decided to take a walk.
오늘 저녁 진짜 좋다. 산책하길 잘했네.

B Yeah, it feels peaceful.
I love it when you hold my hand while we walk.
응, 진짜 평화롭다. 걸으면서 네가 내 손 잡아 줄 때 너무 좋아.

A Aww, really? I didn't even notice I grabbed it. It just feels natural.
정말? 나도 모르게 잡았네. 그냥 자연스럽게 손이 가.

B That's what I love about it. It means a lot, even without words.
그래서 더 좋아. 말 안 해도 마음이 전해지잖아.

take a walk 산책하다   hold hands 손을 잡다

PRACTICE 패턴 활용

문장을 써 보고 음원을 들으며 소리 내어 말하세요. 제시어 중 기본형 동사는 패턴에 맞게 바꾸고, 제시어의 // 앞까지만이라도 완성해 말하세요.

▶ 정답 312쪽

- 아침에 함께 커피 마시는 게 정말 좋아. I / we have coffee / together / in the morning
  I love it when we have coffee together in the morning.

1. 계획대로 일이 잘 풀릴 때 너무 좋아. I / a plan comes together / smoothly

2. 누군가 내가 한 사소한 말을 기억해 줄 때 너무 좋아. I / someone remembers the little things I say

3. 사람들이 내 말 가로챌 때 정말 싫어. I / people talk over me

4. 사람들이 내 유머를 못 알아들을 때 너무 싫어. I / people don't get my sense of humor

5. 우린 인터넷 연결이 느릴 때 정말 싫어해. we / the Internet connection is slow

6. 그들은 계획이 마지막 순간에 취소될 때 정말 싫어해.
   they / their plans get canceled / at the last minute

7. 그 선생님은 학생들이 숙제를 안 해 올 때 정말 싫어해. 응용
   the teacher / students don't do their homework

8. 그는 할머니가 어린 시절 이야기를 해 주실 때 정말 좋아해. 응용
   he / his grandmother tells him stories / from her childhood

---

have coffee 커피를 마시다   **come together** (계획이나 일이) 완성되다   **little things** 사소한 것들
talk over ~의 말을 가로채다   **sense of humor** 유머 감각   **Internet connection** 인터넷 연결
do one's homework 숙제를 하다   **childhood** 어린 시절

걸으면서 네가 내 손 잡아 줄 때 너무 좋아.

주어 + love it when + 절
  | |
  I   you hold my hand while we walk

105

UNIT 34

be supposed to + 동사원형
~하기로 되어 있다, ~해야 한다

be supposed to는 예정, 의무, 약속, 기대, 추측 등 다양하게 활용되어 일상 속에서 자주 사용돼요. 동사 suppose는 '추측하다, 가정하다, ~라고 생각하다'라는 뜻으로 추측이나 가정을 나타내고, 해야 하는 의무나 규범을 나타낼 때도 사용해요.

be supposed to 뒤에는 현재 해야 할 일을 나타내는 동사원형을 사용합니다.

 My package **was supposed to** arrive yesterday.
제 택배가 어제 도착하기로 했는데요.

be supposed to의 다양한 쓰임

1 미리 정해진 일이나 계획을 말할 때
   I'm supposed to meet my friend at 8 PM.
   저녁 8시에 친구를 만나기로 되어 있어요.

2 사회적으로 지켜야 하는 어떤 규칙이나 약속, 행동을 말할 때
   You're supposed to always wear a seatbelt while driving.
   운전할 때는 항상 안전벨트를 착용해야 해요.

3 원래 일어났어야 하는 일인데 그 일이 일어나지 않아 당혹스럽거나 놀라움을 표현할 때
   The bus was supposed to be here 20 minutes ago!
   버스가 20분 전에 여기 왔어야 했어요!

실생활 대화

A My package was supposed to arrive yesterday, but it's still not here.
   제 택배가 어제 도착하기로 했는데, 아직 안 왔어요.

B Did you check the tracking info? Maybe it's delayed.
   배송 조회해 보셨어요? 아마 지연됐을 수도 있어요.

A Yeah, it says "out for delivery" since this morning.
   네, 오늘 아침부터 '배송 중'이라고만 뜨네요.

B Hmm, sometimes it arrives late in the evening.
   음, 가끔 저녁 늦게 올 때도 있더라고요.

be delayed 지연되다   out for delivery 배송 중   late in the evening 저녁 늦게

PRACTICE 패턴 활용

문장을 써 보고 음원을 들으며 소리 내어 말하세요. 제시어 중 기본형 동사는 패턴에 맞게 바꾸고, 제시어의 // 앞까지만이라도 완성해 말하세요.

▶ 정답 312쪽

• 주말마다 부모님께 **전화드리기로 했어요.** I / call my parents / every weekend
  ### I'm supposed to call my parents every weekend.

1 다음 주 월요일에 뉴욕으로 **출발할 예정이에요.** I / fly to New York / next Monday

2 내일 오후 2시에 치과 **예약이 되어 있어요.** I / have a dentist appointment / at 2 PM / tomorrow

3 오늘 **쉬는 날**인데, 상사가 출근하라고 했어요. I / be off / today // but my boss just called me in

4 지금쯤 휴가 중이어야 하는데. 야근이 아니라. I / be on vacation / right now // not working overtime

5 여기 레스토랑에서는 웨이터에게 팁을 **줘야 해요.** 응용 you / tip waiters / in restaurants / here

6 이 커피는 **뜨거워야 하는데,** 미지근해요. 응용 this coffee / be hot // but it's lukewarm

7 승객들은 이륙과 착륙 시 안전벨트를 **매야 해요.** 응용
   passengers / fasten their seatbelts / during takeoff and landing

8 한국에서는 다른 사람의 집에 들어갈 때 신발을 **벗어야 해요.** 응용
   you / take off your shoes // before entering someone's home in Korea

---

appointment 약속, 예약   be off 쉬는 날이다   call ~ in ~를 출근하라고 부르다   be on vacation 휴가 중이다
tip 팁을 주다   lukewarm 미지근한   fasten one's seatbelt 안전벨트를 매다   during ~ 동안에
takeoff and landing 이륙 및 착륙   take off ~를 벗다

제 택배가 어제 도착하기로 했는데요.

주어 + be supposed to + 동사원형

My package was   arrive yesterday

UNIT 35

What + 주어 + be trying to say is (that) + 절

[주어]가 하려는 말은 ~라는 것이다

이 패턴은 이야기를 나누다가 상대방이 말을 잘 이해하지 못하거나, 지금까지 말했던 내용의 핵심을 말해 줄 때 사용할 수 있는 굉장히 유용한 표현이에요. 예를 들어, "내가 말하려는 것은 우리가 더 많은 준비가 필요하다는 거야."라고 말하고 싶다면 What I'm trying to say is that we need more preparation, "내 말은 우리랑 같이 공부해 줘서 고맙다는 거야."라고 말하고 싶다면 What we are trying to say is thank you so much for studying with us.라고 하면 돼요.

[What + 주어 + be trying to say is (that)] 뒤에는 핵심이나 요지를 나타내는 절(주어+동사)이 옵니다.

 What I'm trying to say is that we don't really need to replace it.
내가 하고 싶은 말은 그걸 바꿀 필요는 없다는 거야.

실생활 대화

A I don't think we should buy that new sofa right now.
지금 새 소파를 사는 건 별로인 것 같아.

B But it looks so nice! Didn't you say you wanted to buy a new sofa?
하지만 정말 예뻐 보여! 새 소파를 사고 싶다고 하지 않았어?

A **What I'm trying to say is that we don't really need to replace it.**
내가 하고 싶은 말은 그걸 바꿀 필요는 없다는 거야.

B I get it. Let's wait until we think it's the right time.
알겠어. 때가 됐다고 생각할 때까지 기다리자.

---

replace 교체하다, 바꾸다

PRACTICE 패턴 활용

문장을 써 보고 음원을 들으며 소리 내어 말하세요. 제시어 중 기본형 동사는 패턴에 맞게 바꾸고, 제시어의 // 앞까지만이라도 완성해 말하세요.

▶ 정답 312쪽

• 내가 하고 싶은 말은 나는 너를 아낀다는 거야.　　　　　　　　　　　　　　　　I / I care about you
  What I'm trying to say is that I care about you.

1　내가 말하려는 것은 이건 너 혼자만의 책임이 아니라는 거야.　　I / this isn't just your responsibility

2　내 말은, 더 이상 기다릴 여유가 없다는 거야.　　　　　　I / we can't afford to wait / any longer

3　내가 말하고 싶은 건 관계에서는 소통이 정말 중요하다는 거야.
　 I / communication is crucial / in a relationship

4　내 말은, 네 감정을 상하게 하려던 게 아니라는 거야.　　　I / I didn't mean to hurt your feelings

5　그들이 말하려는 건 행사가 연기될 수도 있다는 거야. 〔응용〕　they / the event might be postponed

6　의사 선생님이 말하려는 건 당분간 무리하지 말라는 거야. 〔응용〕
　 the doctor / you should take it easy / for a while

7　부모님이 말씀하시려는 건 내 건강이 걱정된다는 거야. 〔응용〕
　 my parents / they're worried about my health

8　그녀가 말하려는 건 프로젝트를 끝내려면 시간이 좀 더 필요하다는 거야. 〔응용〕
　 she / she needs more time // to finish the project

---

care about ~를 아끼다　　responsibility 책임　　afford to ~할 여유가 있다　　communication 의사소통
crucial 결정적인, 중요한　　relationship 관계　　postpone 연기하다　　take it easy 무리하지 않다
be worried about ~에 대해 걱정하다

> **내가 하고 싶은 말은 그걸 바꿀 필요는 없다는 거야.**
>
> **What + 주어 + be trying to say is that + 절**
> 　　　　　I'm　　　　　　　　　　　we don't really need to replace it

REMINDER 패턴 강화

이제 내 이야기를 해 봐요! 나에게 있음 직한 일들을 적고, 소리 내어 말해 보는 거예요.
주어가 별도로 제시되지 않으면, 주어는 항상 I(나)예요.

▶ 정답 312쪽

UNIT 31 That new superhero moive **is likely to** sell out fast.

> **be likely to + 동사원형**
> ~할 것 같다, ~할 가능성이 높다

1 지연될 것 같아.   it / be delayed

2 또 일어날 것 같아.   it / happen again

3 붐빌 것 같아.   it / be crowded

UNIT 32 **I'm really happy** with my new phone.

> **be really happy with + 명사[동명사]**
> ~에 매우 만족하다

4 요즘 시간을 더 잘 관리하게 되어 정말 만족스러워.
   managing my time better these days

5 프로젝트의 최종 결과에 정말 만족스러워.   the final outcome of the project

6 내가 예산을 잘 지키는 것에 정말 만족스러워.   sticking to my budget

UNIT 33 I **love it when** you hold my hand while we walk.

> **love[hate] it when + 절**
> ~할 때 너무 좋다[싫다]

7 비 오는데 밖에 안 나가도 될 때 정말 좋아.   it rains and I don't have to go out

8 낡은 코트에서 돈을 발견하면 정말 좋아.   I find money in my old coat

9 양말 신고 물 밟을 때 정말 싫어.   I step in water with socks on

UNIT 34 My package **was supposed to** arrive yesterday.

> be supposed to + 동사원형
> ~하기로 되어 있다, ~해야 한다

10 이걸 내일까지 끝내야 해.   finish this by tomorrow

11 오늘 밤에 친구를 만났어야 했는데. 응용   meet my friend tonight

12 넌 답을 알고 있어야지. 응용   you / know the answer

UNIT 35 **What I'm trying to say is that** we don't really need to replace it.

> What + 주어 + be trying to say is (that) + 절
> [주어]가 하려는 말은 ~라는 것이다

13 내가 말하려는 건 너는 나에게 중요하다는 거야.   you matter to me

14 내가 말하려는 건 시간이 좀 필요하다는 거야.   I need some time

15 내가 말하려는 건 이건 나한테 정말 중요한 일이라는 거야.
this means a lot to me

REMINDER 맥락 적용

이제 앞에서 연습한 패턴을 실생활 대화 맥락에 적용해 보세요. 패턴을 일상적인 대화에 넣어서 직접 소리 내어 말해 보는 거예요. 빈칸에 들어갈 말이 기억이 나지 않는다면 다시 앞으로 가서 확인해 보세요.

UNIT 31

A I heard you're planning an overseas trip next month.
다음 달에 해외여행 간다며?

B Yeah, the weather 🐱 _____ be perfect. I can't wait!
응, 날씨가 딱 좋을 것 같아. 너무 기대돼!

A Wow, sounds amazing! Where are you headed?
진짜 좋겠다! 어디로 가?

B I'm off to Bali. Can't wait to chill on those beautiful beaches.
발리로 갈 거야. 아름다운 해변에서 푹 쉬고 싶어.

UNIT 32

A How do you like your new job?
새 직장은 어떠세요?

B I'm really 🐱 _____ it. The work environment is great.
정말 만족하고 있어요. 근무 환경이 아주 좋아요.

A That's awesome! What do you like most about it?
좋네요! 가장 마음에 드는 점이 뭐예요?

B I love the team spirit that everyone has. Everyone is so supportive, friendly, and passionate.
모두가 갖고 있는 협동심이 정말 마음에 들어요. 모두들 서로 돕고 친절하고 열정적이에요.

UNIT 33

A I 🐱 _____ you surprise me with little gifts.
네가 작은 선물들로 나를 놀래킬 때가 좋아.

B It's just my way of showing how much you mean to me.
그냥 네가 나에게 얼마나 소중한지를 보여주는 방법인걸.

A That's so sweet of you. You always make me feel special.
넌 정말 다정해. 나를 언제나 특별하게 만들어 주니까.

B And you deserve to feel that way every single day.
넌 매일 그렇게 느낄 자격이 있어.

UNIT 34

A Wasn't this restaurant 🐱 _____ be open until 10 PM?
이 식당 밤 10시까지 영업하는 거 아니었어?

B Maybe they changed their hours.
영업 시간이 바뀌었나 봐.

A I was looking forward to eating here.
나 여기서 먹고 싶었는데.

B Yeah, it's disappointing. How about we try that new place down the street?
아쉽네. 길 아래 새로 생긴 식당 가 볼래?

UNIT 35

A Who are you going to invite to your birthday party?
생일 파티에 누구 초대할 거야?

B Hmm, I'm not sure yet. Who do you want to invite?
아직 잘 모르겠어. 넌 누구 부르고 싶어?

A Well, 🐱 _____, how about inviting our old high school friends too?
저기, 내가 하고 싶은 말은 우리 옛날 고등학교 친구들도 불러보면 어떨까 하는 거야.

B That's a great idea! I'll start making a list. Do you have their contact information?
좋은 생각이야! 명단을 만들어 볼게. 걔네 연락처 있어?

어휘 head 향하다 | team spirit 협동심 | supportive 도와주는 | disappointing 실망스러운 | contact information 연락처

정답 is likely to | happy with | love it when | supposed to | what I'm trying to say is

UNIT 36

There's no better time to + 동사원형 + than now
지금이 ~하기 가장 좋은 때다, 지금보다 ~하기 좋은 시기는 없다

이 패턴은 특정 행동을 하기에 지금이 가장 좋은 때임을 강조할 때 사용해요. 예를 들어, "지금이 여행을 떠날 가장 좋은 때야."라고 말하고 싶다면 There's no better time to go on a trip than now, 또는 "지금보다 영어 공부를 시작하기 더 좋을 때는 없어."라고 말하고 싶다면 There's no better time to start learning English than now.라고 말할 수 있어요.

There's no better time to 뒤에 동사원형을 사용해 어떤 행동을 하기에 지금이 가장 좋다는 것을 표현합니다.

 There's no better time to declutter **than now**.
지금이야 말로 정리하기 딱 좋을 때야.

실생활 대화

A I need to organize my closet this weekend.
   이번 주말에 옷장 정리를 좀 해야 겠어.

B That's a good plan! There's no better time to declutter than now.
   좋은 생각이야! 지금이야 말로 정리하기 딱 좋을 때야.

A I have so many clothes I never wear anymore.
   한 번도 안 입은 옷이 너무 많아.

B You could donate what you don't need anymore!
   더 이상 필요 없는 옷은 기부하는 건 어때?

organize 정리하다   declutter 물건을 정리하다   donate 기부하다

PRACTICE 패턴 활용

문장을 써 보고 음원을 들으며 소리 내어 말하세요. 제시어 중 기본형 동사는 패턴에 맞게 바꾸고, 제시어의 // 앞까지만이라도 완성해 말하세요.

▶ 정답 313쪽

- 습관을 고치기엔 지금이 좋은 때야.　　　　　　　　　　　　　　　　　　　　　fix your habits

  There's no better time to fix your habits than now.

1 지금보다 운동을 시작하기에 더 좋은 때는 없어.　　　　　　　　　　　　　　　start exercising

2 나이 상관없이 새 언어 배우기엔 지금이 딱이야.　　learn a new language // regardless of your age

3 지금처럼 집 사기 좋은 때가 없어, 특히 요즘 이자율이 많이 낮거든.
  buy a house // especially with current interest rates being so low

4 지금이 부업 시작하기 딱 좋은 때야. 주 수입원이 될 수도 있어.
  start a side hustle // it could become your main source of income

5 간단한 안부 인사라도 좋으니, 부모님께 전화드리기엔 지금이 가장 좋은 때야.
  call your parents // even if it's just to say hi and ask how they're doing

6 지금 그녀가 기분이 좋으니까, 말 걸기엔 지금이 최고야.　　talk to her // since she's in a good mood

7 시간이 조금 더 있을 때, 새로운 기술을 배우기에는 지금만큼 좋은 때가 없어.
  learn a new skill // when you have a bit more free time

8 더 큰 문제가 되기 전에, 지금 고치는 게 가장 좋아.　　fix it // before it turns into a bigger problem

fix 고치다　regardless of ~와 상관없이　interest rate 이자율　side hustle 부업
main source of income 주요 수입원　be in a good mood 기분이 좋다　have free time 자유 시간이 있다
turn into a bigger problem 더 큰 문제로 악화되다

지금이야 말로 정리하기 딱 좋은 때야.

There's no better time to + 동사원형 + than now
　　　　　　　　　　　　　　declutter

UNIT 37

Let's say (that) + 절
~라고 치자, ~라고 가정해 보자

이 패턴은 어떤 상황을 가정하면서 예시와 함께 말을 할 때 사용해요. 예를 들어, "내가 백만 달러를 가진다고 가정해 보자."라고 말하고 싶다면 Let's say that I have a million dollars, "우리가 내일 떠난다고 가정해보자."라고 말하고 싶다면 Let's say that we leave tomorrow. 등으로 말이죠. 일상 생활에서는 보다 자연스럽게 '~라고 치자!'라는 뉘앙스로 많이 사용돼요.

Let's say (that) 뒤에 가정하거나 예를 들어 설명하는 절(주어+동사)을 씁니다.

 Let's say that we go on a trip next week.
다음 주에 여행을 간다고 가정해 보자.

실생활 대화

A Let's say that we go on a trip next week. Where do you want to go?
다음 주에 여행을 간다고 가정해 보자. 어디로 가고 싶어?

B Hmm, I'd prefer to go to the beach. I want to relax by the sea.
음, 나는 해변에 가는 게 좋겠어. 바닷가에서 쉬고 싶어.

A That's a good idea. How about Malibu?
We can enjoy both the ocean and mountains there.
좋은 생각이네. 말리부는 어때? 그곳에서는 바다와 산 모두를 즐길 수 있어.

B Oh, Malibu sounds great! Let's look up some good restaurants there, too. A trip is all about good food, right?
아, 말리부 좋다! 거기 좋은 음식점도 찾아보자. 여행은 맛있는 음식이 중요하잖아, 그치?

---

go on a trip 여행을 가다   prefer 선호하다   relax 쉬다   look up 찾아보다   all about ~가 전부인, 핵심인

PRACTICE 패턴 활용

문장을 써 보고 음원을 들으며 소리 내어 말하세요. 제시어 중 기본형 동사는 패턴에 맞게 바꾸고, 제시어의 // 앞까지만이라도 완성해 말하세요.

▶ 정답 313쪽

- **내년 여름에 유럽 여행을 가기로 했다고 치자. 어떤 나라를 갈 거야?**
  you decide to travel to Europe next summer // what countries would you visit

  Let's say you decide to travel to Europe next summer. What countries would you visit?

1. **새로운 취미를 시작한다고 가정해 보자. 어떤 취미를 고를 거야?**
   you want to start a new hobby // what hobby would you choose

2. **새 노트북을 좋은 가격에 발견했다고 치자. 바로 살 거야?**
   you find a great deal on a new laptop // will you buy it immediately

3. **우리가 이사를 간다고 가정해 보자. 어느 도시로 가고 싶어?**
   we move to a new place // which city would you want to move to

4. **우리가 내년에 가족여행을 간다고 치자. 어디로 가면 좋을까?**
   we go on a family trip next year // where should we go

5. **복권에 당첨됐다고 해 보자. 제일 먼저 뭘 살 거야?** you won the lottery // what would you buy first

6. **어떤 연예인이든 만날 수 있다고 해 보자. 누구를 고를래?**
   you could meet any celebrity // who would you choose

7. **외딴곳에서 차가 고장 났다고 해 보자. 어떻게 할 거야?**
   your car broke down in the middle of nowhere // what would you do

8. **누가 너에게 직장을 그만두는 대가로 백만 달러를 준다고 해 보자. 할 거야?** `응용`
   someone offered you a million dollars to leave your job // would you do it

---

find a great deal 좋은 가격을 발견하다   win the lottery 복권에 당첨되다   celebrity 유명인사
break down 고장 나다   in the middle of nowhere 외딴곳에   offer 제안하다

다음 주에 여행을 간다고 가정해 보자.

Let's say that + 절

we go on a trip next week

UNIT 38

That's a great way to + 동사원형
그건 ~할 수 있는 정말 좋은 방법이다

이 패턴은 어떤 행동에 대해 상대를 칭찬해 주거나 그런 방식을 추천해 줄 때 활용할 수 있는 표현이에요. 그리고 먼저 자신이 어떤 좋은 방법에 대해서 이야기를 할 때는 that 대신에 it을 써서 It's a great way to로 활용할 수 있어요. 화자나 문맥에 따라 that 이나 it을 선택하면 돼요. 예를 들어, 친구가 매일 한 시간씩 영어 패턴 공부를 한다고 했을 때 그건 영어 실력을 향상시키는 좋은 방법이라고 말하고 싶다면 That's a great way to improve your English skills.가 되겠죠?

That's a great way to 뒤에 동사원형을 사용합니다.

 That's a great way to reduce plastic waste.
그건 플라스틱 쓰레기를 줄이는 정말 좋은 방법이야.

실생활 대화

A I've started using reusable shopping bags and containers for my groceries.
장 볼 때 에코백이랑 다회용기 쓰기 시작했어.

B **That's a great way to reduce plastic waste and help the environment.**
그건 플라스틱 쓰레기도 줄이고 환경을 보호할 수 있는 정말 좋은 방법이야.

A It feels good to make a difference. Have you tried any eco-friendly practices?
작은 변화라도 도움이 된다는 게 좋아. 너도 친환경적인 방법 시도해 본 적 있어?

B I've been carrying a tumbler. It's amazing how much plastic it saves.
나는 요즘 텀블러 들고 다녀. 그게 얼마나 많은 플라스틱을 줄일 수 있는지 놀랄 정도야.

---

reusable containers 다회용 용기   reduce 줄이다   plastic waste 플라스틱 쓰레기
help the environment 환경을 보호하다   make a difference 변화를 만들다
eco-friendly practices 친환경적인 실천

PRACTICE 패턴 활용

문장을 써 보고 음원을 들으며 소리 내어 말하세요. 제시어 중 기본형 동사는 패턴에 맞게 바꾸고, 제시어의 // 앞까지만이라도 완성해 말하세요.   ▶ 정답 313쪽

- 그건 시야를 넓힐 수 있는 정말 좋은 방법이야.   expand your horizons

  That's a great way to expand your horizons.

1. **A** I make coffee at home instead of buying it every day.
   난 매일 커피 사는 대신 집에서 만들어.
   B 돈을 아끼는 정말 좋은 방법이야.   save money

2. **A** I walk to work instead of taking the bus. 난 버스 대신 걸어서 출근해.
   B 건강을 유지하는 정말 좋은 방법이야.   stay healthy

3. **A** I try to watch English movies with subtitles. 난 영어로 된 영화를 자막 켜고 보려고 해.
   B 듣기 실력 늘리는 데 정말 좋은 방법이야.   improve your listening skills

4. **A** I put my phone on airplane mode whenever I have to get something done.
   난 일해야 할 땐 핸드폰을 비행기 모드로 바꿔 놔.
   B 집중력을 유지하고 방해 요소를 차단하는 데 딱이네.   stay focused / and cut out distractions

5. **A** When my thoughts are all over the place, I just start journaling.
   머릿속이 복잡할 땐 그냥 일기부터 써.
   B 마음을 비우고 생각을 정리하는 데 좋은 방법이지.   clear your mind / and organize your thoughts

6. **A** I send a quick message to my friends every weekend.
   주말마다 친구들한테 짧은 메시지를 보내.
   바빠도 계속 연결돼 있는 느낌이라서 정말 좋아. 응용   stay connected / even when we're busy

   B That's such a good habit. I really need to start doing that too.
   그거 진짜 좋은 습관이다. 나도 진짜 그렇게 좀 해야겠다.

   expand one's horizons 시야를 넓히다   put one's phone on airplane mode 휴대폰을 비행기 모드로 전환하다
   get ~ done ~을 해내다, 끝내다   stay focused 집중력을 유지하다   cut out distractions 방해 요소를 없애다
   all over the place 생각이 정리되지 않은   journal 일기를 쓰다   clear one's mind 마음을 비우다, 생각을 정리하다
   organize one's thoughts 생각을 체계적으로 정리하다

   그건 플라스틱 쓰레기를 줄이는 정말 좋은 방법이야.

   That's a great way to + 동사원형
                              reduce plastic waste

UNIT 39

It's no wonder (that) + 절

~하는 게 당연하다, ~는 놀랄 일도 아니다

이 패턴은 어떤 일이 당연하다고 느껴질 때 사용해요. '어쩐지 ~하더라', '~하는 게 당연해' 이렇게 말할 때가 있죠? 예를 들어서 복권에 당첨됐다고 말하는 친구에게 I knew it! It's no wonder you look so happy recently!(그럴 줄 알았어! 어쩐지 요즘 행복해 보이더라!)라며 이 패턴을 사용해 말할 수 있어요. 이렇게 어떤 일이 발생했을 때 그 예상이 맞았거나, 그 이유가 충분히 이해될 때 사용하는 표현이에요. It's no wonder 뒤에 that은 써도 되지만 생략하는 것이 원어민에게 더욱 자연스럽게 들리는 편이에요.

It's no wonder (that) 뒤에 당연하다고 느끼는 이유를 설명하는 절(주어+동사)이 옵니다.

 It's no wonder she's getting better.
그녀의 실력이 점점 느는 게 당연해.

실생활 대화

A Jane's English has improved so much lately.
제인의 영어 실력이 최근에 많이 좋아졌어.

B It's no wonder she's getting better.
She practices every day with native speakers.
그녀의 실력이 점점 느는 게 당연해. 매일 원어민들과 연습하잖아.

A Right. I wish I could study that hard, but it's not easy.
맞아. 나도 그렇게 열심히 공부하고 싶은데, 쉽지 않네.

B You can do it, too. If you keep at it like Jane, your skills will improve.
너도 할 수 있어. 제인처럼 꾸준히 하다 보면 실력이 늘 거야.

---

get better 실력이 늘다   native speaker 원어민   keep at it 꾸준히 하다, 계속 노력하다

PRACTICE 패턴 활용

문장을 써 보고 음원을 들으며 소리 내어 말하세요. 제시어 중 기본형 동사는 패턴에 맞게 바꾸고, 제시어의 // 앞까지만이라도 완성해 말하세요.

▶ 정답 313쪽

- 그가 살이 찌는 건 당연해. 하루 종일 패스트푸드만 먹거든.
  he's gaining weight // he eats junk food all day

  It's no wonder he's gaining weight. He eats junk food all day.

1. 네가 배고픈 건 당연해, 아침을 안 먹었잖아.   you're hungry // you didn't have any breakfast

2. 시장이 북적거렸던 건 당연해. 추수감사절이 다가오고 있으니까.
   the market was bustling / thanksgiving is coming

3. 너는 정말 좋은 사람이야. 그래서 모든 사람이 너를 좋아하는 건 당연해.
   you are such a nice person / everyone likes you

4. 네가 피곤한 것도 당연하지. 어젯밤에 거의 못 잤잖아.   you're tired // you barely slept last night

5. 걔네가 헤어진 것도 당연하지. 맨날 싸웠잖아.   they broke up // they were always arguing

6. 침대가 불편했던 건 당연해. 매트리스가 20년 넘었으니까.
   the bed was uncomfortable // the mattress is over 20 years old

7. 이곳이 인기 있는 것도 당연하지. 음식이 정말 맛있잖아.   this place is popular // the food is amazing

8. 그녀가 그렇게 쉬지 않고 헌신하는데, 자기 분야에서 뛰어나지 않을 수가 없지.
   she excels in her field // because she puts in non-stop dedication

---

bustling 부산한   break up 헤어지다   argue 다투다   uncomfortable 불편한   excel 뛰어나다   field 분야   non-stop 멈추지 않고   dedication 헌신

그녀의 실력이 점점 느는 게 당연해.

It's no wonder + 절
　　　　　　　　she's getting better

UNIT 40

Nothing can beat + 명사[동명사]

~만큼 좋은 게 없다

이 패턴은 어떤 것이 최고이며 다른 어떤 것도 그것을 능가할 수 없다는 것을 표현할 때 사용해요. 여기서 beat는 '이기다, 통제하다'라는 뜻이 있어서 '그 어떤 것도 ~를 이길 수 없다' '~가 최고다' 혹은 '~만큼 좋은 게 없다'라는 뉘앙스를 가지고 있어요. 예를 들어, 주말에 가족들과 함께 시간을 보내는 것만큼 좋은 게 없을 때 이 표현을 활용할 수 있겠죠? Nothing can beat quality time with family on the weekend. 이렇게 말이죠. 또는 엄청 추울 겨울날 벽난로 옆에 앉아 있을 때 Nothing can beat sitting by the fireplace in winter.라고 표현할 수 있어요.

Nothing can beat 뒤에는 주로 명사나 동명사를 씁니다.

Nothing can beat that for a good night's sleep.
숙면하는 데 그만한 게 없어.

실생활 대화

A I'm having trouble sleeping lately. Do you have any advice?
요즘 잠이 잘 안 와. 뭐 좋은 방법 없을까?

B Try drinking a warm glass of milk before bed.
Nothing can beat that for a good night's sleep.
자기 전에 따뜻한 우유 한 잔 마셔 봐. 숙면하는 데 그만한 게 없어.

A I'll definitely give that a try!
I heard that herbal tea is also good for sleep. What do you think?
꼭 그렇게 볼게! 허브차도 숙면에 좋다던데, 너는 어떻게 생각해?

B Absolutely! Herbal teas like chamomile can help you relax, too.
Nothing can beat a combination of warm milk and herbal tea for a peaceful night.
맞아! 카모마일 같은 허브차도 몸을 풀어 주는 데 좋지. 편안한 밤을 위해서는 따뜻한 우유랑 허브차만한 게 없어.

---

have trouble -ing ~하는데 어려움을 겪다　herbal tea 허브차　chamomile 카모마일　combination 조합
a peaceful night 평화로운 밤

PRACTICE 패턴 활용

문장을 써 보고 음원을 들으며 소리 내어 말하세요. 제시어 중 기본형 동사는 패턴에 맞게 바꾸고, 제시어의 // 앞까지만이라도 완성해 말하세요.

▶ 정답 313쪽

• 아침에 마시는 커피보다 좋은 건 없어. a cup of coffee / in the morning

  Nothing can beat a cup of coffee in the morning.

1 엄마가 해 주신 집밥보다 좋은 건 없어. mom's home-cooked meals

2 누군가를 도와줬을 때의 기분만큼 좋은 건 없어. the feeling of helping someone

3 힘든 하루 끝에 따뜻한 샤워만큼 좋은 건 없어. a hot shower / after a long day

4 오랜 친구와 나누는 진심 어린 대화보다 좋은 건 없어. a heartfelt conversation / with an old friend

5 해 질 무렵 해변을 걷는 것보다 더 좋은 건 없지. a walk / on the beach / at sunset

6 오랫동안 열심히 해 온 걸 드디어 끝냈을 때 느끼는 그 기분만큼 좋은 건 없어.
  the feeling you get / when you finally finish something // you've been working hard on

7 가족과 시간을 보내는 것보다 좋은 건 없어. 응용 spend time with family

8 진심으로 날 이해해 주는 사람과 깊은 대화를 나누는 것만큼 좋은 건 없어. 응용
  have a deep conversation // with someone who truly understands me

---

mom's home-cooked meals 엄마의 집밥   a heartfelt conversation 진심 어린 대화   at sunset 해 질 무렵에
work hard on ~를 열심히 하다

숙면하는 데 그만한 게 없어.

Nothing can beat + 명사
that for a good night's sleep

REMINDER 패턴 강화

이제 내 이야기를 해 봐요! 나에게 있음 직한 일들을 적고, 소리 내어 말해 보는 거예요.
주어가 별도로 제시되지 않으면, 주어는 항상 I(나)예요.

▶ 정답 313쪽

UNIT 36 There's no better time to declutter than now.

> There's no better time to + 동사원형 + than now
> 지금이 ~하기 가장 좋은 때다, 지금보다 ~하기 좋은 시기는 없다

1 지금이 목소리를 내기(의견을 말하기) 가장 좋을 때야.   speak up

2 지금이 자기 계발을 하기 가장 좋을 때야.   invest in yourself

3 지금이 저축을 시작하기 가장 좋을 때야.   start saving money

UNIT 37 Let's say that we go on a trip next week.

> Let's say (that) + 절
> ~라고 치자, ~라고 가정해 보자

4 인터넷이 끊긴다고 해 보자.   the Internet goes out

5 아무도 안 온다고 해 보자.   nobody comes

6 네가 시험에 합격한다고 해 보자.   you pass the exam

UNIT 38 That's a great way to reduce plastic waste.

> That's a great way to + 동사원형
> 그건 ~할 수 있는 정말 좋은 방법이다

7 그건 하루를 시작하는 좋은 방법이야.   start the day

8   그건 친구를 사귀는 정말 좋은 방법이야.   make friends

9   그건 사람들과 연결되는 좋은 방법이야.   connect with people

UNIT 39 It's no wonder she's getting better.

> It's no wonder (that) + 절
> ~하는 게 당연하다, ~는 놀랄 일도 아니다

10   그녀가 인기가 많은 것도 당연해.   she's popular

11   그가 기분이 안 좋은 것도 이해돼.   he's in a bad mood

12   그가 지친 것도 당연해.   he's exhausted

UNIT 40 Nothing can beat that for a good night's sleep.

> Nothing can beat + 명사[동명사]
> ~만큼 좋은 게 없다

13   엄마의 요리만큼 좋은 건 없어.   mom's cooking

14   좋아하는 노래를 듣는 것보다 좋은 건 없어.   listening to your favorite song

15   목표를 달성하는 것보다 좋은 건 없어.   accomplishing a goal

REMINDER 맥락 적용

이제 앞에서 연습한 패턴을 실생활 대화 맥락에 적용해 보세요. 패턴을 일상적인 대화에 넣어서 직접 소리 내어 말해 보는 거예요. 빈칸에 들어갈 말이 기억이 나지 않는다면 다시 앞으로 가서 확인해 보세요.

UNIT 36

A   I've been thinking about starting a blog.
블로그를 시작해 볼까 고민 중이야.

B   That sounds exciting! _____ to share your thoughts than now.
재밌겠다! 지금이야 말로 네 생각을 나누기에 딱 좋은 때야.

A   I agree! I just need to figure out what topics to write about.
맞아! 이제 어떤 주제로 글을 쓸지만 정하기만 하면 돼.

B   Maybe start with your hobbies or interests!
네 취미나 관심사부터 시작해 봐.

UNIT 37

A   _____ we decide to buy a house next year. What area would be good?
우리가 내년에 집을 사기로 했다고 가정해 보자. 어떤 지역이 좋을까?

B   I think it would be nice to be near a school. It's good for the kids' education.
나는 학교 근처가 좋을 것 같아. 아이들 교육에 좋잖아.

A   Right, that's important. And I think a place with good public transportation would be nice too. It'd be convenient for commuting.
맞아, 중요하지. 그리고 대중교통이 편리한 곳도 좋을 것 같아. 출퇴근하기 편하잖아.

B   Good thinking. Let's also look for a place near parks. It'd be nice for weekend walks.
좋은 생각이야. 공원이 가까운 곳도 찾아보자. 주말에 산책하기 좋을 것 같아.

UNIT 38

A   I make sure to study English for an hour right after I wake up.
아침에 일어나자마자 1시간 동안 꼭 영어 공부를 하고 있어.

B   _____ to improve your English skills.
영어 실력 향상에 정말 좋은 방법이야.

A   Waking up in the morning was tough at first, but now my eyes open up naturally!
처음엔 아침에 일어나는 게 힘들었는데, 지금은 눈이 자연스럽게 딱 떠져!

B   That's impressive! I think I should give it a try, too.
대단한데? 나도 한번 도전해 봐야지!

UNIT 39

A Lisa won the swimming competition again this year.
리사가 올해도 수영 대회에서 우승했어.

B It's no wonder she won. She trains for hours every day and is really dedicated.
당연해. 매일 몇 시간씩 훈련하고 정말 열심히 하잖아.

A Yeah, it's amazing to see how hard she works.
맞아. 노력하는 모습을 보면 대단해.

B Definitely. Lisa seems to be giving her all for her dream.
그러게. 정말 자기 꿈을 위해 모든 걸 바치는 것 같아.

UNIT 40

A How do you like to start your day?
하루의 시작을 어떻게 하는 걸 좋아해?

B Nothing can beat a quiet moment with a cup of coffee before everyone wakes up.
모두가 일어나기 전에 조용히 잠깐 커피 한 잔 마시는 것만한 게 없어.

A That sounds peaceful. How early do you wake up for this?
평화롭다. 그럴려면 얼마나 일찍 일어나는 거야?

B Usually around 5AM. It's worth it for that moment of tranquility.
보통 새벽 5시쯤. 그 고요한 순간을 위해서라면 충분히 그럴 가치가 있어.

어휘 public transportation 대중교통   naturally 자연스럽게   dedicated 진념하는   tranquility 평온, 차분함
정답 There's no better time | Let's say that | That's a great way | It's no wonder | Nothing can beat

REMINDER 패턴 정착

앞에서 배운 20개 패턴을 머릿속에 새기는 시간이에요.
문장을 보고 패턴을 이용해 영어로 소리 내어 말해 보세요.

21 전화 안 해서 미안해요.

22 꼭 제시간에 갈게.

23 미안하지만 그에게 연락할 방법이 없어요.

24 그래서 도로에 차가 이렇게 많은 거구나.

25 내가 제일 먼저 할 일은 설탕을 끊는 거야.

26 어쩔 수 없이 룸메이트를 구해야 할 것 같아.

27 마라톤을 완주할 줄은 상상도 못 했어.

28 설마 또 야근하는 건 아니겠지?

29 도움이 필요하면 언제든지 말씀하세요.

30 기분 상하게 하려던 건 아니었어.

31   이번에 그 히어로 영화는 금방 매진될 것 같아.

32   새 폰이 정말 마음에 들어.

33   걸으면서 네가 내 손 잡아 줄 때 너무 좋아.

34   제 택배가 어제 도착하기로 했는데요.

35   내가 하고 싶은 말은 그걸 바꿀 필요는 없다는 거야.

36   지금이야 말로 정리하기 딱 좋을 때야.

37   다음 주에 여행을 간다고 가정해 보자.

38   그건 플라스틱 쓰레기를 줄이는 정말 좋은 방법이야.

39   그녀의 실력이 점점 느는 게 당연해.

40   숙면하는 데 그만한 게 없어.

UNIT 41

be no joke

~가 장난이 아니다, ~는 만만치 않다

어떤 일이 쉽지 않거나 어렵다는 것을 강조할 때 '~는 장난 아니야, 만만치 않아'라는 말을 하죠? 그 뉘앙스를 살려서 쓸 수 있는 표현이 바로 이 패턴이에요. 또는 어떤 상황이 정말 심각하다는 것을 강조할 때도 사용해요. 예를 들어, "오늘 추운 날씨 정말 장난 아니야."라고 한다면 The cold weather today is no joke.라고 말할 수 있어요. 이 표현은 캐주얼하고 편한 사이에서 사용해요.

be no joke 앞에는 어떤 중요하거나 심각한 상황이나 일을 나타내는 명사(구)나 동명사를 씁니다.

> The housing prices in New York **are no joke**.
> 뉴욕 집값이 장난 아니야.

실생활 대화

A I heard you're looking for a place in New York. How's that going?
뉴욕에서 집 구하고 있다면서? 어떻게 돼 가?

B **The housing prices in New York are no joke.**
It's hard to manage on just a salary.
뉴욕 집값이 장난 아니야. 월급으로는 감당하기 힘들더라고.

A That's tough. Have you considered looking in the suburbs?
힘들겠다. 외곽도 알아봤어?

B Yeah, I've found some great options in the suburbs that offer more space and a quieter environment. I'm debating what to do.
응, 외곽에 더 넓고 조용한 곳들을 몇 군데 찾았어. 어떻게 할지 고민 중이야.

---

housing prices 집값   consider 고려하다   suburb 외곽, 교외   quiet environment 조용한 환경
debate 고민하다(unit 95 패턴)

PRACTICE 패턴 활용

문장을 써 보고 음원을 들으며 소리 내어 말하세요. 제시어 중 기본형 동사는 패턴에 맞게 바꾸고, 제시어의 // 앞까지만이라도 완성해 말하세요.

▶ 정답 314쪽

- 이 회사의 업무량은 장난이 아니야. the workload / in this company

  The workload in this company is no joke.

1. 결혼식을 준비하는 스트레스는 장난이 아니야. the stress / of planning a wedding

2. 요즘 아이를 키우는 비용은 정말 만만치 않아. the cost / of raising a child / these days

3. 새로운 언어를 마스터하는 건 정말 만만치 않아. the difficulty / of mastering a new language

4. 캐나다 겨울은 정말 장난 아니야. 기온이 영하 30도 밑으로 떨어질 수도 있어.
   winter in Canada // temperatures can drop below minus 30 degrees Celsius

5. 그 대학에 들어가는 건 정말 쉽지 않아. 응용 get into that university

6. 출근하려고 매일 아침 일찍 일어나는 거 진짜 장난 아니야. 에너지가 쫙 빠져. 응용
   wake up early / every day / for work // it really drains your energy

7. 아기를 하루 종일 돌보는 건 진짜 쉽지 않아. 너무 힘들지만 그만한 가치는 있어. 응용
   take care of a baby / 24/7 // it's exhausting but worth it

8. 영어 관용구 배우는 건 쉽지 않아. 직역하면 말이 안 되는 경우가 많거든. 응용
   learn English idioms // they don't always make sense literally

---

workload 업무량   cost of raising a child 아이 양육 비용   difficulty 어려움   temperature 기온, 온도
drop below (온도가) ~ 이하로 떨어지다   Celsius 섭씨(Fahrenheit 화씨)   drain energy 에너지를 고갈시키다
24/7 하루 종일   exhausting 매우 힘든   worth it 그만한 가치가 있는   idiom 관용구   literally 글자 그대로

뉴욕 집값이 장난 아니야.

주어 + be no joke

The housing prices in New York are

UNIT 42

can't bring oneself to + 동사원형
도저히 ~할 수 없다, ~하기 어렵다

이 패턴은 특정한 이유로 인해 어떤 행동을 도저히 할 수 없거나 마음이 내키지 않을 때 사용하는데 단순히 '~할 수 없다'보다 더 강한 감정적 어려움을 나타낼 때 써요. 예를 들어, "그에게 도저히 진실을 말할 수가 없어."라고 말하고 싶다면 I can't bring myself to tell him the truth, "그 일을 도저히 포기할 수 없어."라고 말하고 싶다면 I can't bring myself to give up on that task. 등으로 말이죠.

can't bring oneself to 뒤에 마음이 내키지 않는 행동을 나타내는 동사원형을 씁니다.

 I **can't bring myself to** disappoint them.
도저히 실망시켜 드릴 수 없어.

실생활 대화

A Have you told your parents about your career change?
부모님께 직업 바꾼 거 말씀드렸어?

B I can't bring myself to disappoint them.
They were so proud of my old job.
도저히 부모님을 실망시켜 드릴 수 없어. 예전 일을 많이 자랑스러워하셨거든.

A But aren't you happier now?
하지만 지금이 더 행복하지 않아?

B You're right. I should focus on that when I tell them.
맞아. 말씀드릴 때 그 점을 강조해야겠어.

career change 진로 변경   disappoint 실망시키다   focus on ~에 집중하다

PRACTICE 패턴 활용

문장을 써 보고 음원을 들으며 소리 내어 말하세요. 제시어 중 기본형 동사는 패턴에 맞게 바꾸고, 제시어의 // 앞까지만이라도 완성해 말하세요.

▶ 정답 314쪽

- 그녀에게 헤어지자고 도저히 말할 수가 없어.   I / break up with her

  I can't bring myself to break up with her.

1. 도저히 여동생에게 산타가 진짜가 아니라고 말할 수가 없어.
   I / tell my little sister that Santa isn't real

2. 도저히 고수가 들어간 음식은 먹을 수 없어.   I / eat anything / with cilantro in it

3. 도저히 상사에게 퇴사하겠다고 말할 수 없어.   I / tell my boss that I'm quitting

4. 도저히 엄마한테 엄마가 아끼는 꽃병을 깼다고 말할 수 없어.
   I / tell Mom that I broke her favorite vase

5. 우린 아이들을 키운 그 집을 도저히 팔 수가 없어. 〔응용〕
   we / sell the house // where we raised our kids

6. 그는 강아지가 너무 귀여워서 도저히 혼을 낼 수가 없어. 〔응용〕
   he / discipline the puppy // it's just too cute

7. 우린 저건 도저히 못 먹겠어. 도대체 뭘로 만든 거야? 〔응용〕   we / eat that // what is it even made of

8. 그녀는 전 애인의 사진을 도저히 버릴 수가 없어. 〔응용〕   she / throw away the photos / of her ex

---

break up with ~와 헤어지다   cilantro 고수   vase 꽃병   raise kids 아이를 키우다   discipline 훈육하다
puppy 강아지   be made of ~로 만들어지다   throw away 버리다   ex 전 애인

도저히 실망시켜 드릴 수 없어.

주어 + can't bring oneself to + 동사원형
   I   myself   disappoint them

UNIT 43

feel better after + 동명사[명사]

~하고 나니까 기분이 나아지다

시험 때문에 스트레스를 받고 있다가 밖에 나가 바람도 쐴 겸 운동을 하고 나면 기분이 나아지죠? 이렇게 어떤 일을 한 후에 기분이 나아졌다는 것을 표현할 때 이 패턴을 사용해요. 예를 들어, "운동하고 나니까 기분이 나아졌어."라고 말하고 싶다면 I feel better after exercising, "잠을 자고 나니 기분이 나아졌어."라고 말하고 싶다면 I feel better after sleeping. 등으로 말이죠.

feel better after 뒤에는 기분을 나아지게 만든 행동이나 상태를 나타내는 동명사나 명사를 씁니다.

 I feel better after having a cup of coffee.
커피 한 잔 마시니까 기분이 한결 나아졌어.

실생활 대화

A You looked tired this morning. How are you holding up?
오늘 아침에 엄청 피곤해 보이던데, 괜찮아?

B Much better now.
I feel better after having a cup of coffee and some fresh air.
응, 지금은 훨씬 나아. 커피 한 잔 마시고 바람 좀 쐬니까 기분이 한결 나아졌어.

A That's good. Have you been getting enough sleep lately?
다행이네. 요즘 잠은 충분히 자고 있어?

B Not really, but I feel better after taking a short nap during lunch.
I should probably adjust my sleep schedule.
사실 그렇진 않아. 하지만 점심시간에 잠깐 낮잠 자고 나니까 좀 나아졌어.
수면 패턴을 조절해야 할 것 같아.

How are you holding up? 요즘 잘 지내?, 괜찮아?   take a short nap 짧게 낮잠을 자다
adjust 조절하다

PRACTICE 패턴 활용

문장을 써 보고 음원을 들으며 소리 내어 말하세요. 제시어 중 기본형 동사는 패턴에 맞게 바꾸고, 제시어의 // 앞까지만이라도 완성해 말하세요.

▶ 정답 314쪽

- 헬스장에서 운동하고 나니까 기분이 나아졌어요.   I / exercise at the gym
  I feel better after exercising at the gym.

1. 샤워하고 나니까 상쾌해졌어.   I / the shower

2. 낮잠을 좀 자고 나니까 기분이 나아졌어.   I / the nap

3. 조금 울고 나니까 마음이 좀 편해졌어.   I / cry / a little

4. 마음속에 담아둔 말을 꺼내고 나니까 속이 후련해졌어.   I / get things off my chest

5. 아기는 기저귀 갈고 나면 기분이 좋아져. 응용   the baby / a diaper change

6. 우리 강아지는 산책하고 나면 한결 나아져. 응용   our dog / go for a walk

7. 사람들은 감정을 털어놓고 나면 대체로 기분이 나아져. 응용   people / usually / express their feelings

8. 그는 피곤해도 운동하고 나면 항상 기분이 좋아져. 응용   he / always / exercise // even if he's tired

exercise 운동하다   get things off one's chest 마음속 이야기를 꺼내다   a diaper change 기저귀 갈기   go for a walk 산책하다

커피 한 잔 마시니까 기분이 한결 나아졌어.

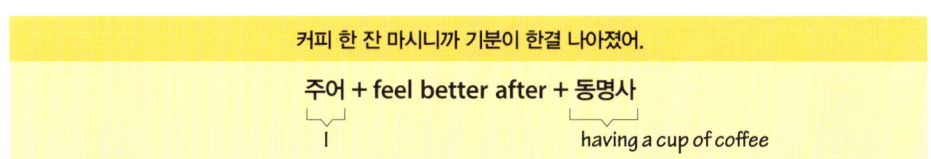

주어 + feel better after + 동명사
        ↳ I   ↳ having a cup of coffee

UNIT 44

Don't get me wrong, + 절
오해하지 마, ~

이 패턴은 "오해하지 마, 내 말을 잘못 받아들이지 마."라는 뜻으로 일상생활에서 대화 중에 상대방이 나의 말을 이해하지 못하거나 다른 방향으로 오해하고 있는 것 같은 느낌이 들 때 사용해요. 또는 의견을 물어 오는 상대방의 감정을 상하지 않게 하기 위해 "오해하지 마세요. 제 말 뜻은~" 이렇게 말을 할 때도 사용해요.

Don't get me wrong 뒤에는 절(주어+동사)을 써서 하고 싶은 말을 씁니다.

 Don't get me wrong, I thought it was visually stunning.
오해하지 마, 영상미는 정말 대단했어.

실생활 대화

A I heard you didn't enjoy the movie.
영화 별로였다며?

B Don't get me wrong, I thought it was visually stunning, but the plot was a bit weak.
오해하지 마, 영상미는 정말 대단했는데 줄거리가 좀 약했어.

A I see what you mean. The story could have been better.
무슨 말인지 알겠어. 스토리가 더 탄탄했으면 좋았을 텐데.

B Exactly! I just expected more from it.
그러니까! 난 그냥 기대를 너무 많이 했나 봐.

get ~ wrong ~를 오해하다   visually stunning 시각적으로 매우 인상적인   plot 줄거리

PRACTICE 패턴 활용

문장을 써 보고 음원을 들으며 소리 내어 말하세요. 제시어 중 기본형 동사는 패턴에 맞게 바꾸고, 제시어의 // 앞까지만이라도 완성해 말하세요.

▶ 정답 314쪽

- **오해하지 마**, 난 전혀 그런 뜻이 아니었어.　　　　　　　　　　　I didn't mean that at all

  Don't get me wrong, I didn't mean that at all.

1. **오해하지 마**, 나 아이들 좋아해. 근데 아직 낳을 준비는 안 됐어.
   I love kids // but I'm not ready to have one yet

2. **오해하지 마**, 네가 잘 된 거 진심으로 기뻐. 근데 솔직히 좀 부럽기도 해.
   I'm happy for you // but I'm also a bit jealous

3. **오해하지 마**, 온라인 수업은 편리해. 근데 사람들을 직접 보는 게 그리워.
   online classes are convenient // but I miss seeing people in person

4. **오해하지 마**, 너랑 시간 보내는 거 좋아. 근데 나도 혼자 있는 시간이 좀 필요해.
   I enjoy spending time with you // but I need some space, too

5. **오해하지 마**, 그는 좋은 사람이야. 다만 이 일에는 적합하지 않은 것 같아.
   he's a nice person // but I don't think he's right for this job

6. **오해하지 마**, 음식은 맛있었어. 다만 음식에 비해 가격이 좀 비싼 것 같아서 말이야.
   the food was delicious // but I thought it was a bit pricey for what it was

7. **오해하지 마**, 그녀는 좋은 관리자야. 다만 가끔 의사소통 방식이 좀 불명확할 때가 있어.
   she's a good manager // but her communication style can be a bit unclear at times

8. **오해하지 마**, 네 새 헤어스타일 정말 멋져. 다만 평소 스타일과 너무 달라서 그래.
   your new haircut looks great // but it's just so different from your usual style

---

be happy for ~의 일이 잘 되어 기쁘다　　jealous 부러운　　convenient 편리한　　in person 직접, 몸소
need some space 혼자만의 시간이 필요하다　　right for ~에 잘 맞는　　pricey 비싼　　unclear 불명확한
at times 때때로

오해하지 마, 영상미는 정말 대단했어.

Don't get me wrong, + 절
　　　　　　　　　　　　I thought it was visually stunning

UNIT 45

If + 주어 + happen to come across + 명사(구), + 절

[주어]가 우연히 ~를 발견하면[마주치면]

이 패턴은 우연히 어떤 것을 발견하거나 누군가를 마주칠 때 사용해요. come across는 '마주치다, 발견하다'라는 뜻으로, 여기에 우연한 일이라는 의미를 더 추가하고 예의 바르게 표현하고 싶을 때 happen to(혹시, 우연히)를 넣어서 활용해요. 예를 들어, '우연히 우리 강아지를 발견하면'이라고 말하고 싶다면 if you happen to come across my dog, '우연히 내 친구를 만난다면'이라고 말하고 싶다면 if you happen to come across my friend 등으로 말이죠.

If + 주어 + happen to come across 뒤에는 명사나 명사구를 씁니다.

 If I happen to come across a nice one, I'll let you know.
혹시나 괜찮은 데 발견하면 알려 줄게.

실생활 대화

A Do you know any good cafés nearby?
혹시 근처에 좋은 카페 알고 있어?

B I can't think of any right now, but if I happen to come across a nice one, I'll let you know.
지금은 딱 떠오르는 데가 없네. 혹시나 괜찮은 데 발견하면 알려 줄게.

A Thanks. I hope it's a quiet place with a good atmosphere.
고마워. 조용하고 분위기 좋은 곳이면 좋겠어.

B Got it. I'll let you know as soon as I find one.
알겠어. 그런 데 찾으면 바로 알려 줄게.

---

atmosphere 분위기   as soon as ~하자 마자

PRACTICE 패턴 활용

문장을 써 보고 음원을 들으며 소리 내어 말하세요. 제시어 중 기본형 동사는 패턴에 맞게 바꾸고, 제시어의 // 앞까지만이라도 완성해 말하세요.

▶ 정답 314쪽

• 너 혹시 괜찮은 카페를 발견하면 나한테 알려 줘.   you / a good café / let me know

  If you happen to come across a good café, let me know.

1 오늘 톰을 우연히 보게 되면 내가 전화했다고 전해 줘.   you / Tom / today / tell him I called

2 혹시 내 잃어버린 노트북을 발견하면 꼭 가져다 줘.   you / my lost notebook / please bring it to me

3 공부하기 조용한 장소를 발견하면 나한테 꼭 알려 줘.   you / a quiet place / to study / I'd love to know

4 혹시 가게에서 이 과자를 우연히 보면, 대신 사다 줄 수 있어?
  you / this snack / in a store / can you buy it for me

5 혹시 내 핸드폰 충전기를 발견하면 올 때 가져다 줘.
  you / my phone charger / please bring it back when you visit

6 혹시 우리 찍은 사진 있으면 보내 줘. 프로필 사진 바꾸고 싶어.
  you / any photos of us / send them to me // I want to change my profile picture

7 오늘 밤 행사에서 혹시 제인을 만나면 내가 조금 늦는다고 전해 줘.
  you / Jane / at the event / tonight / please tell her I'll be a bit late

8 서점에서 혹시 이 책을 보면 정말 읽을 만하니까 읽어 봐. 응용
  you / this book / in a bookstore / it's totally worth reading

---

lost 잃어버린   quiet 조용한   phone charger 휴대폰 충전기   worth -ing ~할 가치가 있는, ~해 볼 만한

혹시나 괜찮은 데 발견하면 알려 줄게.

If + 주어 + happen to come across + 명사
         ㅣ   a nice one, I'll let you know
         I

REMINDER 패턴 강화

이제 내 이야기를 해 봐요! 나에게 있음 직한 일들을 적고, 소리 내어 말해 보는 거예요.
주어가 별도로 제시되지 않으면, 주어는 항상 I(나)예요.

▶ 정답 315쪽

UNIT 41 The housing prices in New York **are no joke**.

> **be no joke**
> ~가 장난이 아니다, ~는 만만치 않다

1 아이 키우는 것은 만만치 않아.   raising kids

2 야간 근무는 만만하지 않아.   working night shifts

3 대도시에서 사는 거 장난 아니다.   living in a big city

UNIT 42 I **can't bring myself to** disappoint them.

> **can't bring oneself to + 동사원형**
> 도저히 ~할 수 없다, ~하기 어렵다

4 도저히 그 영화를 다시 볼 수 없어.   watch that movie again

5 도저히 도움을 요청할 수 없어.   ask for help

6 도저히 작별 인사를 할 수 없어.   say goodbye

UNIT 43 I **feel better after** having a cup of coffee.

> **feel better after + 동명사[명사]**
> ~하고 나니까 기분이 나아지다

7 바깥 공기 좀 쐬고 나니까 기분이 나아졌어.   getting some fresh air

8 일을 끝내고 나니까 기분이 나아졌어.　finishing my work

9 친구와 이야기를 하고 나니까 기분이 나아졌어.　talking to a friend

UNIT 44 **Don't get me wrong**, I thought it was visually stunning.

> **Don't get me wrong, + 절**
> 오해하지마, ~

10 오해하지 마. 난 그 애들이랑 시간 보내는 거 좋아해.
   I like spending time with them

11 오해하지 마. 이 일은 나한테 정말 중요해.　this job means a lot to me

12 오해하지 마. 난 네 의견을 존중해.　I respect your opinion

UNIT 45 **If I happen to come across** a nice one, I'll let you know.

> **If + 주어 + happen to come across + 명사(구), + 절**
> [주어]가 우연히 ~를 발견하면[마주치면]

13 혹시 우리 옛날 사진을 발견하면 나에게 보내 줘.
   you / an old photo of us / send it to me

14 혹시 내 잃어버린 열쇠를 발견하면 나에게 알려 줘.
   you / my missing keys / let me know

15 혹시 아담하고 괜찮은 카페를 발견하면 나에게 말해 줘.
   you / a nice little café / tell me about it

REMINDER 맥락 적용

이제 앞에서 연습한 패턴을 실생활 대화 맥락에 적용해 보세요. 패턴을 일상적인 대화에 넣어서 직접 소리 내어 말해 보는 거예요. 빈칸에 들어갈 말이 기억이 나지 않는다면 다시 앞으로 가서 확인해 보세요.

UNIT 41

A How's living abroad going?
외국 생활은 어때?

B Living in a new country is _____. I have to adapt to a new culture and language every day.
새로운 나라에서 사는 건 정말 쉬운 일이 아니야. 매일 새로운 문화와 언어에 적응해야 하거든.

A That must be quite an adjustment! How long have you been there?
진짜 큰 변화겠다! 거기 얼마나 있었지?

B It's been six months now. It's been challenging, but I love pushing myself to learn and grow every day!
이제 6개월 됐어. 힘들긴 하지만 매일 배우고 성장하려고 스스로 노력하는 게 정말 좋아!

UNIT 42

A Are you going to change your hairstyle?
헤어스타일을 바꿀 건가요?

B I want to, but I can't _____ cut my hair short.
바꾸고 싶긴 한데, 도저히 짧게 자를 용기가 안 나요.

A It could look really good on you! Why don't you sleep on it and decide tomorrow?
당신에게 정말 잘 어울릴 수도 있어요! 고민해 보고 내일 결정해 보는 거 어때요?

B Thank you! I'll let you know what I decide tomorrow.
고마워요! 어떻게 할지 내일 말해 줄게요.

UNIT 43

A How's your headache?
두통은 좀 어때?

B I _____ taking some painkillers. It's almost gone now.
진통제 먹고 나니까 한결 낫네. 거의 다 나은 것 같아.

A That's great to hear. Do you think it was stress-related?
다행이다. 스트레스 때문인 것 같아?

B Probably. I feel better overall after finishing that big project at work.
아마도. 회사에서 큰 프로젝트 끝내고 나니까 전반적으로 컨디션이 좋아졌어.

UNIT 44

A What do you think of Sarah's new boyfriend?
사라 새 남자친구 어때?

B _____, he's a nice person, but I feel like they are moving too fast.
오해하지 마. 좋은 사람 같긴 한데 둘이 너무 서두르는 것 같아.

A I agree; it seems like they're rushing into things.
나도 그렇게 생각해. 너무 급하게 진행되는 것 같아.

B Right? I just hope she takes her time and thinks it through.
그치? 사라가 좀 더 시간을 갖고 신중히 생각해 봤으면 좋겠어.

UNIT 45

A Have you seen my blue laptop?
내 파란 노트북 봤어?

B No, I haven't. But if I _____ it, I'll let you know.
아니, 못 봤어. 우연히라도 발견하면 알려줄게.

A Thanks! It has some important files on it.
고마워! 중요한 파일들이 들어 있어서.

B Don't worry. I'll contact you right away if I find it.
걱정 마. 찾으면 바로 연락할게.

어휘 adapt to ~에 적응하다   adjustment 적응   sleep on 하룻밤 자면서 생각해 보다   painkiller 진통제
     stress-related 스트레스와 관련된   rush into things 서두르다

정답 no joke | bring myself to | feel better after | Don't get me wrong |
     happen to come across

143

UNIT 46

have a hunch that + 절

~라는 예감이 들다[촉이 오다]

여러분은 무언가 확실하지는 않지만 가끔씩 '촉'이 올 때가 있죠? 그때 이 패턴을 사용해요. 예를 들어 날씨가 정말 화창한데, 왠지 모르게 눈이 올 것 같은 예감이 들 때 I have a hunch that it will snow today.라고 표현하면 돼요. 이렇게 어떤 일이 일어날 것이라는 강한 예감이나 직감을 표현할 때 이 패턴을 사용해요.

have a hunch that 뒤에 예감하는 상황을 나타내는 절(주어+동사)이 옵니다.

 I **have a hunch that** it's going to rain this evening.
오늘 저녁은 비가 올 것 같은 예감이 들어.

실생활 대화

A I have a hunch that it's going to rain this evening.
오늘 저녁은 비가 올 것 같은 예감이 들어.

B Really? What's the weather forecast say?
정말? 날씨 예보는 뭐래?

A It's not certain yet. Just a feeling I have.
아직 확실하진 않아. 그냥 그런 느낌이 있어.

B Got it. We should probably take umbrellas, just in case.
알겠어. 혹시 모르니까 우산 챙기는 게 좋겠다.

hunch 예감, 직감   weather forecast 날씨 예보   certain 확실한

PRACTICE 패턴 활용

문장을 써 보고 음원을 들으며 소리 내어 말하세요. 제시어 중 기본형 동사는 패턴에 맞게 바꾸고,
제시어의 // 앞까지만이라도 완성해 말하세요. ▶ 정답 315쪽

- 이 책이 베스트셀러가 될 것 같은 촉이 와.   I / this book will become a bestseller
  I have a hunch that this book will become a bestseller.

1 잃어버린 핸드폰이 집 어딘가에 있을 것 같은 예감이 들어.
   I / my lost phone is somewhere / in the house

2 우리가 곧 좋은 소식을 듣게 될 것 같은 예감이 들어.   I / we're going to get good news / soon

3 내일 경기에서 우리가 이길 것 같은 느낌이 들어.   I / we'll win the game / tomorrow

4 다음 달에 주식 시장이 좋아질 것 같은 예감이 들어.   I / the stock market will improve / next month

5 우리는 회의가 취소될 것 같은 느낌이 들어.   we / the meeting will be canceled

6 그는 그녀가 자기한테 마음이 있는 것 같다는 예감을 갖고 있어. 응용   he / she likes him

7 그는 식당에 핸드폰을 두고 온 것 같다는 예감을 갖고 있어. 응용
   he / he left his phone / at the restaurant

8 그녀는 누군가 몰래 자기 노트북을 쓴 것 같다는 예감을 갖고 있어. 응용
   she / someone has been using her laptop

stock market 주식 시장   improve 나아지다, 개선되다   laptop 노트북

오늘 저녁은 비가 올 것 같은 예감이 들어.

주어 + have a hunch that + 절
 I   it's going to rain this evening

UNIT 47

The bottom line is (that) + 절
결론적으로[핵심은] ~이다

이야기를 나누다가 가장 중요한 요점이나 결론을 강조하고 싶을 때가 있죠? 예를 들어, 수입에 비해 지출이 너무 많을 때 여러 가지 해결 방법 중에서도 "결론적으로 가장 중요한 건 지출을 줄여야 해!"라는 말은 The bottom line is that we need to cut our expenses!라고 할 수 있어요. 또는 이야기의 요점을 말하고 싶을 때도 사용해요. "핵심은 저희가 더 많은 시간이 필요하다는 것입니다."라고 말하고 싶다면 The bottom line is that we need more time.이라고 하면 돼요. 이때 The bottom line is 뒤의 that은 써도 되지만 생략하는 것이 원어민의 귀에는 훨씬 자연스럽게 들려요.

The bottom line is (that) 뒤에 요점을 나타내는 절이 나옵니다.

 The bottom line is eating healthy and exercising are what really matter.
핵심은 건강하게 먹고 운동하는 게 진짜 중요하다는 거야.

실생활 대화

A Have you tried any new diet methods?
새로운 다이어트 방법 시도해 본 적 있어?

B Yeah, I've tried a few, but none of them seemed very effective.
응, 몇 가지 해 봤는데 다 별로 효과 없더라.

A Really? **The bottom line is,** no matter what method you try, eating healthy and exercising are what really matter.
그래? 결국 어떤 방법을 쓰든, 핵심은 건강하게 먹고 운동하는 게 진짜 중요하다는 거군.

B True. That's what it really comes down to.
맞아. 결국 그게 핵심이지.

method 방법   effective 효과적인   it really comes down to 결국 중요한 건 ~이다

PRACTICE 패턴 활용

문장을 써 보고 음원을 들으며 소리 내어 말하세요. 제시어 중 기본형 동사는 패턴에 맞게 바꾸고, 제시어의 // 앞까지만이라도 완성해 말하세요.

▶ 정답 315쪽

- 핵심은 우리에게 시간이 더 필요하다는 거야.   we need more time

   The bottom line is we need more time.

1. 핵심은 네가 결정을 내려야 한다는 거야.   you need to make a decision

2. 요점은 우리가 이 일을 이번 주 금요일까지 끝내야 한다는 거야.
   we need to get this done / by this Friday

3. 결국 웃음이야말로 스트레스에 만병통치약이라는 거야. laughter really is the best medicine / for stress

4. 핵심은 서로 솔직하게 소통하는 것이 중요하다는 거야.
   it's important to communicate / openly / with each other

5. 핵심은 너는 네 행동에 책임을 져야 한다는 거야.   you have to take responsibility / for your actions

6. 결국 네가 규칙적으로 연습하지 않으면 실력은 늘지 않는다는 거야.
   if you don't practice regularly, you won't improve

7. 핵심은 우리가 마감일을 맞춰야 한다는 거야. 야근을 하더라도 말이야.
   we have to meet the deadline // even if it means working overtime

8. 핵심은 우리는 시간이 부족하니까, 가장 중요한 일들에 집중해야 해.
   we don't have enough time // so we need to focus on the most important tasks

---

get ~ done ~를 끝내다   by (기간) ~까지   laughter 웃음   medicine 약   communicate 소통하다
take responsibility for ~에 책임지다   regularly 정기적으로   meet the deadline 마감일을 지키다
even if ~일지라도   task 일, 과업

핵심은 건강하게 먹고 운동하는 게 진짜 중요하다는 거야.

The bottom line is (that) + 절

eating healthy and exercising are what really matter.

UNIT 48

All + 주어 + be saying is (that) + 절

[주어]의 말은 ~라는 것이다

이 패턴은 하려는 말을 더 강조하고 요점을 명확히 하고 싶을 때 사용해요. saying 대신에 suggesting(제안하다), asking(요청하다), explaining(설명하다) 등을 넣어서 활용할 수도 있어요. 예를 들어, "내가 말하고 싶은 건 네가 휴식이 필요하다는 거야. 하루 종일 일했잖아."라고 말하고 싶다면 All I'm saying is that you need to take a break. You've been working all day, 또는 "제가 요청드리는 건 더 많은 시간이 필요하다는 것뿐입니다."라고 말하고 싶다면 All I'm asking is that we need more time. 등으로 말이죠.

is (that) 뒤에 절을 써서 강조하고 싶은 말을 쓰면 됩니다.

 All I'm saying is that you'll do great.
내 말은 넌 잘할 거라는 거야.

실생활 대화

A I'm not sure if I'm ready for the presentation tomorrow.
내일 발표할 준비가 된 건지 모르겠어.

B You've practiced a lot. All I'm saying is that you'll do great.
너 연습 많이 했잖아. 내 말은 넌 잘할 거라는 거야.

A Thanks, that really helps.
고마워, 그 말 들으니까 힘이 난다.

B Anytime. I believe in you.
언제든지. 난 널 믿어.

---

believe in ~를 믿다

PRACTICE 패턴 활용

문장을 써 보고 음원을 들으며 소리 내어 말하세요. 제시어 중 기본형 동사는 패턴에 맞게 바꾸고, 제시어의 // 앞까지만이라도 완성해 말하세요.

▶ 정답 315쪽

- 내 말은 한 번 더 시도해 **보자는 거야**. I / we give it another try
  All I'm saying is that we give it another try.

1 내가 진짜 말하고 싶은 건 남들과 너 자신을 비교하지 말아야 **한다는 거야**.
  I / you need to stop comparing yourself to others

2 내 말은 가끔은 거절해도 괜찮다는 거야. I / it's okay to say no / sometimes

3 내 말은 어떤 관계에서든 의사소통이 핵심이라는 거야. I / communication is key / in any relationship

4 내 말은 너의 노력이 결국에는 반드시 보상받을 것이라는 거야.
  I / your efforts will definitely pay off / in the end

5 내가 말하고 싶은 건, 무슨 일이 있어도 넌 존중받을 자격이 있다는 거야.
  I / you deserve to be treated with respect // no matter what

6 의사 선생님이 말씀하시는 건 네가 더 쉬어야 한다는 거야. 응용 the doctor / you need more rest

7 그가 말하는 건 네가 너무 자책하지 말라는 거야. 응용 he / you shouldn't blame yourself

8 그녀가 요청하는 건 가끔 전화 좀 해 달라는 거야. 네 소식을 듣고 싶어 해. 응용
  she / ask / you call her / once in a while // she misses hearing from you

---

definitely 반드시   pay off 보상받다   in the end 결국에   deserve ~할 자격이 있다
be treated with respect 존중받다   no matter what 무슨 일이 있어도   blame oneself 자책하다
once in a while 가끔씩   hear from ~의 소식을 듣다

내 말은 넌 잘할 거라는 거야.

All + 주어 + be saying is that + 절
         I'm   you'll do great

UNIT 49

have always wanted to + 동사원형

항상 ~하고 싶었다

이 패턴은 오랫동안 해 보고 싶었던 것, 꿈꿔 왔던 것을 표현할 때 사용해요. 예를 들어, "나는 항상 제주에서 살아 보고 싶었어."라고 말하고 싶다면 I've always wanted to live in Jeju, 또는 "나는 항상 기타를 배워 보고 싶었어."라고 말하고 싶다면 I've always wanted to learn how to play the guitar. 등으로 말이죠.

have always wanted to 뒤에 하고 싶었던 행동을 나타내는 동사원형을 씁니다.

 I've always wanted to travel around Europe.
난 항상 유럽으로 여행 가고 싶었어.

실생활 대화

A What's something you've always wanted to do?
네가 예전부터 항상 해 보고 싶었던 게 뭐야?

B I've always wanted to travel around Europe.
난 항상 유럽으로 여행 가고 싶었어.

A That sounds like an amazing experience! Where would you go first?
정말 멋진 경험이 될 것 같아! 어디서부터 가고 싶어?

B I'd probably start in Italy and check out all the historic sites.
아마 이탈리아에서 시작해서 역사적인 장소들을 둘러보고 싶어.

experience 경험   historic site 역사적인 장소

PRACTICE 패턴 활용

문장을 써 보고 음원을 들으며 소리 내어 말하세요. 제시어 중 기본형 동사는 패턴에 맞게 바꾸고, 제시어의 // 앞까지만이라도 완성해 말하세요.

▶ 정답 316쪽

- 항상 책을 써 보고 싶었어.   I / write a book.
  I've always wanted to write a book.

1. 항상 스카이다이빙을 해 보고 싶었어.   I / try skydiving

2. 항상 케이크를 처음부터 손수 만들어 보고 싶었어.   I / bake a cake / from scratch

3. 항상 내 사업을 시작해 보고 싶었어.   I / start my own business

4. 항상 미국의 50개 주를 모두 가 보고 싶었어.   I / visit all 50 states / in the US

5. 우리는 항상 바닷가 근처에 살면서 파도 소리에 깨고 싶었어.
   we / live by the beach // and wake up to the sound of waves

6. 그들은 항상 미국 전역을 자동차 여행으로 돌아다니고 싶어 했어.
   they / take a road trip / across the United States

7. 그녀는 항상 파리에 가서 에펠탑을 직접 보고 싶어 했어. `응용`
   she / visit Paris // and see the Eiffel Tower in person

8. 내 여동생은 항상 강아지를 입양하고 싶어 했지만 부모님이 허락하지 않으셨어. `응용`
   my sister / adopt a dog // but our parents wouldn't allow it

---

bake a cake 케이크를 만들다   from scratch 처음부터   start one's own business 자신의 사업을 시작하다
state (미국의) 주   live by ~ 근처에 살다   take a road trip 자동차로 여행하다   adopt 입양하다

난 항상 유럽으로 여행 가고 싶었어.

주어 + have always wanted to + 동사원형
     I   travel around Europe

UNIT 50

All + 주어 + have to do is + 동사원형

[주어]는 ~하기만 하면 된다

이 패턴은 복잡해 보이는 일을 단순화하거나, 쉬운 해결책을 제시할 때 사용해요. 예를 들어, "이 버튼만 누르면 기계가 작동할 거야."라고 말하고 싶다면 All you have to do is press this button, and the machine will start, "너는 그냥 그에게 전화하기만 하면 돼." 라고 말하고 싶다면 All you have to do is call him. 등으로 말이죠.

is 뒤에는 동사원형을 써서 간단한 행동을 나타내는 말이나 쉬운 해결책을 제시합니다.

 All you have to do is get started.
그냥 넌 시작만 하면 돼.

do는 '행동하다'라는 의미를 포함하고 있기 때문에, 동사 is 다음에 나오는 동작은 to 없이 동사원형을 쓰는 것이 자연스러워요.

All you have to do is <u>start</u>. (자연스러운 표현)

All you have to do is <u>to start</u>. (가능하지만 부자연스러운 표현)

실생활 대화

A Your room is such a mess. When are you going to clean it?
방이 너무 엉망이야. 언제 청소할 거야?

B Ugh... Cleaning is such a hassle.
으… 청소 너무 귀찮아.

A It's really not that hard. All you have to do is get started.
Once you start, everything else will fall into place.
그렇게 어렵지 않아. 그냥 넌 시작만 하면 돼. 시작하면 나머지는 알아서 풀릴 거야.

B Okay, okay. I'll start now.
알겠어, 알겠어. 지금 시작할게.

such a hassle 정말 귀찮은 일   get started 시작하다   fall into place 제자리를 찾다, 일이 자연스럽게 풀리다

PRACTICE 패턴 활용

문장을 써 보고 음원을 들으며 소리 내어 말하세요. 제시어 중 기본형 동사는 패턴에 맞게 바꾸고, 제시어의 // 앞까지만이라도 완성해 말하세요.

▶ 정답 316쪽

- 넌 공부를 열심히 하기만 하면 돼. *you / study hard*
  All you have to do is study hard.

1. 여기 이 서류에 서명하기만 하면 돼. 그러면 계약을 마무리할 수 있어.
   you / sign this document // and we can finalize the agreement

2. 설거지를 도와주기만 하면 돼. 내가 디저트를 준비할게.
   you / help me with the dishes // and I'll take care of dessert

3. 그에게 전화해서 상황을 설명하기만 하면 돼. 분명 이해할 거야.
   you / call him / and explain the situation // I'm sure he'll understand

4. 집에 도착하면 문자만 보내 주면 돼. 그러면 네가 안전하게 도착했다는 걸 알 수 있어.
   you / text me / when you get home // so I know you got home safely

5. 이 버튼을 누르기만 하면 나머지는 커피 머신이 다 해 줘.
   you / press this button // and the coffee machine does the rest

6. 학생들이 해야 할 건 금요일 전까지 과제를 제출하는 거야.
   the students / submit the assignment / by Friday

7. 그는 그냥 그렇게 웃기만 해도 방 안에 있는 사람들이 다 웃기 시작해. 응용
   he / smile / like that // and everyone in the room starts laughing

8. 내 남동생은 그냥 "제발"이라고만 하면 엄마가 뭐든 다 주셔. 응용
   my little brother / say "Please" // and my mom gives him whatever he wants

---

finalize 마무리 짓다   agreement 계약   help with the dishes 설거지를 도와주다
explain the situation 상황을 설명하다   text 문자를 보내다   do the rest 나머지를 하다   assignment 과제

그냥 넌 시작만 하면 돼.

All + 주어 + have to do is + 동사원형

you   get started

REMINDER 패턴 강화

이제 내 이야기를 해 봐요! 나에게 있음 직한 일들을 적고, 소리 내어 말해 보는 거예요.
주어가 별도로 제시되지 않으면, 주어는 항상 I(나)예요.

▶ 정답 316쪽

UNIT 46 I **have a hunch that** it's going to rain this evening.

> **have a hunch that + 절**
> ~라는 예감이 들다[촉이 오다]

1 그녀가 뭔가 숨기고 있는 것 같은 예감이 들어.   she's hiding something

2 그들이 깜짝 이벤트를 준비 중인 것 같은 예감이 들어.   they're planning a surprise

3 뭔가 일이 벌어지고 있는 것 같은 촉이 와.   something's going on

UNIT 47 **The bottom line is** eating healthy and exercising are what really matter.

> **The bottom line is (that) + 절**
> 결론적으로[핵심은] ~이다

4 결론적으로 우리는 비용을 줄여야 한다는 거야.   we need to cut costs

5 결론적으로 시간이 얼마 남지 않았다는 거야.   time is running out

6 핵심은 그녀는 더 나은 대우를 받을 자격이 있다는 거야.   she deserves better

UNIT 48 **All I'm saying is that** you'll do great.

> **All + 주어 + be saying is (that) + 절**
> [주어]의 말은 ~라는 것이다

7 내 말은 커피가 필요하다는 거야.   I need coffee

8   내 말은 이 쇼가 진짜 재밌다는 거야.   this show is amazing

9   내 말은 내가 네 감자튀김을 안 먹었다는 거야.   I didn't eat your fries

UNIT 49 I've always wated to travel around Europe.

have always wanted to + 동사원형
항상 ~하고 싶었다

10   난 항상 직접 피자를 만들어 보고 싶었어.   try making my own pizza

11   난 항상 혼자 여행해 보고 싶었어.   travel alone

12   난 항상 저 사람이랑 말 한 번 해 보고 싶었어.   talk to that person

UNIT 50 All you have to do is get started.

All + 주어 + have to do is + 동사원형
[주어]는 ~하기만 하면 된다

13   너 자신을 믿기만 하면 돼.   you / believe in yourself

14   시간 맞춰 오기만 하면 돼.   you / show up on time

15   레시피만 따라 하면 돼.   you / follow the recipe

REMINDER 맥락 적용

이제 앞에서 연습한 패턴을 실생활 대화 맥락에 적용해 보세요. 패턴을 일상적인 대화에 넣어서 직접 소리 내어 말해 보는 거예요. 빈칸에 들어갈 말이 기억이 나지 않는다면 다시 앞으로 가서 확인해 보세요.

UNIT 46

A I _____ that this restaurant will be good.
이 레스토랑은 맛있을 것 같은 촉이 와.

B Why do you think so?
왜 그렇게 생각해?

A I saw people lining up outside.
밖에 사람들이 줄 서 있는 걸 봤거든.

B I see. Let's try it out then.
그렇구나. 그럼 한번 가 보자.

UNIT 47

A I'm thinking about deleting my social media accounts.
SNS 계정을 삭제할까 봐.

B Why? Don't you enjoy staying connected with friends?
왜? 친구들이랑 연락하는 걸 좋아하지 않아?

A I do, but _____ that it's taking up too much of my time.
좋아하긴 하지만, 핵심은 내 시간을 너무 많이 뺏고 있다는 거야.

B I understand. Maybe you could just limit your usage instead?
이해해. 그러면 대신 사용 시간을 줄이는 건?

UNIT 48

A Do you want to go out for a bite tonight?
오늘 저녁은 간단히 밖에 나가서 먹을래?

B I'm not sure. I'm pretty tired from work.
글쎄. 일 때문에 꽤 피곤해.

A _____ that we treat ourselves after a long week.
내가 제안하는 건 힘든 한 주를 보낸 우리 자신에게 보상을 하자는 거야.

B You know what? You're right. Let's go to that new Italian place.
알겠어. 네 말이 맞아. 새로 문 연 이탈리안 식당에 가자.

UNIT 49

A What's a skill you've always wanted to learn?
항상 배우고 싶었던 기술이 뭐였어?

B **I've always wanted** to learn how to speak Japanese.
난 항상 일본어를 배우고 싶었어.

A That's cool! Why Japanese in particular?
멋지다! 특별히 일본어를 고른 이유가 있어?

B I love anime and I'd love to watch it without subtitles.
애니메이션을 좋아하는데, 자막 없이 보고 싶어.

UNIT 50

A Are you planning to attend the workshop next week?
다음 주 워크숍에 참석할 건가요?

B I want to, but I'm not sure how to register online.
그러고 싶지만, 어떻게 온라인 등록을 할지 잘 모르겠어요.

A No worries! **All you have to do** is visit their website and fill out the registration form.
걱정 마세요! 그냥 웹사이트에 가서 신청서를 작성하기만 하면 돼요.

B That sounds simple! I'll try and let you know if I have questions.
간단한 것 같네요! 한번 해 보고 질문 있으면 물어볼게요.

어휘 line up 줄을 서다   delete 삭제하다   take up 차지하다   limit 제한하다
go out for a bite 밖에 나가서 간단히 먹다   without subtitles 자막 없이   register 등록하다
registration form 신청서

정답 have a hunch | the bottom line is | All I'm suggesting is | I've always wanted |
All you have to do

UNIT 51

might as well + 동사원형

이왕 이렇게 된 거 ~할까 보다, 차라리 ~하는 게 낫겠다

이 패턴은 현재 상황에서 별다른 대안이 없으니 차라리 그 행동을 하겠다고 할 때 사용해요. 대개 "별다른 대안이 없어서 차라리 그렇게 하겠다."라는 뉘앙스를 주죠. 예를 들어서, 햄버거가 너무 먹고 싶은데 지금 내가 고를 수 있는 음식은 피자, 치킨, 파스타일 때 이 모든 선택지가 내가 가장 원하는 최선의 선택은 아니지만, 그중에서도 어쩔 수 없이 차선책을 고르면서 I might as well have pasta for lunch. (이왕 이렇게 된 거 난 점심으로 파스타 먹을래.)라고 말할 수 있어요.

might as well 뒤에는 동사원형을 사용합니다.

 I guess we **might as well** buy pork then.
이왕 이렇게 된 거 돼지고기나 살까 봐.

실생활 대화

A The grocery store is out of chicken.
마트에 닭고기가 다 팔렸대.

B Oh no, what should we do? I was really craving chicken today.
아, 어쩌지? 오늘 꼭 닭고기 먹고 싶었는데.

A Me, too. What a shame. We need some kind of protein for dinner…
나도. 정말 아쉽네. 저녁에 단백질이 필요한데….

B I guess we might as well buy pork then. It is what it is.
이왕 이렇게 된 거 돼지고기나 살까 봐. 어쩔 수 없지 뭐.

What a shame. 정말 아쉽다.　　It is what it is. 어쩔 수 없지. 그러니 해야지.

PRACTICE 패턴 활용

문장을 써 보고 음원을 들으며 소리 내어 말하세요. 제시어 중 기본형 동사는 패턴에 맞게 바꾸고, 제시어의 // 앞까지만이라도 완성해 말하세요.

▶ 정답 316쪽

- 버스가 늦었으니 그냥 걸어가는 게 낫겠어.   I / walk // since the bus is late

  I might as well walk since the bus is late.

1 우리 차도 안 막히니까 그냥 일찍 가자.   we / leave early // since there's no traffic

2 우리 오늘 저녁은 차라리 외식하는 게 낫겠어. 냉장고에 아무것도 없거든.
   we / eat out / tonight // there's nothing in the fridge

3 어차피 여기 왔으니 쇼핑이나 할까 봐.   since I'm already here / I / do some shopping

4 이미 벌어진 일은 바꿀 수 없으니 그냥 잊고 넘어가는 게 낫겠어.
   I can't change what happeend / so / I / move on

5 정말 외출하고 싶었는데 비가 오네. 그냥 집에서 영화나 볼까 봐.
   I really wanted to go out but it's raining / so / I / stay home / and watch a movie

6 TV에 마땅히 볼 게 없으니, 차라리 이 다큐멘터리나 볼까 봐.
   there's nothing else to watch on TV / so / I / watch this documentary

7 우산도 안 가져왔고 이미 다 젖었으니, 기다리기보다 그냥 걸어서 집에 가는 게 낫겠어.
   I forgot my umbrella and I'm already soaked / so / I / walk home / instead of waiting

8 헬스장에 등록도 해 놨으니까, 최소한 일주일에 몇 번은 가는 게 낫겠어.
   I already paid for the gym membership / so / I / try to go / at least a few times a week

do some shopping 쇼핑하다   walk home 집까지 걸어 가다   instead of ~ 대신에
pay for ~에 대해 돈을 지불하다. (행동에 대한) 대가를 치르다   gym membership 헬스장 회원권
a few times 두세 번

이왕 이렇게 된 거 돼지고기나 살까 봐.

주어 + might as well + 동사원형

I guess   we   buy pork then

UNIT 52

Don't be too hard on + (대)명사
너무 ~에게 엄격하지 마

이 패턴은 누군가에게 너무 엄격하거나 가혹하게 대하지 말라고 조언할 때 사용해요. 예를 들어, "너무 자책하지 마."라고 말하고 싶다면 Don't be too hard on yourself, "그에게 너무 엄격하게 하지 마."라고 말하고 싶다면 Don't be too hard on him. 등으로 말이죠.

Don't be too hard on 뒤에는 그 대상을 지칭하는 명사 또는 대명사를 씁니다.

 Don't be too hard on yourself.
너무 자책하지 마.

추가로 대상 뒤에 이유를 덧붙이고 싶다면 [for + 동명사] 형태를 활용하면 돼요. 예를 들어, "실수한 것에 대해 너무 자책하지 마."라고 말할 경우에는 Don't be too hard on yourself for making a mistake.로 이유까지 설명할 수 있어요.

실생활 대화

A I yelled at my kids this morning. I feel like such a bad parent.
오늘 아침에 아이들에게 소리를 질렀어. 난 정말 나쁜 부모인 것 같아.

B Parenting can be really stressful sometimes.
가끔 육아가 정말 스트레스일 때가 있어.

A But they didn't do anything to deserve that. I just feel so guilty.
근데 아이들이 그만한 짓을 한 게 아니었어. 너무 죄책감 들어.

B **Don't be too hard on yourself.**
Just apologize and do your best to move forward.
너무 자책하지 마. 그냥 사과하고 앞으로 잘 해나가면 돼.

---

hard on ~에게 가혹한   parenting 육아   feel guilty 죄책감을 느끼다   move forward 앞으로 나아가다

PRACTICE 패턴 활용

문장을 써 보고 음원을 들으며 소리 내어 말하세요. 제시어 중 기본형 동사는 패턴에 맞게 바꾸고, 제시어의 // 앞까지만이라도 완성해 말하세요.

▶ 정답 316쪽

- 아이들에게 너무 엄격하게 하지 마. 그들은 아직 배우는 중이잖아. your kids / they're still learning
  Don't be too hard on your kids. They're still learning.

1 네 첫 발표였잖아. 잘했어! 스스로에게 너무 박하게 굴지 마.
  it was your first presentation and you did great / yourself

2 자신에게 너무 엄격하게 하지 마. 누구나 가끔 실수를 해.
  yourself / everyone makes mistakes sometimes

3 팀에 너무 엄격하지 마. 팀원들, 일주일 내내 초과 근무 했어.
  the team / they've been working overtime all week

4 그 친구 요즘 힘든 일 많았대. 너무 냉정하게 대하지 마. she's been going through a lot lately / so / her

5 프로젝트를 제시간에 끝내지 못했다고 너무 자책하지 마. 그런 일도 있는 거야. 응용
  yourself / for not finishing the project on time // it happens

6 하루 쉬었다고 자신을 너무 몰아세우지 마. 누구나 가끔은 휴식이 필요해. 응용
  yourself / for taking a day off // everyone needs a break sometimes

7 걔는 아직 어려. 한 번 실수했다고 그렇게 뭐라고 하면 안 돼. 응용
  he's just a kid / him / for making one mistake

8 사소한 걸 잊었다고 배우자를 너무 몰아세우지 마. 완벽한 사람은 없어. 응용
  your partner / for forgetting small things // nobody's perfect

go through a lot 많은 일을 겪다, 힘든 시간을 보내다   take a day off 하루 쉬다
make one mistake 한 번 실수하다

너무 자책하지 마.

Don't be too hard on + 대명사
                              yourself

UNIT 53

It's okay to + 동사원형

~해도 괜찮다, ~해도 문제없다

이 패턴은 어떤 행동을 해도 괜찮다고 말할 때 사용해요. 예를 들어, "늦어도 괜찮아."라고 말하고 싶다면 It's okay to be late, "실수해도 괜찮아."라고 말하고 싶다면 It's okay to make mistakes. 등으로 말이죠.

It's okay to 뒤에는 해도 괜찮은 행동을 나타내는 동사원형을 씁니다.

 It's okay to take some time to explore your options.
천천히 네 길을 찾아보는 것도 괜찮아.

실생활 대화

A I'm thinking of taking a gap year before starting college.
대학 가기 전에 일 년을 쉴까 생각 중이야.

B It's okay to take some time to explore your options.
What are you thinking of doing?
천천히 네 길을 찾아보는 것도 괜찮아. 뭐 해 보고 싶은데?

A I'm not sure yet. Maybe travel or get a part-time job for a while.
아직 잘 모르겠어. 당분간 여행을 가거나 알바를 좀 할까 싶어.

B It's okay not to have everything figured out.
This time could really help you grow as a person.
모든 걸 다 계획하지 않아도 괜찮아. 이 시간이 진짜 네가 성장하는 데 도움이 될 거야.

---

take a gap year 1년간 학업을 중단하다   explore 탐험하다, 탐구하다   part-time job 아르바이트
figure out 생각해 내다

PRACTICE 패턴 활용

문장을 써 보고 음원을 들으며 소리 내어 말하세요. 제시어 중 기본형 동사는 패턴에 맞게 바꾸고, 제시어의 // 앞까지만이라도 완성해 말하세요.

▶ 정답 317쪽

- 솔직하게 네 감정을 표현해도 괜찮아. 　　　　　　　　　express your feelings / honestly
  It's okay to express your feelings honestly.

1 가끔 혼자만의 시간을 가져도 괜찮아. 　　　　　　　　　take time for yourself / every now and then

2 너무 힘들 때는 쉬어 가도 괜찮아. 　　　　　　　　　take a break // when you're feeling overwhelmed

3 뭔가 이해가 안 되면 질문해도 괜찮아. 　　　　　　　　　ask questions // if you don't understand something

4 뭔가 불편하면 거절해도 괜찮아. 　　　　　　　　　say no // if you're not comfortable with something

5 어떤 걸 모른다고 솔직하게 말해도 괜찮아. 아는 척하는 것보다 솔직함이 훨씬 중요해.
admit / you don't know something // being honest is more valuable than pretending

6 밤새 시즌을 다 몰아 보는 거 괜찮아. 다들 한 번쯤은 해 봤잖아.
binge-watch an entire season / in one night // we've all been there

7 피곤하고, 혼란스럽고, 길을 잃은 것 같은 기분이 들어도 괜찮아. 항상 완벽할 필요는 없어.
feel tired, confused, or even lost // you don't have to have it all together all the time

8 너무 힘들면 우는 것도 괜찮아. 그건 약하다는 뜻이 아니라, 네가 인간이라는 뜻이야.
cry / if you're feeling overwhelmed // it doesn't make you weak // it just means you're human

---

take time for oneself 혼자만의 시간을 갖다　　overwhelmed 주체를 못 하는　　admit 인정하다　　valuable 소중한
pretend ~인 척하다　　have it all together 완벽하게 해내다

천천히 네 길을 찾아보는 것도 괜찮아.

It's okay to + 동사원형
　　　　　　　　take some time to explore your options

UNIT 54

be key

~가 핵심이다

여러분도 대화를 하다가 가장 중요한 부분을 '키 포인트'라고 하죠? 이렇게 특정한 내용이 매우 중요하다고 강조할 때 이 패턴을 사용해요. 예를 들어, "소통이 핵심이야."라고 말하고 싶다면 Communication is key, "일관성이 가장 중요해."라고 말하고 싶다면 Consistency is key. 등으로 말이죠.

be key 앞에 주어로는 중요한 대상을 나타내는 동명사나 명사를 씁니다.

> Practicing a little every day **is key**.
> 매일 조금씩 연습하는 게 핵심이야.

key 뒤에 무엇의 핵심인지 나타내기 위해서 전치사 in이나 to를 쓰기도 해요. 예를 들어, "창의성은 성공적인 마케팅 전략의 핵심이야."는 Creativity is key in successful marketing strategies, "건강한 식습관은 건강 유지의 핵심이야."는 Healthy eating is key to maintaining good health.라고 말할 수 있어요. to는 전치사이기 때문에 뒤에 명사나 동명사를 써요. 그 외에도 '~할 때'를 의미하는 when, if 등의 다양한 구와 절이 이어질 수 있어요.

실생활 대화

A I really want to do well on the English test next week.
나 다음 주 영어 시험 잘 보고 싶어.

B Then practicing a little every day is key.
그럼 매일 조금씩 연습하는 게 핵심이야.

A Yeah, I always try to study the night before, and it never works.
맞아, 난 항상 전날에 벼락치기 하니까, 잘 안 돼.

B Exactly. Just 20 minutes a day can make a big difference.
맞아. 하루 20분만 투자해도 정말 달라질 수 있어.

---

do well on ~를 잘하다, 잘 해내다 study the night before (시험 등) 전날 밤에 벼락치기를 하다
Exactly. 정확해, 바로 그거야.

PRACTICE 패턴 활용

문장을 써 보고 음원을 들으며 소리 내어 말하세요. 제시어 중 기본형 동사는 패턴에 맞게 바꾸고, 제시어의 // 앞까지만이라도 완성해 말하세요.

▶ 정답 317쪽

• 어떤 관계이든 신뢰는 핵심이야.　　　　　　　　　　　trust / in any relationship
  Trust is key in any relationship.

1　신뢰를 쌓는 데는 정직이 핵심이야.　　　　　　　　　honesty / in building trust

2　효과적인 의사소통의 핵심은 경청이야.　　　　　　listening / to effective communication

3　새로운 기술을 배울 때는 인내심이 핵심이야.　　　patience / when learning a new skill

4　몸을 만들고 싶다면 꾸준함이 핵심이야.　　　　consistency / if you want to get in shape

5　월요병을 버티려면 커피가 핵심이지.　　　　　coffee / to surviving the Monday blues

6　사람 이름을 기억하는 건 좋은 첫인상을 주는 데 핵심이야. 응용
　remember people's names / to giving a good first impression

7　충분히 자는 게 하루 종일 집중력을 유지하는 데 핵심이야. 응용
　get enough sleep / to staying focused throughout the day

8　발표할 때는 자신감이 정말 중요해. 자신감 있는 태도가 청중이 네 말을 믿게 만들거든.
　confidence / when giving a presentation // it helps your audience believe in what you're saying

---

listening 경청　patience 인내심　consistency 꾸준함　get in shape 건강한 체형이 되다, 몸을 만들다　survive 살아남다, 버티다　the Monday blues 월요병　give a good first impression 좋은 첫인상을 주다　throughout the day 하루 종일　confidence 자신감

매일 조금씩 연습하는 게 핵심이야.

주어 + be key
Practicing a little every day is

UNIT 55

What are the odds of + 명사[동명사]?
~할 확률이 얼마나 될까?

이 패턴은 어떤 일이 발생할 확률이나 가능성에 대해 물을 때 사용해요. odds는 '확률, 가능성'이라는 뜻으로 질문과 대답 모두에 쓰일 수 있으니 알아 두면 정말 유용하게 사용할 수 있어요. 예를 들어, "내일 비가 올 확률이 얼마나 될까?"는 What are the odds of rain tomorrow?이고, 이에 대한 대답으로 "일기 예보를 확인했는데, 비가 올 확률이 높대."는 I checked the weather forecast, and it says the odds are high.라고 말하면 돼요.

[What are the odds of + 명사/동명사]가 질문이고, 그에 대한 대답이 [The odds are + 형용사]입니다.

 What are the odds of rain this weekend?
이번 주말에 비가 올 확률은 얼마나 될까?

The odds are high.
확률이 높아.

실생활 대화

A What are the odds of rain this weekend?
이번 주말에 비가 올 확률은 얼마나 될까?

B The odds are high.
There's an 80% chance, according to the forecast.
확률이 높아. 일기 예보에 의하면 80% 확률이래.

A Ugh, that ruins our plans for a picnic!
어휴, 그러면 소풍 계획을 망치겠네!

B Let's have a backup plan just in case.
만약을 대비해 대안을 세우자.

according to ~에 의하면   ruin 망치다   backup plan 대안

PRACTICE 패턴 활용

문장을 써 보고 음원을 들으며 소리 내어 말하세요. 제시어 중 기본형 동사는 패턴에 맞게 바꾸고,
제시어의 // 앞까지만이라도 완성해 말하세요.

▶ 정답 317쪽

- **A** 우리 팀이 올해 우승할 확률이 얼마나 될까?   our team / win the championship / this year
  What are the odds of our team winning the championship this year?

  B With our new star player, the odds are better than ever!
  새로 들어온 스타 선수 덕분에, 그 어느 때보다 높아졌지!

1. **A** 우리 비행기 지연될 확률은 얼마나 돼?   our flight / be delayed

   B Given the weather forecast, the odds are pretty high, unfortunately.
   일기 예보를 보면, 안타깝지만 확률이 꽤 높아.

2. **A** 네가 영화 시작 전에 숙제를 끝낼 확률이 얼마나 돼?
   you / finish your homework / before the movie starts

   B Pretty high. I only have a few math problems left. 꽤 높아. 수학 문제 몇 개만 남았거든.

3. **A** 내가 냉장고에서 남은 피자를 찾을 확률이 얼마나 될까?
   me / find the leftover pizza / in the fridge

   B 확률은 희박하지. 너도 알잖아, 네 동생이 얼마나 빨리 먹는지.
   slim // you know how fast your brother eats

4. **A** 공부 안 하고 이 시험 통과할 확률 얼마나 돼?   pass this test / without studying

   B 확률은 거의 0에 가깝지만, 기적이란 게 있긴 하지.   close to zero // but miracles happen

5. **A** 내가 사라한테 데이트 신청하면, 수락해 줄 확률이 얼마나 될까? 응용
   Sarah / say yes / if I ask her out

   B 솔직히? 확률은 꽤 괜찮아. 요즘 너한테 자주 웃어 주더라. 응용
   honestly / pretty good // she's been smiling at you a lot lately

flight 비행편   leftover 남은 음식, 먹다 남은   slim (확률이) 희박한

이번 주말에 비가 올 확률은 얼마나 될까?

What are the odds of + 명사?
rain this weekend

REMINDER 패턴 강화

이제 내 이야기를 해 봐요! 나에게 있음 직한 일들을 적고, 소리 내어 말해 보는 거예요.
주어가 별도로 제시되지 않으면, 주어는 항상 I(나)예요.

▶ 정답 317쪽

UNIT 51 I guess we **might as well** buy pork then.

> might as well + 동사원형
> 이왕 이렇게 된 거 ~할까 보다, 차라리 ~하는 게 낫겠다

1 이왕 이렇게 된 거 우리 아이스크림이나 사러 가는 게 낫겠어.
   we / go get some ice cream

2 이왕 이렇게 된 거 우리 낮잠이나 자는 게 낫겠어.　we / take a nap

3 이왕 이렇게 된 거 우리 다른 에피소드를 볼까 봐.　we / watch another episode

UNIT 52 **Don't be too hard on** yourself.

> Don't be too hard on + (대)명사
> 너무 ~에게 엄격하게 하지 마

4 처음 시도한 거에 너무 실망하지 마.　your first try

5 너의 춤 실력을 너무 엄격하게 평가하지 마.　your dance moves

6 그 바리스타한테 너무 심하게 굴지 마.　that barista

UNIT 53 **It's okay to** take some time to explore your options.

> It's okay to + 동사원형
> ~해도 괜찮다, ~해도 문제없다

7 모든 걸 다 알지 않아도 괜찮아.　not / have all the answers

8 오늘이 무슨 요일인지 까먹어도 돼. 그래서 달력이 있는 거니까.
   forget what day it is // that's what calendars are for

9 도움을 요청해도 괜찮아. ask for help

UNIT 54 Practicing a little every day **is key**.

> **be key**
> ~가 핵심이다

10 연습이 핵심이야. practice

11 자기 자신이 되는 것은 가장 중요해. being yourself

12 타이밍이 가장 중요해. timing

UNIT 55 **What are the odds of** rain this weekend?

> **What are the odds of + 명사[동명사]? The odds are + 형용사**
> ~할 확률이 얼마나 될까? 확률은 ~이다

13 A 전 애인을 마주칠 확률은 얼마나 될까? running into your ex
    B 불가능하지는 않아. not impossible

A
B

14 A 주차할 자리 찾을 확률은 얼마나 될까? finding a parking spot
    B 오늘은 평소보다 나아. better than usual today

A
B

15 A 오늘 비 올 확률은 얼마나 될까? it / raining today
    B 반반 정도야. about fifty-fifty

A
B

REMINDER 맥락 적용

이제 앞에서 연습한 패턴을 실생활 대화 맥락에 적용해 보세요. 패턴을 일상적인 대화에 넣어서 직접 소리 내어 말해 보는 거예요. 빈칸에 들어갈 말이 기억이 나지 않는다면 다시 앞으로 가서 확인해 보세요.

UNIT 51

A The flight is delayed for three hours.
비행기가 3시간 지연됐어.

B That's frustrating. What can we do at the airport?
짜증 나네. 공항에서 뭘 하지?

A There's a duty-free shop we haven't visited yet.
아직 안 가 본 면세점이 있어.

B _____ do some shopping then.
그럼 이왕 이렇게 된 거 차라리 쇼핑이나 하는 게 낫겠어.

UNIT 52

A I feel heavy-hearted because I haven't been able to visit my grandparents often.
할머니, 할아버지를 자주 찾아 뵙지 못해서 마음이 무거워.

B _____ on yourself. You still call them three times a week.
너무 자책하지 마. 그래도 일주일에 3번씩 전화드리잖아.

A But I still want to visit them and make them something delicious.
그래도 직접 찾아 뵙고 맛있는 것도 만들어 드리고 싶어.

B Let's plan to visit them together during the next holiday!
이번 휴가 때 같이 뵈러 가자!

UNIT 53

A I'm really upset that I didn't get the job.
그 회사에 못 들어가서 정말 속상해.

B _____ be upset. Anyone would feel the same.
속상한 건 당연해. 누구나 그럴 거야.

A I thought I did really well in the interview.
난 면접 잘 본 줄 알았거든.

B It's okay, I'm sure you did your best and there will be better opportunities.
괜찮아. 넌 분명 최선을 다했을 거고 더 좋은 기회가 올 거야.

UNIT 54

A I've been practicing my guitar every day.
나 매일 기타 연습하고 있어.

B That's fantastic! Practice **is key** to improving your skills.
멋지다! 실력 향상을 위해서는 연습이 가장 중요하지.

A I can already play a few songs!
벌써 몇 곡은 연주할 수 있어!

B That's amazing! Having fun while learning **is key** to enjoying music.
대단해! 음악을 즐기는 데는 배우면서 즐기는 게 핵심이야.

UNIT 55

A **What are the odds** we'll get tickets to the concert?
콘서트 티켓을 구할 확률이 얼마나 될까?

B The odds are pretty slim; it's sold out everywhere.
확률은 꽤 낮아. 모두 매진됐어.

A That's disappointing. I really wanted to see them live!
아쉽네. 정말로 직접 보고 싶었는데!

B I know! Maybe we can catch their next tour instead.
그러게! 다음에 투어할 때 가자.

어휘 heavy-hearted 마음이 무거운   opportunity 기회
정답 I might as well | Don't be too hard | It's okay to | is key, is key | What are the odds

UNIT 56

Don't even think about + 동명사[명사]
~할 생각은 꿈도 꾸지 마

이 패턴은 어떤 행동이나 생각을 절대 하지 말라는 경고나 강한 권고를 나타낼 때 사용해요. 예를 들어, 집에 케이크가 딱 한 조각 남았을 때 "마지막 케이크 조각 먹을 생각은 꿈도 꾸지 마!"라고 말하고 싶다면 Don't even think about eating the last slice of cake.라고 하면 돼요. 또는 친구가 비가 와서 헬스장에 안 간다고 핑계를 댈 때 "건너뛸 생각은 꿈도 꾸지 마! 넌 할 수 있어!"라고 말하고 싶다면 Don't even think about skipping the gym today! You've got this! 이렇게 말할 수 있어요.

Don't even think about 뒤에는 동명사나 명사를 써서 하지 말아야 할 행동을 나타냅니다.

 Don't even think about giving up.
포기는 꿈도 꾸지 마.

실생활 대화

A I'm really struggling with my diet. I'm thinking about quitting.
   다이어트하는 게 너무 힘들어. 그만둘까 봐.

B Don't even think about giving up! You've already lost a lot of weight.
   포기는 꿈도 꾸지 마! 벌써 많이 감량했잖아.

A But I still have a long way to go to reach my goal.
   근데 아직 목표까지 멀었는 걸.

B No way! You've been sticking to your diet for three months without missing a day. I'm so proud of you!
   아니야! 너는 하루도 안 빼먹고 3달 동안 다이어트를 하고 있어. 난 네가 너무 자랑스러워!

---

struggle with ~와 씨름하다   have a long way to go 갈 길이 멀다   stick to ~를 계속하다

PRACTICE 패턴 활용

문장을 써 보고 음원을 들으며 소리 내어 말하세요. 제시어 중 기본형 동사는 패턴에 맞게 바꾸고, 제시어의 // 앞까지만이라도 완성해 말하세요.

▶ 정답 317쪽

- 술 마시고 운전하는 건 꿈도 꾸지 마. 내가 택시 불러 줄게.   drive after drinking // I'll call you a taxi
  Don't even think about driving after drinking. I'll call you a taxi.

1. 내 간식 건드릴 생각도 하지 마. 아껴 둔 거야.   my snacks // I've been saving them

2. 디저트는 생각도 하지 마. 저녁부터 먹어.   dessert // eat your dinner first

3. 이번 주말에 파티는 생각도 하지 마. 우리 이미 여행 계획이 있잖아.
   a party / this weekend // we already have a trip planned

4. 내 노트북 건드릴 생각도 하지 마. 오늘 업무에 꼭 필요해.   my laptop // I need it for work today

5. 알람 끌 생각도 하지 마. 이번 주에 벌써 두 번이나 늦잠 잤잖아. 〔응용〕
   turn off the alarm // we've already overslept twice this week

6. 지금 포기하려고 생각도 하지 마. 여기까지 왔는데, 나중에 후회할 거야. 〔응용〕
   quit / now // you've already come so far // and you'll regret it later

7. 이번 일로 나를 원망할 생각하지 마. 너도 그 결정에 관여했잖아. 〔응용〕
   blame me for what happened // you were part of the decision, too

8. 다시 나한테 거짓말할 생각하지 마. 한 번은 믿었지만, 두 번은 안 돼. 〔응용〕
   lie to me / again // I trusted you once and I won't make that mistake twice

---

driving after drinking 음주 운전   snack 간식, 주전부리   turn off the alarm 알람을 끄다
oversleep 늦잠 자다   lie to ~에게 거짓말하다(lie + -ing = lying)

포기는 꿈도 꾸지 마.

Don't even think about + 동명사
                                  └ giving up

UNIT 57

tend to + 동사원형
~하는 편이다, ~하는 경향이 있다

이 패턴은 어떤 행동이나 습관을 자주 하게 되는 경향이 있을 때 사용해요. 이 패턴으로 자신이 무의식적으로 반복하거나 자주 하는 행동을 자연스럽게 설명할 수 있어요. 예를 들어 친구 중에 긴장을 하면 말을 많이 하는 습관이 있는 경우 She tends to talk a lot when she's nervous. (그녀는 긴장하면 말을 많이 하는 경향이 있어.)라고 말할 수 있죠.

tend to 뒤에는 동사원형을 써서 자주 하는 행동이나 습관을 나타냅니다.

 I **tend to** spend money impulsively.
난 돈을 충동적으로 쓰는 편이야.

실생활 대화

A **I tend to spend money impulsively.**
난 돈을 충동적으로 쓰는 편이야.

B **That could be problematic in the long run.**
그건 결국에는 문제가 될 수 있어.

A **True. How can I manage my money more wisely?**
맞아. 어떻게 하면 더 현명하게 돈을 관리할 수 있을까?

B **Making a budget and tracking your expenses would help.**
예산을 세우고 지출을 기록하는 게 도움이 될 거야.

---

impulsively 충동적으로   problematic 문제가 있는   in the long run 결국에는   budget 예산

PRACTICE 패턴 활용

문장을 써 보고 음원을 들으며 소리 내어 말하세요. 제시어 중 기본형 동사는 패턴에 맞게 바꾸고, 제시어의 // 앞까지만이라도 완성해 말하세요.

▶ 정답 318쪽

- 나는 집안일 할 때 음악을 듣는 편이야. I / listen to music / while doing chores
  I tend to listen to music while doing chores.

1. 나는 이름은 잘 잊어버리는 편이지만 얼굴은 잘 기억해.
   I / forget names // but I always remember faces

2. 나는 아침에 정신 차리려고 커피를 마시는 편이야. I / drink coffee / in the morning // to help me wake up

3. 나는 아침에 일어나자마자 휴대폰을 확인하는 편이야. I / check my phone / as soon as I wake up

4. 집에서 공부하면 나는 쉽게 집중력이 흐트러지는 편이야.
   I / get distracted / easily // when I study at home

5. 아이들은 주위 어른들, 특히 부모의 행동을 따라 하는 경향이 있어.
   children / imitate the behavior of adults / around them // especially their parents

6. 사람들은 소문을 여러 번 들으면 더 쉽게 믿는 경향이 있어.
   people / believe rumors / more easily // when they hear them from multiple sources

7. 나이가 많은 사람들은 문자나 메신저보다는 직접 대화하는 걸 더 선호하는 경향이 있어.
   older people / prefer face-to-face communication / over texting or messaging apps

8. 우리 개는 누가 집 앞을 지나가기만 해도 크게 짖는 편이야. 응용
   my dog / bark / loudly // whenever someone walks past our house

get distracted 산만해지다   imitate 따라하다   behavior 행동   adult 어른   rumor 소문
face-to-face communication 직접적인 의사소통   bark loudly 크게 짖다

> 난 돈을 충동적으로 쓰는 편이야.
>
> 주어 + tend to + 동사원형
> I   spend money impulsively

UNIT 58

I thought to myself, + "절"
속으로 ~라고 생각했다

이 패턴은 자신이 생각이나 마음속으로 떠오른 생각을 표현할 때 사용해요. 보통 속으로 생각한다고 하죠? 예를 들어, "나는 이건 말이 안 된다고 속으로 생각했어."라고 말하고 싶다면 I thought to myself, "This doesn't make sense."라고 할 수 있어요.

글로 쓸 때는 I thought to myself, 뒤에 큰따옴표 안에 절(주어+동사)로 생각을 나타냅니다.

 I thought to myself, "Wow, he's really tall."
'와, 키 진짜 크다.'고 속으로 생각했어.

영어 수업 시간에 배운 직접 화법과 간접 화법 기억하나요? 위의 문장을 간접 화법으로 말한다면 I thought to myself 다음에 쉼표를 삭제하고 that을 넣고, 그다음에 생각한 내용을 그대로 말하면 돼요. 단, 시제를 thought와 같은 과거형으로 맞춰 줘야 해요. I thought to myself that this didn't make sense. 이렇게요.

실생활 대화

A What was your impression when you first met him?
처음 그를 만났을 때 어떤 인상이었어?

B I thought to myself, "Wow, he's really tall."
'와, 키 진짜 크다.'고 속으로 생각했어.

A I thought to myself, "He seems a lot kinder than I expected."
나는 '생각보다 훨씬 더 친절하네.'라고 생각했어.

B First impressions really do vary from person to person.
첫인상은 정말 사람마다 다 다르지.

---

impression 인상   kinder than expected 예상보다 더 친절한   vary 다양하다

PRACTICE 패턴 활용

문장을 써 보고 음원을 들으며 소리 내어 말하세요. 제시어 중 기본형 동사는 패턴에 맞게 바꾸고, 제시어의 // 앞까지만이라도 완성해 말하세요.

▶ 정답 318쪽

- **속으로** '여기는 내가 상상한 것보다 훨씬 아름답네.'라고 생각했어.
  this place is more beautiful than I imagined

  ### I thought to myself, "This place is more beautiful than I imagined."

1. 그녀가 웃는 걸 보고 '오늘 정말 행복해 보이네.'라고 생각했어.
   when I saw her smile / she's really happy today

2. 마라톤을 완주하고 나서 **속으로** '내가 정말 해냈다!'라고 생각했어.
   finishing the marathon / I can't believe I did it

3. 시험 결과를 보며 **속으로** 생각했어. '그동안 공부한 보람이 있었네.'
   looking at the test results / all that studying paid off

4. 비가 쏟아지기 시작하자 **속으로**, '우산 가져올 걸.'이라고 생각했어.
   as the rain poured down / I should have brought an umbrella

5. 영화 보고 나서 '생각보다 꽤 괜찮은데.'라고 생각했어.
   after watching the movie / it was actually pretty good

6. 규칙적으로 운동을 해야겠다고 마음먹었어. 〔응용〕   that I should start exercising more regularly

7. 일이 더 커지기 전에 사과해야겠다고 **속으로** 생각했어. 〔응용〕
   I needed to apologize / before things got worse

8. 진짜 돈을 좀 아껴야겠다고 **속으로** 생각했어. 〔응용〕   that I should really start saving more money

---

pay off 보람이 있다   **get worse** 더 나빠지다

'와, 키 진짜 크다.'고 속으로 생각했어.

I thought to myself, + "절"

Wow, he's really tall

UNIT 59

It's no use + 동명사

~해도 소용없다, ~하는 건 무의미하다

이 패턴은 어떤 행동을 하는 것이 쓸모없거나 효과가 없다는 것을 표현할 때 사용해요. 예를 들어, 아무리 말을 해도 말이 통하지 않을 때 "그에게 이야기하는 것은 소용이 없어."라고 말하고 싶다면 It's no use talking to him.이라고 할 수 있어요.

It's no use 뒤에는 동명사(-ing)를 써서 쓸모없는 행동을 나타냅니다.

 It's no use trying to do it alone.
그걸 혼자 하려는 건 무의미해.

실생활 대화

A I'm trying to move this furniture by myself, but it's too heavy.
이 가구를 혼자 옮기려고 하는데 너무 무거워.

B **It's no use trying to do it alone.**
Why don't you ask someone for help?
그걸 혼자 하려는 건 무의미해. 누군가에게 도움을 요청해 봐.

A I just don't want to bother anyone...
그냥 다른 사람들한테 민폐 끼치기 싫어서...

B Come on, I'll help you!
에이, 내가 도와줄게!

by oneself 혼자   bother 괴롭히다

PRACTICE 패턴 활용

문장을 써 보고 음원을 들으며 소리 내어 말하세요. 제시어 중 기본형 동사는 패턴에 맞게 바꾸고, 제시어의 // 앞까지만이라도 완성해 말하세요.

▶ 정답 318쪽

- 엎질러진 우유를 두고 울어 봤자 <u>소용없어</u>. 이미 지나간 일이야.
  cry over spilled milk // what's done is done.

  It's no use crying over spilled milk. What's done is done.

1. 날씨 걱정해도 <u>소용없어</u>. 어차피 우리가 통제할 수 없는 거잖아.
   worry about the weather // we can't control it anyway

2. 진실을 숨기려고 해도 <u>소용없어</u>. 결국엔 드러나게 될 거야.
   try to hide the truth // it will come out eventually

3. 이 오래된 컴퓨터를 고치려고 해도 <u>소용없어</u>. 그냥 새로 사는 게 낫겠어.
   try to fix this old computer // we should just buy a new one

4. 완벽한 순간을 기다려 봐도 <u>소용없어</u>. 때로는 그냥 시작해야 해.
   wait for the perfect moment // sometimes you just need to start

5. 그를 설득하려고 해 봐야 <u>소용없어</u>. 그는 이미 결심을 했어.
   try to persuade him // he's made up his mind

6. 생일 파티에 들떠 있는 게 뻔한데 시크한 척해도 <u>소용없어</u>. 〔응용〕
   act cool // when you're obviously super excited about your birthday party

7. 버스를 기다려 봐야 <u>소용없어</u>. 이미 30분이나 늦었으니 택시를 부르는 게 좋겠어.
   wait for the bus // it's already 30 minutes late // so we should probably call a taxi

8. 너 노래방 안 좋아하는 척해도 <u>소용없어</u>. 첫 곡 시작하기 전에 마이크 먼저 잡았잖아!
   pretend you don't love karaoke // you grabbed the mic before the first song even started

---

cry over spilled milk 엎질러진 우유를 두고 울다   hide the truth 진실을 숨기다   eventually 결국에는
perfect moment 완벽한 순간   persuade 설득하다   make up one's mind 결심하다   act cool 시크한 척하다

그걸 혼자 하려는 건 무의미해.

It's no use + 동명사
　　　　　　└─ trying to do it alone

UNIT 60

make every effort to + 동사원형

~를 하기 위해 노력[최선]을 다하다

이 패턴은 어떤 목표를 이루기 위해 모든 노력을 다한다는 것을 표현할 때 사용해요. do one's best보다 더 강하게 목표 달성을 위한 모든 노력을 하고 있다는 것을 강조하지요. 예를 들어, 시험에 합격하기 위해 모든 노력을 다하겠다는 다짐은 I will make every effort to pass the exam.이라고 말할 수 있어요. 또한, 프로젝트를 완성하기 위해 모든 노력을 다하겠다는 의지는 We will make every effort to complete the project.와 같이 말할 수 있어요.

make every effort to 뒤에는 동사원형을 써서 목표를 나타냅니다.

 I'm **making every effort to** stick with them consistently.
꾸준히 지키려고 정말 노력 중이야.

실생활 대화

A How are you doing with your New Year's resolutions?
새해 목표는 잘 지키고 있어?

B I'm making every effort to stick with them consistently.
꾸준히 지키려고 정말 노력 중이야.

A Oh yeah? Which one's going best?
아 진짜? 뭐가 제일 잘되고 있어?

B Daily meditation! I've been working hard to make it a regular habit.
매일 하는 명상! 그걸 습관으로 만들려고 열심히 실천 중이야.

New Year's resolution 새해 결심   stick with ~를 지키다   consistently 꾸준히   meditation 명상
make it a regular habit 규칙적인 습관으로 만들다

PRACTICE **패턴 활용**

문장을 써 보고 음원을 들으며 소리 내어 말하세요. 제시어 중 기본형 동사는 패턴에 맞게 바꾸고,
제시어의 // 앞까지만이라도 완성해 말하세요.   ▶ 정답 318쪽

- 그녀는 그 일자리를 얻기 위해 모든 노력을 다했어.   she / get the job

    She made every effort to get the job.

1. 그는 새 동료들과 잘 지내기 위해 최선을 다했어.   he / get along with his new coworkers

2. 나는 제시간에 도착하려고 정말 애썼는데, 교통이 너무 막혔어요.
    I / arrive on time // but the traffic was terrible

3. 그녀는 여행 전에 영어 실력을 향상시키려고 열심히 노력했어.
    she / improve her English / before the trip

4. 우리는 이 프로젝트를 제시간에 끝내려고 최선을 다하고 있어.   we / get this project done / on time

5. 나는 집에서 플라스틱 사용을 줄이기 위해 최선을 다하고 있어.   I / reduce plastic use / at home

6. 나는 다정한 아빠가 되어 자녀가 하는 모든 일을 응원하기 위해 최선을 다하고 있어.
    I / be a loving father // and support my children / in everything they do

7. 그 시험에 합격하려고 정말 온 힘을 다할 거야. 응용   I / pass that exam

8. 제시간에 도착하려고 최대한 노력하겠지만, 확신은 못 해. 응용
    I / be there / on time // but I can't promise

---

get the job 일자리를 얻다   get along with ~와 잘 지내다   coworker 동료   reduce 줄이다
a loving father 다정한 아빠   support 지지하다, 응원하다

> 꾸준히 지키려고 정말 노력 중이야.
>
> 주어 + make every effort to + 동사원형
>   I'm making   stick with them consistently

181

REMINDER 패턴 강화

이제 내 이야기를 해 봐요! 나에게 있음 직한 일들을 적고, 소리 내어 말해 보는 거예요.
주어가 별도로 제시되지 않으면, 주어는 항상 I(나)예요.

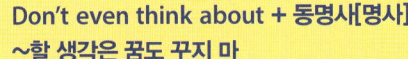 정답 318쪽

UNIT 56 **Don't even think about** giving up.

> **Don't even think about + 동명사[명사]**
> ~할 생각은 꿈도 꾸지 마

1 일찍 갈 생각은 꿈도 꾸지 마.   leaving early

2 내 후드티 입을 생각은 꿈도 꾸지 마.   wearing my hoodie

3 내 초콜릿 먹을 생각은 꿈도 꾸지마.   eating my chocolates

UNIT 57 I **tend to** spend money impulsively.

> **tend to + 동사원형**
> ~하는 편이다, ~하는 경향이 있다

4 나는 너무 많이 생각하는 경향이 있어.   overthink things

5 내 농담에 내가 웃는 경향이 있어.   laugh at my own jokes

6 나는 폰을 너무 자주 보는 경향이 있어.   check my phone too often

UNIT 58 **I thought to myself**, "Wow, he's really tall."

> **I thought to myself, + "절"**
> 속으로 ~라고 생각했다

7 '집에 있어야 했어.'라고 속으로 생각했어.   I should've stayed home

8 '그가 길을 잃은 게 확실해.'라고 속으로 생각했어.   he's definitely lost

9 '내가 과잉 반응을 하고 있는 것 같아.'라고 속으로 생각했어.
   maybe I'm overreacting

UNIT 59 **It's no use** trying to do it alone.

> **It's no use + 동명사**
> ~해도 소용없다, ~하는 건 무의미하다

10 그 사람이랑 말싸움해 봐야 소용없어.   arguing with him

11 그녀의 마음을 바꾸려 해 봐야 소용없어.   trying to change her mind

12 그 일로 스트레스 받아 봐야 소용없어.   stressing over it

UNIT 60 I'm **making every effort to** stick with them consistently.

> **make every effort to + 동사원형**
> ~를 하기 위해 노력[최선]을 다하다

13 침착하려고 정말 애썼어.   stay calm

14 마감일을 맞추려고 온 힘을 다했어.   meet the deadline

15 그의 입장을 이해하려고 정말 노력했어.   understand his point of view

REMINDER 맥락 적용

이제 앞에서 연습한 패턴을 실생활 대화 맥락에 적용해 보세요. 패턴을 일상적인 대화에 넣어서 직접 소리 내어 말해 보는 거예요.
빈칸에 들어갈 말이 기억이 나지 않는다면 다시 앞으로 가서 확인해 보세요.

UNIT 56

A I'm thinking about going on a working holiday to Australia.
호주로 워킹 홀리데이를 갈지 말지 고민 중이야.

B _____ backing out! It could be a really great opportunity for you.
빠질 생각은 하지도 마! 너에게 정말 좋은 기회가 될 거야.

A Do you really think so? I'm worried about my English skills.
정말 그렇게 생각해? 영어 때문에 걱정이야.

B You can start studying English now! Once you're there, you'll definitely broaden your horizons.
영어 공부는 지금부터 하면 되지! 다녀오면 분명 시야를 넓힐 수 있을 거야.

UNIT 57

A _____ overeat when I'm stressed.
나는 스트레스 받으면 과식하는 경향이 있어.

B Really? _____ lose sleep when I'm stressed.
그래? 나는 스트레스 받으면 잠을 설치는 편인데.

A So how do you relieve your stress?
넌 어떻게 스트레스를 풀어?

B I usually exercise or listen to music. You should try to find alternatives to overeating.
주로 운동을 하거나 음악을 들어. 넌 과식 대신 다른 방법을 찾아봐야 할 것 같다.

UNIT 58

A What did you think when the plane took off?
비행기 이륙할 때 무슨 생각 했어?

B _____ excitedly, "Finally, it's vacation time!"
나는 들떠서 속으로 '드디어 휴가다!'라고 생각했지.

A I worried, "What if the plane isn't safe?"
난 '비행기가 안전할까?'라고 걱정했는데.

B We really do have different thoughts in the same situation.
우리는 진짜 같은 상황에서도 생각하는 게 다르네.

UNIT 59

A I'm thinking of texting that person again.
그 사람한테 또 문자를 보낼까 생각 중이야.

B 🐱 _____ texting repeatedly. It's better to wait for a reply.
계속 연락하는 건 무의미해. 차라리 답장이 올 때까지 기다려.

A But I'm feeling anxious about it.
그래도 불안해서 어쩔 줄 모르겠어.

B I understand, but let's give it some time.
이해해. 하지만 조금 여유를 가지고 기다려보자.

UNIT 60

A I heard you're writing a book. How's it coming along?
너 요새 책 쓴다면서? 잘돼 가?

B It's exciting! 🐱 _____ write a little bit every day.
재밌어! 매일 조금씩이라도 쓰려고 최선을 다하고 있어.

A Wow, that's cool! What's it about?
와, 멋지다! 뭐에 관한 책이야?

B It's a travel essay. I'm putting a lot of thought into vividly conveying my experiences.
여행 에세이야. 내 경험을 생생하게 전달하고 싶어서 많이 고민하고 있어.

어휘 back out (하기로 했던 일에서) 손을 떼다 | broaden one's horizons 시야를 넓히다 | overeat 과식하다 | relieve 없애다, 완화하다 | alternative 대안 | repeatedly 반복해서 | anxious 불안해하는 | put thought into 고민하다 | vividly 생생하게 | convey 전달하다

정답 Don't even think about | I tend to, I tend to | I thought to myself | It's no use | I'm making every effort to

REMINDER 패턴 정착

앞에서 배운 20개 패턴을 머릿속에 새기는 시간이에요.
문장을 보고 패턴을 이용해 영어로 소리 내어 말해 보세요.

41 뉴욕 집값이 장난 아니야.

42 도저히 실망시켜 드릴 수 없어.

43 커피 한 잔 마시니까 기분이 한결 나아졌어.

44 오해하지 마, 영상미는 정말 대단했어.

45 혹시나 괜찮은 데 발견하면 알려 줄게.

46 오늘 저녁은 비가 올 것 같은 예감이 들어.

47 핵심은 건강하게 먹고 운동하는 게 진짜 중요하다는 거야.

48 내 말은 넌 잘할 거라는 거야.

49 난 항상 유럽으로 여행 가고 싶었어.

50 그냥 넌 시작만 하면 돼.

51 이왕 이렇게 된 거 돼지고기나 살까 봐.

52 너무 자책하지 마.

53 천천히 네 길을 찾아보는 것도 괜찮아.

54 매일 조금씩 연습하는 게 핵심이야.

55 이번 주말에 비가 올 확률은 얼마나 될까?

56 포기는 꿈도 꾸지 마.

57 난 돈을 충동적으로 쓰는 편이야.

58 '와, 키 진짜 크다.'고 속으로 생각했어.

59 그걸 혼자 하려는 건 무의미해.

60 꾸준히 지키려고 정말 노력 중이야.

UNIT 61

be here to + 동사원형 / be here for + 명사

~를 하러 오다

이 패턴은 어떤 목적을 가지고 왔다는 것을 표현할 때 사용해요. 예를 들어 James를 도와주기 위해 왔을 때는 I'm here to help James.라고 말하고, 회의에 참석하려고 왔을 때는 I'm here for the meeting.이라고 말하면 돼요. [be here to + 동사원형]과 [be here for + 명사]는 둘 다 자연스러운 형태니까 자유롭게 쓰면 돼요.

be here 뒤에는 [to + 동사원형]이나 [for + 명사]를 씁니다.

 I'm here to pick up my prescription.
처방약 받으러 왔어요.

실생활 대화

A   Hi, how can I help you today?
   안녕하세요. 무엇을 도와드릴까요?

B   Hello, **I'm here to pick up my prescription.**
   안녕하세요. 처방약 받으러 왔어요.

A   Certainly. May I have your name and date of birth, please?
   네, 알겠습니다. 성함과 생년월일을 알려 주시겠어요?

B   Sure, it's Jacob Shin, born on June 19, 1991.
   네, 제이콥 신이고, 1991년 6월 19일생입니다.

---

pick up one's prescription 처방약을 받다

PRACTICE 패턴 활용

문장을 써 보고 음원을 들으며 소리 내어 말하세요. 제시어 중 기본형 동사는 패턴에 맞게 바꾸고, 제시어의 // 앞까지만이라도 완성해 말하세요.

▶ 정답 319쪽

- 김 선생님 진료 예약 있어서 왔어요. 　　　　　　　　I / my appointment with Dr. Kim
  I'm here for my appointment with Dr. Kim.

1. 오전 10시에 있는 면접 보러 왔어요. 　　　　　　　　I / the job interview / at 10 AM

2. 오후 2시에 있는 회의에 참석하러 왔어요. 　　　　　　I / the meeting / that's happening at 2 PM

3. 온라인으로 주문한 물건을 가지러 왔어요. 확인해 주실 수 있나요?
   I / pick up my order / that I got online // can you check it for me

4. 지난주에 했던 검사 결과를 받으러 왔어요. 　　　　　I / get my test results / from last week

5. 당신은 배우고 성장하러 온 거니까 실수하는 걸 두려워하지 마세요. [응용]
   you / learn and grow // so don't be afraid to make mistakes

6. 그가 와이파이를 고치러 왔으니까 우리가 공유기 위치를 알려 줘야 해요. [응용]
   he / fix the Wi-Fi // so we should let him know where the router is

7. 의사 선생님은 당신의 질문에 답변하러 오신 거니까, 뭐든 편하게 물어보세요. [응용]
   the doctor / answer your questions // so feel free to ask anything

8. 그녀는 할머니 생신 때문에 왔고, 온 가족이 모일 거예요. [응용]
   she / her grandmother's birthday // and the whole family is getting together

---

appointment 예약　　job interview 취직 면접　　pick up one's order 주문한 물건을 찾다
get one's test results 검사 결과를 받다　　Feel free to 편하게 ~ 하세요.(unit 29 패턴)

처방약 받으러 왔어요.

주어 + be here to + 동사원형
　　I'm　　　　　　pick up my prescription

UNIT 62
to see if + 절
~인지 알아보려고

이 패턴은 어떤 상황이나 조건이 맞는지 확인하기 위한 행동을 할 때 사용해요. 예를 들어 친구가 집에 있는지 확인하려고 방문했을 때 I went to his house to see if he was home, 또는 냉장고에 우유가 남아 있는지 확인하기 위해 냉장고를 열었을 때는 I opened the fridge to see if there was any milk left.라고 말할 수 있어요. 여기서 see는 '알아보다'라는 뜻으로 쓰였어요. 이 패턴은 다양한 상황에서 많이 활용되니까 꼭 익혀 두세요.

이 패턴은 주절과 if절로 이루어져 있습니다.

 I'm going to the store **to see if** they have any fresh strawberries.
신선한 딸기가 있는지 보러 마트에 갈 거야.

실생활 대화

A I'm going to the store to see if they have any fresh strawberries.
신선한 딸기가 있는지 보러 마트에 갈 거야.

B Oh, could you check if they have blueberries, too?
오, 블루베리도 있는지 확인해 줄 수 있어?

A Sure, no problem. Do you need anything else?
물론이지. 다른 거 필요한 거 있어?

B No, that's it. Thanks for asking!
아니, 그게 다야. 물어봐 줘서 고마워!

see 알아보다, 확인하다

PRACTICE 패턴 활용

문장을 써 보고 음원을 들으며 소리 내어 말하세요. 제시어 중 기본형 동사는 패턴에 맞게 바꾸고, 제시어의 // 앞까지만이라도 완성해 말하세요.

▶ 정답 319쪽

- 그가 괜찮은지 확인하려고 문자를 보냈어. I texted him / he was okay
  I texted him to see if he was okay.

1 우린 아직 비가 <u>오는지 보려고</u> 밖을 내다봤어. we looked outside / it was still raining

2 우린 그가 집에 <u>있는지</u> 확인하려고 연락했어. we reached out to him / he was home

3 결과가 올라왔는지 확인하려고 그는 페이지를 새로 고침 했어.
   he refreshed the page / the results had been posted

4 나는 변경 사항이 있는지 확인하려고 일정을 살펴봤어.
   I checked the schedule / there were any changes

5 나는 자리가 있는지 확인하려고 식당에 전화했어.
   I called the restaurant / they had any tables available

6 결제가 완료됐는지 확인하려고 그녀는 은행 계좌를 확인했어.
   she checked her bank account / the payment had gone through

7 나는 차를 사기 전에 정말 마음에 드는지 보려고 시운전을 할 거야. **응용**
   before buying the car / I'm going to test-drive it / I really like it

8 나는 마스크를 써야 할지 알아보려고 항상 공기질과 미세먼지 수치를 확인해.
   I always check the air quality / and fine dust levels / I need to wear a mask

---

reach out to ~에게 연락하다   refresh the page 페이지를 새로 고침 하다   available 이용할 수 있는
bank account 은행 계좌   payment 결제   go through 통과되다   test-drive 시운전하다   air quality 공기질
fine dust level 미세먼지 수치   wear a mask 마스크를 쓰다

신선한 딸기가 있는지 보러 마트에 갈 거야.

to see if + 절
I'm going to the store   they have any fresh strawberries

UNIT 63

When [If] you get a chance, + 절
시간 날 때[시간이 되면]

이 패턴은 '시간이 있으면' 또는 '기회가 된다면'이라는 뜻으로 상대방에게 어떤 행동을 부탁할 때 사용해요. get a chance는 '기회를 얻다, 시간이 나다'라는 뜻이며 그 앞에 When과 If를 사용할 수 있는데, 두 단어의 뉘앙스 차이를 비교해 보고 활용하세요. When you get a chance는 상대방에게 기회가 생길 걸 전제로 하는 부드러운 요청인 한편, If you get a chance는 상대방이 시간이 생길지 아닐지 확신이 없을 때 하는 조심스러운 제안이며 시간이 안 나도 괜찮다는 배려가 포함되어 있어요.

When[If] you get a chance에 이어지는 절에는 주로 요청하는 내용이 이어집니다. 따라서 평서문(주어+동사) 외에도, 명령문, 의문문 등 다양한 형태가 옵니다.

 When you get a chance, you should try it.
시간 날 때 한번 가 봐.

When[If] you get a chance는 문장 앞뒤에 모두 올 수 있는데, 문장 앞에 올 경우에는 쉼표를 붙여야 해요.

When you get a chance, call me. / Call me when you get a chance.

실생활 대화

A Have you been to that new lunch buffet near the office?
회사 근처에 새로 생긴 점심 뷔페 가 봤어?

B Not yet. I've been so busy lately that even lunch breaks feel rushed.
아직 못 가 봤어. 요즘 너무 바빠서 점심시간도 빠듯하게 느껴져.

A It's really good. The salad bar is super fresh and has a great variety.
When you get a chance, you should try it.
진짜 괜찮더라. 샐러드바가 엄청 신선하고 종류도 다양해. 시간 날 때 한번 가 봐.

B Oh, really? I'll definitely try it sometime next week.
It'd be even better if we go together!
오, 그래? 다음 주쯤 꼭 한번 가 봐야겠다. 같이 가면 더 좋겠다!

---

buffet 뷔페   **lunch break** 점심시간   **a great variety** 다양한 종류

PRACTICE 패턴 활용

문장을 써 보고 음원을 들으며 소리 내어 말하세요. 제시어 중 기본형 동사는 패턴에 맞게 바꾸고, 제시어의 // 앞까지만이라도 완성해 말하세요.

▶ 정답 319쪽

- 시간 될 때 이메일 좀 확인해 줘. when / please check your email

  When you get a chance, please check your email.

1. 시간 되면 전화나 문자 한번 줘. if / just give me a call / or send a message

2. 시간 날 때 나 빨래하는 것 좀 도와줄래? when / can you help me / with my laundry

3. 시간 나면 나중에 커피 마시면서 얘기 좀 하자. if / let's catch up over coffee / sometime

4. 집에 오는 길에 시간 되면 간식 좀 사다 줄 수 있어?
   if / can you pick up some snacks / on your way home

5. 시간 날 때 베란다에 있는 식물에 물 좀 줄 수 있어? 좀 말라 보이더라.
   when / could you water the plants / on the balcony // they're looking a little dry

6. 시간 날 때 어젯밤에 찍은 사진들 좀 보내 줘. 난 하나도 안 찍었거든!
   when / send me the photos / from last night // I forgot to take any

7. 시간 날 때 잠깐 산책이라도 해. 몇 시간째 일만 하고 있잖아.
   when / take a break / and go for a short walk // you've been working for hours

8. 기회 되면 사라 선물 고르는 거 좀 도와줄래? 뭘 사야 할지 모르겠어.
   if / could you help me choose a gift for Sarah // I have no idea what to get her

---

laundry 빨래   catch up over coffee 커피 마시면서 이야기하다   pick up some snacks 간식 좀 사 오다
water the plants 식물에 물을 주다   balcony 베란다   go for a short walk 짧게 산책하다

시간 날 때 한번 가 봐.

When you get a chance, + 절
　　　　　　　　　　　　you should try it

193

UNIT 64

should have p.p.
~했어야 했다, ~할 걸 그랬다

이 패턴은 과거에 일어났어야 했던 일 또는 일어나지 말았어야 했던 일에 대해 말할 때 사용해요. 예를 들어, 어제 결국 야식을 참지 못하고 먹었을 때, 다음 날 후회하며 "어제 야식을 안 먹었어야 했는데."라고 말할 수 있겠죠? 이런 후회나 아쉬움을 표현하는 패턴이 바로 [should/shouldn't have + 과거분사(p.p.)]예요. 예를 들어, "시험 공부 더 열심히 할 걸."이라고 말하고 싶다면 I should have studied harder for the exam, 또는 "너는 그런 말을 하지 말았어야 했어."는 You shouldn't have said that.이라고 할 수 있죠.

should have 뒤에는 동사의 과거분사를 써서 후회되는 일이나 아쉬운 일을 나타냅니다.

 You **should've come** with us.
너도 같이 갔으면 좋았을 텐데.

'~를 하지 말았어야 했다'라는 부정의 의미는 should에 not을 붙여서 shouldn't have p.p.로 말하면 돼요.

실생활 대화

A Have you tried that new restaurant downtown?
시내에 새로 생긴 그 식당 가 봤어?

B Yeah, it was delicious! You should've come with us.
The food was fantastic.
응, 진짜 맛있더라! 너도 같이 갔으면 좋았을 텐데, 음식이 환상적이었어.

A I'll definitely have to check it out! What dish would you recommend?
나도 꼭 가 봐야겠다! 추천 메뉴는?

B The seafood pasta was amazing. You should give it a try.
It's their specialty.
해산물 파스타가 진짜 맛있었어. 꼭 한번 먹어 봐, 거기 대표 메뉴거든.

---

check out 확인하다   **give it a try** 시도해 보다   **specialty** 대표 메뉴, 특별 요리

PRACTICE 패턴 활용

문장을 써 보고 음원을 들으며 소리 내어 말하세요. 제시어 중 기본형 동사는 패턴에 맞게 바꾸고, 제시어의 // 앞까지만이라도 완성해 말하세요.

▶ 정답 319쪽

• 우산을 챙겨 왔어야 했어. 비가 엄청 오네!   I / bring an umbrella // it's pouring

   I should have brought an umbrella. It's pouring!

1 더 편한 신발 신었어야 했어. 발이 너무 아파. I / wear more comfortable shoes // my feet are killing me

2 우리 예약해 둘 걸. 기다리는 줄 엄청 길어.   we / make a reservation // there's a long wait

3 그 디저트 사진 찍을 걸! 진짜 예뻤는데.   I / take a picture of that dessert // it looked amazing

4 회의 전에 커피 마실 걸. 졸려 죽겠어.
   I / grab a coffee / before the meeting // I can barely stay awake

5 너도 카페에 있었으면 말해 주지! 나도 거기 있었어. you / tell me you were at the café // I was there, too

6 장바구니 가져올 걸. 또 비닐봉지 값 내야 하잖아.
   I / bring my reusable bag // now I have to pay for a plastic bag again

7 그걸 온라인에 올리지 말았어야 했어. 이제 모두가 다 알아버렸어. 응용
   I / post that online // now everyone knows

8 어젯밤에 너무 많이 먹지 말았어야 했어. 속이 더부룩해. 응용
   I / eat so much / last night // I feel so bloated

---

pour 마구 쏟아지다, 붓다   grab a coffee 커피를 마시다   stay awake 자지 않고 깨어 있다
reusable bag 재활용이 가능한 장바구니   plastic bag 비닐봉지   bloated 부은, 배가 터질 듯한

너도 같이 갔으면 좋았을 텐데.

주어 + should have p.p.

You   come with us

UNIT 65

could have p.p.
~할 수 있었는데

should have p.p.가 과거에 했어야 했던 일에 대한 후회나 아쉬움을 나타낸다면, could have p.p.는 과거에 어떤 일을 할 수 있었지만 하지 않았기 때문에 그로 인한 후회를 표현할 때 사용해요. 예를 들어, 비트코인이 백만 원일 때 살 수 있는 기회가 있었지만 사지 않았을 경우에 I could have bought Bitcoin when it was at 1 million won, (but I didn't).라고 말할 수 있어요. 또는 숙제를 할 시간이 있었지만 숙제를 끝내지 못한 경우에는 I could have finished my homework, (but I didn't).라고 말할 수 있어요. 이처럼 could have p.p 뒤에는 '결국에는 하지 않았다'라는 의미가 숨어 있어요.

could have 뒤에는 동사의 과거분사를 써서, 할 수 있었지만 하지 못해서 후회되는 일을 나타냅니다.

 You **could've taken** the subway and avoided all that traffic.
지하철을 타서 교통 체증을 다 피할 수 있었을 텐데.

실생활 대화

A I heard the traffic was terrible this morning.
오늘 아침 교통 엄청 막혔다면서?

B Yeah, it was awful!
응, 진짜 끔찍했어!

A You could've taken the subway and avoided all that traffic if only you'd listened to me.
내 말만 들었으면 지하철을 타서 교통 체증을 다 피할 수 있었을 텐데.

B Yeah... I really should've listened to you.
그러게... 진짜 네 말을 들었어야 했어.

---

avoid traffic 교통 체증을 피하다   should've p.p. ~했어야 했다(unit 64 패턴)

PRACTICE 패턴 활용

문장을 써 보고 음원을 들으며 소리 내어 말하세요. 제시어 중 기본형 동사는 패턴에 맞게 바꾸고, 제시어의 // 앞까지만이라도 완성해 말하세요. ▶ 정답 319쪽

- **조금만 더 공부했으면 시험에 통과할 수도 있었어.** I / pass the test // if I had studied just a bit more

  I could have passed the test if I had studied just a bit more.

1. **내가 저녁 만들 수도 있었는데, 네가 이미 음식 시켰더라.**
   I / make dinner // but you already ordered food

2. **더 이른 버스를 탈 수도 있었는데, 잠을 조금 더 자고 싶었어.**
   I / take the earlier bus // but I wanted a few more minutes of sleep

3. **그 주식이 10달러였을 때 살 수도 있었는데, 사지 않았어.**
   I / buy the stock // when it was at 10 dollars // but I didn't

4. **외출할 수도 있었는데, 그냥 집에서 넷플릭스 봤어.**
   I / go out // but I ended up staying in and watching Netflix

5. **그는 기차를 탈 수도 있었는데 운전해서 갔어.** he / take the train // but he chose to drive instead

6. **그들이 더 일찍 출발했다면 공항에 도착할 수도 있었을 텐데.** 응용
   they / make it to the airport // if they had left earlier

7. **우리가 티켓을 조금 더 일찍 예약했다면 돈을 많이 아낄 수도 있었을 텐데.** 응용
   we / save a lot of money // if we had booked our tickets earlier

8. **그녀는 우리와 함께 콘서트에 갈 수도 있었는데, 집에 있기로 했어.** 응용
   she / go to the concert / with us // but she decided to stay home

---

make dinner 저녁을 만들다   go out 외출하다   end up -ing 결국 ~하게 되다   make it to ~에 도착하다
book tickets 티켓을 예약하다

지하철을 타서 교통 체증을 다 피할 수 있었을 텐데.
주어 + could have p.p.
You 　　taken the subway and avoided all that traffic

REMINDER 패턴 강화

이제 내 이야기를 해 봐요! 나에게 있음 직한 일들을 적고, 소리 내어 말해 보는 거예요.
주어가 별도로 제시되지 않으면, 주어는 항상 I(나)예요.

▶ 정답 320쪽

UNIT 61 I'm here to pick up my prescription.

> be here to + 동사원형 / be here for + 명사
> ~를 하러 오다

1 당신을 도와주러 왔어요.   help you out

2 내 친구 응원하러 왔어요.   support my friend

3 그 프로젝트에 대해 이야기하러 왔어요.   talk about the project

UNIT 62 I'm going to the store **to see if** they have any fresh strawberries.

> to see if + 절
> ~인지 알아보려고

4 그녀가 답장했나 보려고 핸드폰을 확인했어.   checked my phone / she replied

5 내가 좋아하는 빵이 있나 보려고 빵집으로 갔어.
   headed to the bakery / they had the bread I like

6 누가 내 지갑을 봤는지 주변에 물어봤어.
   asked around / anyone had seen my wallet

UNIT 63 **When you get a chance**, you should try it.

> When[If] you get a chance, + 절
> 시간 날 때[시간이 되면]

7 시간이 될 때 단톡방 확인해 줘.   when / check the group chat

8 시간이 될 때 전자레인지 좀 닦아 줘.   when / clean the microwave

9 시간이 되면 내가 보낸 영상 좀 봐 줘.   if / watch the video I sent

UNIT 64 You **should've come** with us.

> **should have p.p.**
> ~를 했어야 했다, ~할 걸 그랬다

10 답장했어야 했어.   texted you back

11 네 말을 들었어야 했어.   listened to you

12 휴대폰 충전해 놓을 걸.   charged my phone

UNIT 65 You **could've taken** the subway and avoided all that traffic.

> **could have p.p.**
> ~할 수 있었는데

13 좀 더 일찍 나한테 전화할 수도 있었어.   you / called me earlier

14 그거 어제 끝낼 수 있었는데.   finished it yesterday

15 사진을 더 잘 찍을 수 있었는데.   taken a better photo

REMINDER 맥락 적용

이제 앞에서 연습한 패턴을 실생활 대화 맥락에 적용해 보세요. 패턴을 일상적인 대화에 넣어서 직접 소리 내어 말해 보는 거예요. 빈칸에 들어갈 말이 기억이 나지 않는다면 다시 앞으로 가서 확인해 보세요.

UNIT 61

A Good afternoon! Welcome to our German language school.
안녕하세요! 저희 독일어 학원에 오신 걸 환영합니다.

B Hi, _____ inquire about language classes.
안녕하세요. 독일어 수업 문의하러 왔어요.

A Great! Are you a beginner or do you have some experience with German?
좋습니다! 독일어를 처음 배우시나요, 아니면 조금 경험이 있으신가요?

B I'm a beginner. I'd like to learn German for my upcoming trip to Germany.
초보예요. 곧 독일로 여행 갈 예정이라 독일어를 배우러 온 거예요.

UNIT 62

A I'm checking the weather forecast _____ it's going to rain this weekend.
이번 주말에 비가 올지 알아보려고 일기 예보를 확인하고 있어.

B Good thinking. What does it say?
좋은 생각이야. 뭐라고 되어 있어?

A Looks like it might rain on Saturday, but Sunday should be clear.
토요일에는 비가 올 수 있지만, 일요일은 맑을 거래.

B Perfect, let's plan our picnic for Sunday then.
완벽해. 그럼 소풍은 일요일로 잡자.

UNIT 63

A Mom, I'm having trouble with my math homework.
엄마, 수학 숙제가 어려워요.

B I'm making supper right now, sweetie. _____ later, I'll come help you, okay?
지금 저녁 만들고 있으니까, 이따가 시간이 되면 도와줄게, 알았지?

A Okay, thanks Mom. I'll keep working on it for now.
알겠어요, 엄마. 일단 계속 해 볼게요.

B If you get really stuck, you can ask your older sister for help, too.
정말 막히면, 누나한테도 도와달라고 해 봐.

UNIT 64

A How did your presentation go?
발표는 어땠어?

B It went really well! I wish I had practiced a bit more, but I still felt confident.
진짜 잘됐어! 좀 더 연습했으면 더 좋았겠지만, 그래도 자신 있게 했어.

A That's great! You always do well. How was the audience reaction?
잘됐네! 넌 항상 잘하잖아. 청중들 반응은 어땠어?

B They loved it! 　　　　　　　　　 seen how engaged they were during the Q&A session.
다들 좋아했어! Q&A 시간에 얼마나 열심히 참여하던지, 네가 봤어야 했는데.

UNIT 65

A What did you do with your first paycheck?
첫 월급으로 뭐 했어?

B I saved it. But 　　　　　　　　　 bought a gift for my parents.
저축했어. 사실 부모님께 선물을 사드릴 수도 있었는데.

A You can buy it next month.
다음 달에 사드리면 되잖아.

B Right. I'm planning to give them some cash along with a gift next month.
맞아. 다음 달에 선물이랑 현금도 조금 드리려고 해.

어휘　inquire 문의하다　upcoming 다가오는　have trouble with ~로 고생하다　for now 우선은
　　　get stuck 막히다　confident 자신 있는　paycheck 급여

정답　I'm here to　|　to see if　|　When I get a chance　|　You should have　|　I could have

UNIT 66

would have p.p.
~했을 텐데

이 패턴은 과거에 어떤 일이 일어났을 가능성이나 가정하는 상황을 표현할 때 사용해요. 보통 조건을 나타내는 if절과 함께 쓰여요. 예를 들어, 생각보다 일찍 도착한 딸을 보고 엄마가 "일찍 온다고 미리 말했으면 내가 음식이라도 만들어 놨을 텐데."라고 말하는 상황일 때 "If you had told me you were coming early, I would have made some food for you."라고 말할 수 있어요. 또는 "내가 거기에 있었으면 도와줬을 텐데."라고 말하고 싶다면 I would have helped if I had been there.처럼 말할 수 있어요.

would have 뒤에는 가정하는 상황을 나타내는 과거분사를 씁니다.

> If you'd let me know ahead of time, I **would've made** you something to eat.
> 미리 말했으면, 뭐 먹을 거라도 해 놨을 텐데.

반대로 '~하지 않았을 텐데'는 would에 not을 붙여서 wouldn't have p.p.로 말하면 돼요.

실생활 대화

A Why didn't you tell me you were coming home? If you'd let me know ahead of time, I would've made you something to eat.
왜 집에 온다고 말 안 했어? 미리 말했으면 뭐 먹을 거라도 해 놨을 텐데.

B It's okay, Mom. I just didn't want to trouble you.
괜찮아요, 엄마. 그냥 엄마 힘들게 하고 싶지 않았어요.

A You're never a burden, sweetie.
I could've at least picked you up from the station.
넌 절대 부담 아니야, 얘야. 적어도 역에는 데리러 갈 수 있었을 텐데.

B I really appreciate that, Mom. Next time, I'll make sure to let you know in advance.
고마워요, 엄마. 다음엔 꼭 미리 알려 드릴게요.

---

ahead of time 미리   trouble 귀찮게 하다   burden 짐, 부담   pick ~ up ~를 차에 태우러 가다
appreciate 고마워하다   in advance 미리

PRACTICE 패턴 활용

문장을 써 보고 음원을 들으며 소리 내어 말하세요. 제시어 중 기본형 동사는 패턴에 맞게 바꾸고, 제시어의 // 앞까지만이라도 완성해 말하세요.

▶ 정답 320쪽

- 비만 안 왔으면 우린 그 소풍을 갔을 텐데. if it hadn't rained / we / go on that picnic
  If it hadn't rained, we would've gone on that picnic.

1 이렇게 추운 줄 알았으면 재킷 입고 나왔을 텐데.
   I / wear a jacket // if I had known it was going to be this cold

2 그날 약속만 없었으면 이사를 도와줬을 텐데. I / help you move // if I hadn't had plans that day

3 이렇게 차가 막힐 줄 알았으면 더 일찍 왔을 거야. I / come earlier // if I'd known the traffic was this bad

4 네 생일인 줄 알았다면 케이크를 사 왔을 텐데. If I had known it was your birthday / I / buy you a cake

5 네가 아프다고 말해 줬다면 내가 너를 위해 수프를 만들어 줬을 텐데.
   if you had told me you were feeling sick / I / make you some soup

6 우리가 버스를 놓치지 않았으면 제시간에 도착했을 텐데.
   we / make it on time // if we hadn't missed the bus

7 그가 그렇게 서두르지만 않았으면 휴대폰을 잃어버리진 않았을 텐데. 응용
   he / lose his phone // if he hadn't been in such a rush

8 우리가 미리 예매를 안 했으면 공연을 놓쳤을 거야.
   we / miss the show // if we hadn't booked the tickets in advance

make it on time 제시간에 도착하다   in a rush 서둘러, 급히

미리 말했으면, 뭐 먹을 거라도 해 놨을 텐데.

주어 + would have p.p.

If you'd let me know ahead of time, I made you something to eat

UNIT 67

The minute + 절
~하자마자

이 패턴은 '~하자마자'라는 뜻으로 as soon as와 서로 바꿔 쓸 수 있어요. 여기서 the minute은 실제로 '1분'이라는 시간을 나타내는 것이 아니라, 아주 짧은 시간을 강조하는 표현이에요. 예를 들어, "6시가 되자마자, 바로 칼퇴했다."는 The minute it hit 6 o'clock, I left work, 또는 As soon as it hit 6 o'clock, I left work.로 말할 수 있어요.

The minute 뒤에는 절(주어+동사)이 옵니다.

 The minute we moved in, it already felt like home.
이사하자마자 벌써 집처럼 느껴지더라.

[The minute + 절, 주절]은 콤마(,) 없이 [주절 + the minute + 절]로 쓸 수 있어요. I left work the minute it hit 6 o'clock.과 같이요.

실생활 대화

A I heard you moved to a new apartment.
새 아파트로 이사했다며?

B Yeah, the minute we moved in, it already felt like home.
응, 이사하자마자 벌써 집처럼 느껴지더라.

A Wow, is it that nice?
와, 그렇게 좋아?

B Yeah, the location's great and the neighbors are super friendly.
응, 위치도 좋고 이웃들도 정말 친절해.

location 위치   friendly 친절한

PRACTICE 패턴 활용

문장을 써 보고 음원을 들으며 소리 내어 말하세요. 제시어 중 기본형 동사는 패턴에 맞게 바꾸고, 제시어의 // 앞까지만이라도 완성해 말하세요.

▶ 정답 320쪽

- 새로운 소식 들으면 바로 문자 할게.   I'll text you / I hear any news

  I'll text you the minute I hear any news.

1. 뉴욕에 도착하자마자 알려 줄게.   I arrive / in New York / I'll let you know

2. 그걸 맛보자마자 뭔가 이상하다는 걸 알았어.   I tasted it / I knew something was off

3. 우리가 밖으로 나가자마자 비가 내리기 시작했어.   we stepped outside / it started to rain

4. 그녀가 방에 들어가자마자 모두가 그녀를 바라봤어.
   she walked into the room / everyone turned to look at her

5. 그녀가 상자를 열자마자 얼굴에 기쁨이 가득했어.
   she opened the box / her face lit up with excitement

6. 선생님이 들어오시자마자 교실이 완전히 조용해졌어.
   the teacher walked in / the class went completely silent

7. 어머니가 방을 나가자마자 아기가 울기 시작했어. `응용`
   the baby started crying / his mother left the room

8. 그 말이 입에서 나오는 순간 그는 실수했다는 걸 알았어. `응용`
   he knew he'd made a mistake / the words left his mouth

---

taste 맛보다   off (음식이) 상한   step outside 밖으로 나가다   light up (얼굴이) 환해지다

> 이사하자마자 벌써 집처럼 느껴지더라.
>
> **The minute + 절, + 주절**
>   we moved in   it already felt like home

UNIT 68

By the time + 절
~할 때쯤

이 패턴은 '~할 때쯤'이라는 뜻으로, 어떤 일이 일어났을 때쯤 '이미' 다른 일은 끝났다는 것을 강조할 때 사용해요. 예를 들어 "저녁 다 만들어질 때쯤, 집에 도착할거야!" (I'll be home by the time dinner is ready!)라든지, 아니면 "내가 도착했을 때쯤, 그들은 이미 떠났어." (By the time I arrived, they had already left.)라고 말할 수 있어요. [by the time + 절] 형태로 쓰이고 앞이나 뒤에 주절이 와요.

By the time 뒤에는 절(주어 + 동사)이 옵니다.

 By the time we made our decision, someone else had already taken it.
우리가 결정했을 땐, 이미 다른 사람이 계약했더라고.

실생활 대화

A Did you sign the contract for the new apartment?
새 아파트 계약했어?

B We couldn't. By the time we made our decision, someone else had already taken it.
못 했어. 우리가 결정했을 땐, 이미 다른 사람이 계약했더라고.

A Oh no, that's too bad. Weren't there any other options?
아, 너무 아쉽다. 다른 선택지는 없었어?

B We're still looking. I just hope it's not too expensive by the time we find the right place.
아직 찾는 중이야. 괜찮은 곳 찾을 때쯤 너무 비싸지만 않길 바라고 있어.

---

contract 계약하다   make one's decision 결정하다

PRACTICE 패턴 활용

문장을 써 보고 음원을 들으며 소리 내어 말하세요. 제시어 중 기본형 동사는 패턴에 맞게 바꾸고, 제시어의 // 앞까지만이라도 완성해 말하세요.

▶ 정답 320쪽

- 내가 도착했을 땐, 비가 이미 그쳤어.　　　　　　　　　I arrived / the rain had already stopped

  By the time I arrived, the rain had already stopped.

1. 내가 역에 도착했을 무렵에, 기차는 막 출발했어.　　　I got to the station / the train had just left

2. 우리가 거기에 도착했을 무렵에, 가게는 문을 닫은 상태였어.　　we got there / the store was closed

3. 그가 전화했을 때쯤, 그녀는 이미 잠자고 있었어.　　he called / she had already gone to bed

4. 네가 이 메시지를 읽었을 때쯤, 나는 이미 떠난 뒤일 거야.
   you read this message / I will have already left

5. 이 책을 다 읽을 즈음엔, 아마 속편이 나와 있을 거야.
   I finish this book / the sequel will probably be out

6. 영화가 시작했을 때쯤, 우리는 이미 팝콘을 다 먹었어.
   the movie started / we had already finished our popcorn

7. 우리가 식당에 도착할 무렵엔, 너무 붐빌 수도 있어.
   we get to the restaurant / it might be too crowded

8. 내 실수를 깨달았을 즈음엔, 더 빨리 행동하지 못한 걸 이미 후회하고 있었어.
   I realized my mistake / I was already full of regret for not acting sooner

get to ~에 도착하다　sequel 속편　realize 깨닫다　be full of ~로 가득차다　regret 후회

우리가 결정했을 땐, 이미 다른 사람이 계약했더라고.

By the time + 절, + 주절
we made our decision　someone else had already taken it

UNIT 69

It's a shame (that) + 절
~라니 아쉽다[안타깝다]

이 패턴은 '~라는 게 아쉽다'라는 뜻으로 어떤 상황에 대해 아쉬움을 표현할 때 사용해요. shame은 Shame on you.(부끄러운 줄 아세요.)라는 표현처럼 수치심, 부끄러움이라는 뜻도 있지만 '아쉬움, 안타까움, 유감'의 감정을 나타내기도 해요. 예를 들면, 친구들과 재밌게 놀고 있었는데 갑자기 한 친구가 이제 집에 가야 한다고 할 때, 아쉬운 마음에 You are leaving already? It's a shame that you are leaving so early. (벌써 간다고? 이렇게 빨리 간다니 아쉽다.)라고 말할 수 있어요.

It's a shame (that) 뒤에는 유감스럽거나 안타까운 상황을 나타내는 절(주어+동사)이 옵니다.

 It's a shame that we couldn't stay longer.
더 오래 있지 못해서 아쉬워요.

아쉬움이나 애석한 마음을 더 강조하고 싶을 때는 such를 붙여서 It's such a shame ~ 이라고 해요.

실생활 대화

A How was your trip to Colombia?
콜롬비아 여행은 어땠어요?

B It was great, but it's a shame that we couldn't stay longer.
정말 좋았어요. 그런데 더 오래 있지 못해서 아쉬워요.

A Oh yeah? How long did you stay?
Did you get to see everything you wanted?
아, 그래요? 얼마나 계셨어요? 보고 싶었던 건 다 봤어요?

B We stayed for a week, but it wasn't enough.
It's a shame we missed out on a few places.
일주일 있었는데도 부족했어요. 몇 군데 못 가본 게 아쉬워요.

stay 머무르다   miss out on ~을 놓치다, 못하다

PRACTICE 패턴 활용

문장을 써 보고 음원을 들으며 소리 내어 말하세요. 제시어 중 기본형 동사는 패턴에 맞게 바꾸고, 제시어의 // 앞까지만이라도 완성해 말하세요.

▶ 정답 320쪽

- 당신이 파티에 참석 못 하다니 아쉽네요. you can't come to the party
  It's a shame that you can't come to the party.

1 우리가 단체 사진 찍는 걸 까먹다니 아쉬워요! we forgot to take a group photo

2 콘서트 표가 너무 빨리 매진돼서 아쉬워요. the concert tickets sold out / so fast

3 이제 막 알게 된 최애 카페가 바로 문을 닫다니 아쉬워요. my favorite café closed // right after I discovered it

4 안 좋은 날씨 때문에 콘서트가 취소되어서 안타깝네요.
   the concert was canceled / due to bad weather

5 아이스크림 한 입도 못 먹었는데 녹아버리다니 아쉬워요.
   the ice cream melted // before I even took a bite

6 빵집에 크루아상이 다 떨어졌다니 너무 아쉬워요. 진짜 먹고 싶었는데. [응용]
   the bakery ran out of croissants // I was really craving one

7 벌써 휴가가 끝나다니 너무 아쉬워요. 벌써 또 쉬고 싶어요! [응용]
   my vacation's already over // I need another one

8 그가 승진 못 했다니 너무 안타까워요. 요 몇 달 동안 그렇게 열심히 일했는데. [응용]
   he didn't get the promotion // he's been working so hard these past few months

group photo 단체 사진   sell out 매진되다   discover 발견하다, 알게 되다   melt 녹다   take a bite 한 입 먹다
run out of ~이 다 떨어지다   get the promotion 승진하다   past few months 지난 몇 달 동안

더 오래 있지 못해서 아쉬워요.

It's a shame that + 절
           ↳
     we couldn't stay longer

UNIT 70

It's a relief (that) + 절
~여서 다행[안심]이다

이 패턴은 '~여서 다행이에요, 안심이에요'라는 뜻으로 어떤 상황이 해결되어 안도감을 느낄 때 사용해요. 예를 들어, 시드니에 큰 사고가 나서 거기에 사는 친구에게 전화했는데 아무 일이 없다고 할 때 안도하며 "네가 괜찮아서 다행이야."라고 말하고 싶다면 It's a relief that you're okay, 또는 "늦을 줄 알았는데 제시간에 도착해서 다행이야."라고 말하고 싶을 때 It's a relief that we arrived on time. 등으로 말이죠.

It's a relief (that) 뒤에는 안도감을 느낀 상황을 나타내는 절이 옵니다.

 It's such **a relief that** everyone's okay.
모두가 무사하다니 진짜 다행이야.

안도감을 느끼는 상황은 [It's a relief to + 동사원형] 형태로도 가능해요. 예를 들어, 친구에게 무슨 일이 있을까 걱정했는데 별일이 없는 걸 알게 되었다면 It's a relief to know everything's okay. (다 괜찮다니 안심이야.)라고 말할 수 있겠지요.

실생활 대화

A Did you hear about the storm last night?
어젯밤 폭풍 소식 들었어?

B Yeah, it's such a relief that everyone's okay.
응, 모두 무사해서 진짜 다행이야.

A I know, it was pretty scary. Did you guys have any damage?
그러게, 꽤 무섭더라. 너희 집은 피해 입었어?

B Thankfully, no. It's a relief we were prepared for the worst.
다행히도 없었어. 최악의 상황에 대비해 둔 게 정말 다행이야.

---

scary 무서운, 두려운   damage 손상, 피해   thankfully 다행히도, 고맙게도
prepare for the worst 최악의 상황에 대비하다

PRACTICE 패턴 활용

문장을 써 보고 음원을 들으며 소리 내어 말하세요. 제시어 중 기본형 동사는 패턴에 맞게 바꾸고, 제시어의 // 앞까지만이라도 완성해 말하세요.

▶ 정답 321쪽

- 날씨가 맑아져서 다행이야.   the weather cleared up

  It's a relief that the weather cleared up.

1. 그가 지갑을 찾아서 정말 다행이야.   he found his wallet

2. 기차 안 놓쳐서 다행이야.   we didn't miss the train

3. 시험이 생각만큼 어렵지 않아서 다행이야.   the test wasn't as hard as I expected

4. 차 수리 비용이 너무 많이 들지 않아서 다행이야.   the car repair didn't cost too much

5. 폭풍이 아무 피해 없이 지나가서 다행이야.   the storm passed / without causing any damage

6. 충전기를 가져와서 다행이야. 배터리가 3%밖에 안 남았었거든.
   I brought my charger with me // my phone battery was down to 3%

7. 드디어 그 보고서를 끝내서 정말 다행이야. [응용]   finally finish that report

8. 수술이 잘 됐다는 소식 들으니 정말 다행이야. [응용]   hear that the surgery went well

---

clear up (날씨가) 개다, 맑아지다   repair 수리   cost 비용이 들다   surgery 수술   pass 지나가다
cause 야기하다, 일으키다   battery 배터리

모두가 무사하다니 진짜 다행이야.

It's a relief that + 절
       such   everyone's okay

REMINDER 패턴 강화

이제 내 이야기를 해 봐요! 나에게 있음 직한 일들을 적고, 소리 내어 말해 보는 거예요.
주어가 별도로 제시되지 않으면, 주어는 항상 I(나)예요.

▶ 정답 321쪽

UNIT 66 If you'd let me know ahead of time, I **would've made** you something to eat.

> **would have p.p.**
> ~했을 텐데

1 내가 네 자리 맡아 놨을 텐데.   saved you a seat

2 네가 좋아하는 음료를 사다 줬을 텐데.   got you your favorite drink

3 너에게 회의 있는 거 알려 줬을 텐데.   reminded you about the meeting

UNIT 67 **The minute** we moved in, it already felt like home.

> **The minute + 절**
> ~하자마자

4 연기 냄새가 나자마자 건물 밖으로 나왔어.   I smelled the smoke / I left the building

5 그가 음식 얘기하자마자 배고파졌어.   he mentioned food / I got hungry

6 쇼가 시작되자마자 전화가 울렸어.   the show started / my phone rang

UNIT 68 **By the time** we made our decision, someone else had already taken it.

> **By the time + 절**
> ~할 때쯤

7 그녀가 문자 했을 땐, 난 이미 자고 있었어.   she texted me / I was already asleep

8 그들이 전화했을 땐, 우린 가는 중이었어.   they called us / we were on the way

9 일어났을 땐, 알람이 꺼져 있었어.   I woke up / my alarm had stopped

UNIT 69 **It's a shame that** we couldn't stay longer.

It's a shame (that) + 절
~라니 아쉽다[안타깝다]

10 날씨가 안 받쳐준 게 아쉬워.   the weather didn't hold up

11 그 새로 생긴 라면집을 못 가본 게 아쉽네.   we didn't try that new ramen place

12 콘서트가 취소된 게 아쉬워.   the concert got canceled

UNIT 70 **It's** such **a relief that** everyone's okay.

It's a relief (that) + 절
~여서 다행[안심]이다

13 지갑을 잃어버리지 않아서 다행이야.   I didn't lose my wallet

14 마감이 연기돼서 다행이야.   the deadline was extended

15 버스가 빨리 와서 다행이야.   the bus came quickly

REMINDER 맥락 적용

이제 앞에서 연습한 패턴을 실생활 대화 맥락에 적용해 보세요. 패턴을 일상적인 대화에 넣어서 직접 소리 내어 말해 보는 거예요. 빈칸에 들어갈 말이 기억이 나지 않는다면 다시 앞으로 가서 확인해 보세요.

UNIT 66

A Why didn't you come to the party yesterday?
어제 왜 파티에 안 왔어?

B I didn't know there was a party happening yesterday. If I had known about it, I definitely 🐱_____ come.
어제 파티가 있었는지 몰랐어. 알았으면 분명히 갔을 텐데.

A Oh dear, I thought I had told you. I should have double-checked with you.
아이고, 난 내가 말했다고 생각했는데. 너한테 다시 확인했어야 했네.

B It's not your fault; these things happen!
네 잘못이 아니야; 이런 일은 흔하니까!

UNIT 67

A How's the new puppy you adopted?
새로 입양한 강아지는 어때?

B He's cute. 🐱_____ we brought him home, he started exploring everywhere.
귀여워. 집에 데려다 놓으니까 집 안 곳곳을 탐험하더라.

A Is he adapting well?
적응은 잘 하고 있어?

B Yes, he's adjusting faster than we expected.
응, 생각보다 빨리 적응하고 있어.

UNIT 68

A Did you go to your friend's birthday party?
친구 생일 파티에 갔었어?

B I tried to, but 🐱_____ I arrived, everyone was leaving.
가려고 했는데, 내가 도착했을 때는 모두 자리를 뜨고 있더라.

A Oh, did you go too late?
너무 늦게 간 거 아니야?

B Even though I left home early, I was stuck in traffic for hours. The cars were moving bumper-to-bumper, so 🐱_____ I got through it, the party was over.
집에서 일찍 나왔는데도 몇 시간 동안 차가 막혔어. 차들이 기어가는 바람에, 그 정체를 빠져나왔을 때는 파티가 이미 끝났더라고.

UNIT 69

A How's your grandmother doing?
할머니는 어떠세요?

B Not too well. **It's a shame** that she hasn't been able to travel lately due to her health.
별로 좋지 않아요. 건강 때문에 최근에 여행을 못 가고 계셔서 안타까워요.

A I'm sorry to hear that. Has she been able to do any activities at home?
안타깝네요. 집에서라도 뭔가 활동을 하고 계세요?

B A little, but **it's a shame** she can't do as much as she used to. She especially misses gardening.
조금요. 하지만 예전만큼 못하셔서 안타까워요. 특히 정원 일을 많이 그리워하세요.

UNIT 70

A I passed my driving test on the first try!
운전면허 시험을 한 번에 통과했어!

B **It's a relief** that you won't have to take it again. Congratulations!
다시 볼 필요 없어서 다행이네. 축하해!

A Thanks! I was so nervous, but all that practice paid off, and I think I nailed the test, if I do say so myself!
고마워! 정말 긴장했는데, 연습한 게 다 도움이 됐고, 내 입으로 말하긴 좀 그렇지만 시험을 아주 잘 본 것 같아!

B I'm sure you did! When are you going to take me for a drive?
분명 잘 봤을 거야! 언제 나 드라이브시켜 줄 거니?

어휘   get through ~를 헤쳐나가다   nail 완벽하게 해치우다

정답   would have | The minute | by the time, by the time | It's a shame, it's a shame | It's a relief

UNIT 71

The 비교급 + 절, the 비교급 + 절
~할수록 더 ~하다

일상에서 대화를 하다 보면 '~할수록 더 ~하다'라는 말을 쓸 일이 많죠? "배우자의 말을 잘 들을수록 더 행복한 결혼 생활을 할 수 있어요."는 The more you listen to your partner, the happier your marriage will be.라고 할 수 있어요. 어떤 일을 더 많이 하거나 더 강하게 할수록, 그에 따른 결과도 커지거나 달라진다는 의미를 담고 있어요. 반대로 '덜 ~할수록 덜 ~하다'는 어떻게 표현할까요? more 대신 less를 사용하면 돼요. 예를 들어, "자기 전에 핸드폰을 덜 볼수록 다음 날 덜 피곤해요."는 The less you look at your phone before bed, the less tired you feel the next day.라고 할 수 있어요.

보통 비교급은 형용사나 부사에 -(i)er을 붙이거나, 앞에 more를 씁니다.

 The more I meditate, **the calmer** I feel.
명상을 많이 할수록, 마음이 더 차분해져요.

비교급과 절 사이에는 명사도 올 수 있어요. 형용사인 비교급이 명사를 수식해 주는 것이지요. 예를 들어, "피드백을 많이 받을수록 더 나아질 수 있어."는 The more feedback I get, the more I can improve.라고 할 수 있어요.

실생활 대화

A How do you manage stress so well? You always seem so calm.
스트레스를 어떻게 그렇게 잘 관리하세요? 항상 차분해 보이시던데요.

B The more I meditate, the calmer I feel. It's a great way to clear my mind. You should give it a try sometime.
명상을 많이 할수록 마음이 더 차분해져요. 생각을 정리할 수 있는 정말 좋은 방법이에요. 한번 해 보세요.

A I've never tried meditation before. Is it difficult to start?
명상을 해 본 적이 없어요. 시작하기 어렵나요?

B Not at all! The more you practice, the easier it becomes. Start with just a few minutes a day and gradually increase the time.
전혀 어렵지 않아요! 연습할수록 더 쉬워져요. 하루에 몇 분씩만 시작해서 점차 시간을 늘려 보세요.

---

manage 관리하다　meditate 명상하다　calm 차분한(비교급: calmer)　clear one's mind 마음을 정리하다
gradually 점차　increase 증가시키다

PRACTICE 패턴 활용

문장을 써 보고 음원을 들으며 소리 내어 말하세요. 제시어 중 기본형 동사는 패턴에 맞게 바꾸고, 제시어의 // 앞까지만이라도 완성해 말하세요.

▶ 정답 321쪽

- 영어를 연습할수록 더 잘하게 될 거예요. more you practice English / better you will become
  The more you practice English, the better you will become.

1 웃으면 웃을수록 더 행복해져요. more you smile / happier you feel

2 물을 많이 마실수록 피부가 더 좋아져요. more you drink water / better your skin looks

3 화났을 때 말을 덜 할수록 나중에 덜 후회하더라고요. less I talk / when I'm angry / less I regret later

4 운동은 하면 할수록 몸에 대한 자신감이 더 생겨요.
   more you exercise / more confident you become / in your body

5 정직할수록 사람들은 당신을 더 신뢰해요. 응용 more honest you are / more people will trust you

6 빨리 끝낼수록 여가 시간이 더 많아질 거예요. 응용 faster you finish / more free time you'll have

7 설탕을 덜 먹을수록 피로도 줄더라고요. 응용 less sugar I eat / less tired I feel

8 SNS에 시간을 덜 쓰니까 스트레스도 덜 받아요. 응용
   less time I spend on social media / less stressed I am

better 더 잘(well의 비교급), 더 나은(good의 비교급) **regret** 후회하다 **confident** 자신 있는
free time 여가 시간

명상을 많이 할수록, 마음이 더 차분해져요.

The 비교급 + 절, the 비교급 + 절
　　more I meditate　calmer I feel

UNIT 72

be into + 동명사[명사]

~에 푹 빠져 있다, ~에 관심이 많다

이 패턴은 어떤 것에 관심이 있거나 열중하고 있을 때 사용해요. 예를 들어, "나는 달리기에 푹 빠져 있어. 머리가 맑아지거든."이라고 말하고 싶다면 I'm into running. It helps me clear my mind, "나는 요즘 요리에 빠져 있어. 요리는 정말 좋은 취미야."라고 말하고 싶다면 I'm into cooking these days. It's such a great pastime. 등으로 말이죠.

be into 뒤에는 관심 있는 활동이나 대상을 나타내는 동명사나 명사를 씁니다.

 I'm really **into** swimming.
요즘 수영에 푹 빠져 있어.

어떤 것에 별로 관심 없다고 말하고 싶으면 be not into로 말하면 돼요. I'm not into running, I'm not into cooking.과 같이요.

실생활 대화

A **You look really fit! How do you stay in shape?**
너 진짜 건강해 보여! 어떻게 그렇게 몸매 관리를 해?

B **I'm really into swimming. It's such a great full-body workout.**
요즘 수영에 푹 빠져 있어. 전신 운동으로 완전 최고야.

A **That's cool! Do you usually swim alone or with a group?**
멋지다! 보통 혼자 해? 아니면 같이 해?

B **I actually take a class every morning. It keeps me motivated. You should join me sometime!**
사실 매일 아침 수업을 들어. 진짜 동기부여 돼. 나중에 한번 같이 해.

fit 건강한, 몸매가 좋은   stay in shape 몸매를 유지하다   full-body workout 전신 운동
motivated 동기부여가 된, 의욕이 생긴   join 함께하다

PRACTICE 패턴 활용

문장을 써 보고 음원을 들으며 소리 내어 말하세요. 제시어 중 기본형 동사는 패턴에 맞게 바꾸고, 제시어의 // 앞까지만이라도 완성해 말하세요.

▶ 정답 321쪽

- 난 음악에, 특히 클래식 음악에 빠져 있어.   I / music // especially classical music

  I'm into music, especially classical music.

1. 난 요즘 유튜브에서 요리 영상 보는 거에 완전 빠졌어.
   I / totally / watch cooking videos / on YouTube / lately

2. 난 요즘 걷기에 꽂혔어. 하루에 1만 보는 채우려고 해.
   I / walk / these days // I try to get 10,000 steps a day

3. 난 축구에 푹 빠져 있어. 최근에 지역 팀에 가입해서 주 2회 연습하고 있어.
   I / play soccer // I joined a local team recently // and we practice twice a week

4. 난 요가에 푹 빠져 있어. 요가는 날 유연하게 해 주고 스트레스를 줄여 주는데 도움이 돼.
   I / yoga // it helps me stay flexible // and reduces my stress levels

5. 난 스포츠엔 별로 관심 없는데 월드컵 보는 건 정말 좋아해. 응용
   I / really / sports // but I love watching the World Cup

6. 난 전엔 조깅에 관심이 없었는데 지금은 일상이 됐어. 응용
   I / jogging / before // but now it's part of my routine

7. 그녀는 패션에 관심이 많고 항상 유행하는 옷을 입어. 응용
   she / really / fashion // and always wears trendy clothes

8. 그녀는 스포츠에 그다지 관심이 없지만, 대신에 코딩에 대단히 열정적이야. 응용
   she / that / sports // but instead, she is really passionate about coding

step 걸음   yoga 요가   flexible 유연한   jogging 조깅   routine 일상   trendy 유행하는, 최신 유행의
be passionate about ~에 열정적이다

요즘 수영에 푹 빠져 있어.

주어 + be into + 동명사

I'm　really　swimming

UNIT 73

don't feel like + 동명사[명사]
~할 기분이 아니다

이 패턴은 어떤 일을 하고 싶은 마음이 없다는 것을 표현할 때 사용해요. 예를 들어 오늘 너무 피곤해서 저녁을 만들 기분이 아닐 때 I don't want to make dinner tonight. 보다는 좀 더 부드럽게 I don't feel like making dinner tonight.으로 "오늘 저녁 할 기분이 아니야."라고 말할 수 있어요. 또 다른 예로는 "나는 공부할 기분이 아니야."라고 말하고 싶다면 I don't feel like studying, "나는 외출할 기분이 아니야."는 I don't feel like going out.이라고 하면 돼요.

don't feel like 뒤에는 하고 싶지 않은 행동을 나타내는 동명사나 명사를 씁니다.

 I **don't** really **feel like** cleaning.
청소할 기분이 아니야.

실생활 대화

A Should we clean the house this weekend?
이번 주말에 집 청소할까?

B I don't really feel like cleaning. Can we push it to next week?
청소할 기분이 아니야. 다음 주로 미뤄도 될까?

A That works for me. How about doing a bit of decluttering instead?
난 괜찮아. 대신 물건 좀 정리하는 건 어때?

B Yeah, that sounds better. A little tidying up won't hurt.
그게 더 나을 것 같네. 살짝 정리하는 정도면 괜찮아.

push it to (구어) ~로 미루다   tidy up 정리하다, 깔끔하게 하다   won't hurt 나쁠 것 없다, ~해도 괜찮다

PRACTICE 패턴 활용

문장을 써 보고 음원을 들으며 소리 내어 말하세요. 제시어 중 기본형 동사는 패턴에 맞게 바꾸고, 제시어의 // 앞까지만이라도 완성해 말하세요.

▶ 정답 321쪽

- 오늘 밤 영화 볼 기분이 아니야.   I / a movie tonight
  ### I don't feel like a movie tonight.

1   지금 게임할 기분이 아니야.   I / a game / right now

2   지금 긴 대화를 할 기분이 아니야.   I / a long conversation / right now

3   오늘 저녁은 요리할 기분이 아니야. 그냥 시켜 먹자.   I / cook / tonight // let's just order in

4   오늘 밤 외출할 기분이 아니야. 그냥 집에서 쉬고 싶어.
I / go out / tonight // I just want to relax at home

5   우린 이런 날씨에 나가고 싶지 않아. 그냥 집에서 쉬자.
we / go out / in this weather // let's just chill at home

6   지금 공부할 기분이 아니야. 몇 시간 동안 계속 공부해서 좀 쉬어야 할 것 같아.
I / study / right now // I've been at it for hours / and my brain needs a break

7   그녀는 오늘 꾸미고 싶은 기분이 아니라서 편한 옷 입었대. [응용]
she / dress up / today // that's why she wore sweats

8   걔는 오늘 일하고 싶은 마음이 없어. 완전 번아웃이야. [응용]
he / work / today // he's totally burned out

---

chill 편히 쉬다, 느긋하게 보내다   **at it** 계속해서 하고 있는   **dress up** 꾸미다, 차려입다
sweats 편한 옷 (트레이닝복)   **burned out** 번아웃된, 지친

청소할 기분이 아니야.

주어 + don't feel like + 동명사
  I   really   cleaning

221

UNIT 74

must be + 형용사[명사]

~(하)겠다

must be는 상대방의 상황이나 기분을 어느 정도 확신을 가지고 추측할 때 사용해요. 예를 들어, 친구가 오늘 아침과 점심을 모두 굶은 상태에서 공부를 하고 있다면 "정말 배고프겠다."라고 어느 정도 확신을 가지고 You must be starving.이라고 말할 수 있겠죠? 또는 10시간 동안 비행기를 타고 온 동료에게 "오랫동안 비행해서 피곤하겠다."는 You must be tired after such a long flight.라고 말할 수 있어요.

must be 뒤에는 보어로서 형용사나 명사가 옵니다.

 His day at work **must have been** great.
회사에서 오늘 기분이 좋으셨나 봐.

His day at work must have been great.에서처럼 [must have + p.p.] 패턴으로 과거의 상황을 추측하며 말할 수도 있어요. "정말 배고팠겠다."는 You must have been starving, "오랫동안 비행해서 피곤했겠다."는 You must have been tired after such a long flight.라고 말할 수 있는 거죠.

실생활 대화

A Dad says he's coming home early today.
아빠가 오늘 일찍 집에 오신대.

B His day at work must have been great.
회사에서 오늘 기분이 좋으셨나 봐.

A Yeah, and he said he's bringing home a surprise.
응, 그리고 깜짝 선물도 가져오신다고 했어.

B Maybe he finally got that promotion he's been hoping for.
아마 그동안 원했던 승진을 드디어 하신 걸 수도.

surprise 깜짝 선물, 놀라운 일   hope for ~를 바라다

PRACTICE 패턴 활용

문장을 써 보고 음원을 들으며 소리 내어 말하세요. 제시어 중 기본형 동사는 패턴에 맞게 바꾸고, 제시어의 // 앞까지만이라도 완성해 말하세요.

▶ 정답 322쪽

• 오랫동안 등산해서 피곤하겠다. you / tired / after that long hike
  You must be tired after that long hike.

1 요즘 진짜 바쁘겠구나. you / really busy / these days

2 내일 여행이라 진짜 설레겠다. you / excited / for your trip / tomorrow

3 네가 존의 여동생이구나. 둘이 붕어빵처럼 닮았네. you / John's sister // you are the spitting image of him

4 오랜만에 가족을 봐서 정말 기쁘겠다. you / thrilled / to see your family // after such a long time

5 좋아하는 가수를 만나서 정말 기뻤겠네. 응용 you / absolutely thrilled / to meet your favorite singer

6 그는 승진 못 했을 때 정말 실망했을 거야. 응용
  he / really disappointed // when he didn't get the promotion

7 따님이 대학을 졸업했을 때 정말 자랑스러우셨겠어요. 응용
  you / incredibly proud // when your daughter graduated from college

8 그녀가 바이올린을 시작했을 땐 어렸겠네. 아마 초등학생이었을 거야. 응용
  she / young / when she started playing the violin // probably still in elementary school

---

hike 등산   the spitting image of ~의 붕어빵   absolutely 전적으로, 정말로   thrilled 아주 기쁜
disappointed 실망한   incredibly 엄청나게   graduate from ~를 졸업하다

회사에서 오늘 기분이 좋으셨나 봐.

주어 + must be + 형용사

His day at work   have been great

UNIT 75

be cut out for + 명사[동명사]
~에 소질[재능]이 있다

어떤 일을 처음 했을 때 예상외로 너무 잘하게 되면서 "어? 이 일에 소질이 있는 것 같은데!"라는 말을 할 때가 있죠? be cut out for는 그 느낌을 주기에 딱 맞는 패턴이에요. 어떤 역할이나 직업에 있어서 소질이 있거나 적성에 맞다고 말해 줄 때 You are cut out for it.이라고 해요. 또 다른 예로, "그는 요리에 소질이 있어."라고 말하고 싶다면 He is cut out for cooking, "나는 경영에 소질이 있어."는 I'm cut out for management.라고 말할 수 있어요.

be cut out for 뒤에는 소질이나 재능을 나타내는 명사나 동명사를 사용합니다.

 I think he's really **cut out for** it.
개는 그 일에 소질이 있는 것 같아.

반대로 '~에 소질이 없다'는 말을 하고 싶다면 be not cut out for를 사용해요. 예를 들어, "난 그 일에 맞지 않아."는 I'm not cut out for the work.라고 해요.

실생활 대화

A I heard Minsu wants to become a teacher. What do you think?
민수가 선생님이 되고 싶어 한대. 어떻게 생각해?

B I think he's really cut out for it. He's great with kids.
개는 그 일에 소질이 있는 것 같아. 아이들을 진짜 잘 다뤄.

A That's great to hear. Do you think he can handle the challenges that come with the job?
그거 좋은 소식이네. 그 일이 가진 어려움들을 잘 감당할 수 있을까?

B For sure. He's super patient and has a real knack for breaking things down in a way that's easy to understand.
당연하지. 인내심도 강하고, 복잡한 걸 쉽게 풀어 설명하는 재주가 있어.

---

handle 다루다, 감당하다　**have a knack for** ~하는 재주가 있다　**break down** 쉽게 설명하다, 쪼개서 설명하다

PRACTICE 패턴 활용

문장을 써 보고 음원을 들으며 소리 내어 말하세요. 제시어 중 기본형 동사는 패턴에 맞게 바꾸고, 제시어의 // 앞까지만이라도 완성해 말하세요.

▶ 정답 322쪽

- 넌 정말 사람들 앞에서 공연하는 게 딱 맞는 사람이야.   you / really / perform in front of an audience
  ### You're really cut out for performing in front of an audience.

1. 넌 외국어 배우는 데 천부적 재능이 있어. 발음이 정말 좋더라.
   you / learn foreign languages // your pronunciation is really good

2. 넌 요리에 타고난 재능이 있어! 이게 처음 요리하는 거 맞아?
   you / really / cook // are you sure this is your first-time cooking

3. 금융계 일이 나한테 맞을지 모르겠어. 숫자에 약한 것 같거든.
   I'm not sure / if / I / a career in finance // I don't think I'm good with numbers

4. 그녀는 정말 선생님 체질이야. 인내심도 있고, 창의적이고, 학생들과 소통하는 법도 잘 알아.
   she / really / teach // she's patient, creative / and knows how to connect with students

5. 사무직이 내 적성엔 안 맞는 것 같아. 한 자리에 오래 앉아 있으면 답답해지거든. `응용`
   I don't think / I / a desk job // I get restless sitting in one place for too long

6. 너는 진짜 발표 체질이야. 자신감도 있고, 말도 조리 있게 잘하고, 듣는 사람도 집중하게 해.
   you / totally / public speaking // you are confident, clear, and engaging

7. 그는 군대에 갈까 고민했지만, 그런 규율 있는 생활은 자기랑 안 맞는다고 느꼈어. `응용`
   he considered the military but realized / he / the discipline

8. 도시 생활이 나랑 안 맞는다는 걸 점점 깨닫고 있어. `응용`   I'm beginning to realize / I / city life

---

audience 청중   pronunciation 발음   finance 금융, 재정   be good with numbers 숫자에 밝다[능숙하다]
creative 창의적인   connect with ~와 소통하다   desk job 사무직   restless 가만히 있지 못하는
public speaking 발표   engaging 매력적인, 흥미로운   military 군대   discipline 규율, 훈련

걔는 그 일에 소질이 있는 것 같아.

주어 + be cut out for + 명사

I think   he's   really   it

REMINDER 패턴 강화

이제 내 이야기를 해 봐요! 나에게 있음 직한 일들을 적고, 소리 내어 말해 보는 거예요.
주어가 별도로 제시되지 않으면, 주어는 항상 I(나)예요.

▶ 정답 322쪽

UNIT 71 **The more** I meditate, **the calmer** I feel.

> The 비교급 + 절, the 비교급 + 절
> ~할수록 더 ~하다

1 네가 그와 더 많이 대화할수록 그가 더 마음을 열어.
   more you talk to him / more he opens up

2 네가 닦을수록 또 금방 더 더러워져.   more you clean / more it gets messy again

3 네가 미소 지을수록 사람들이 널 더 좋아해. 응용
   more you smile / more people like you

UNIT 72 I'm really **into** swimming.

> be into + 동명사[명사]
> ~에 푹 빠져 있다, ~에 관심이 많다

4 라떼 아트에 빠져 있어.   coffee art

5 새로운 언어를 배우는 데 푹 빠졌어.   learning new languages

6 숏폼 영상 편집하는 거에 재미 붙였어.   editing short videos

UNIT 73 I **don't** really **feel like** cleaning.

> don't feel like + 동명사[명사]
> ~할 기분이 아니다

7 설거지할 기분 아니야.   doing the dishes

8   잡담할 기분이 아니야.   small talk

9   오늘 밤 나가고 싶은 기분이 아니야.   going out tonight

UNIT 74 His day at work **must have been** great.

> must be + 형용사[명사]
> ~(하)겠다

10   너 진짜 지치겠다. / 너 진짜 지쳤겠다.   you / exhausted

11   너 엄청 배고프겠다. / 너 엄청 배고팠겠다.   you / starving

12   너 신나겠다. / 너 신났겠다.   you / thrilled

UNIT 75 I think he's really **cut out for** it.

> be cut out for + 명사[동명사]
> ~에 소질[재능]이 있다

13   난 도시 생활이 딱 맞아.   life in the city

14   난 스트레스를 다루는 걸 잘 못 해. 응용   handling pressure

15   난 이런 일에 소질이 있어.   this kind of work

REMINDER 맥락 적용

이제 앞에서 연습한 패턴을 실생활 대화 맥락에 적용해 보세요. 패턴을 일상적인 대화에 넣어서 직접 소리 내어 말해 보는 거예요. 빈칸에 들어갈 말이 기억이 나지 않는다면 다시 앞으로 가서 확인해 보세요.

UNIT 71

A How can I improve my English skills?
영어 실력을 어떻게 하면 향상시킬 수 있을까?

B _____ you practice, _____ you get. Just make sure to practice every day.
연습을 많이 할수록, 더 잘하게 되지. 매일 꾸준히 연습해 봐.

A That makes sense. Do you have any specific tips for practicing?
그렇구나. 연습을 위한 구체적인 팁이 있을까?

B Sure! _____ you immerse yourself in English, _____ you'll improve. Try watching English shows with subtitles or reading English books.
물론이지! 영어에 더 많이 몰입할수록, 더 빨리 향상될 거야. 자막과 함께 영어 프로그램을 보거나 영어로 된 책을 읽어 봐.

UNIT 72

A What's been keeping you busy lately?
요즘 뭐 하느라 바빠?

B _____ learning Spanish. It's challenging but fun.
요즘 스페인어 배우기에 푹 빠져 있어. 어렵긴 한데 재미있어.

A That's cool! How long have you been studying?
멋진데! 얼마나 배웠어?

B About three months now. _____ the culture too.
이제 3개월 정도 됐어. 스페인 문화에도 완전히 빠져 있어.

UNIT 73

A How about we prepare dinner together tonight?
오늘 저녁은 같이 요리해 볼까?

B _____ preparing. Can we just order takeout?
난 요리할 기분이 아니야. 그냥 배달시키면 안 돼?

A We could order takeout, but making something together could be fun!
배달도 좋지만, 같이 요리하면 재밌을 것 같은데!

B You have a point. Maybe we can create something simple together.
네 말도 맞아. 간단한 거라도 같이 만들어 볼까?

UNIT 74

A Mom suddenly started cleaning the house thoroughly.
엄마가 갑자기 집을 꼼꼼히 청소하셔.

B Someone coming over. She only does that when we have guests.
누가 오시나 봐. 집에 손님이 올 때만 그러시잖아.

A You're right. I just heard her say something about Grandma visiting.
맞아. 방금 할머니가 오신다는 걸 들었어.

B That explains why, then! Let's help her prepare.
그래서 그러시는구나! 준비하시는 걸 도와드리자.

UNIT 75

A I heard Jane wants to become an actor. What do you think?
제인이 배우가 되고 싶어 한대. 어떻게 생각해?

B She's really acting. She's expressive and natural in front of the camera.
걔는 정말 배우 감이야. 표현력이 뛰어나고 카메라 앞에서도 자연스러워.

A Has she been in any productions yet?
그 애가 뭔가 작품에 출연한 적 있어?

B Yes, she's done a few student films and local theater productions. She's definitely got talent.
응. 학생 영화 몇 편이랑 지역 연극에 출연했었어. 확실히 재능이 있어.

어휘 specific 구체적인 immerse 몰두하게 만들다 challenging 도전적인, 흥미를 돋구는 order takeout 배달을 주문하다 You have a point. 네 말도 일리가 있어. production 상연 작품

정답 The more, the better, The more, the faster | I'm into, I'm really into | I don't feel like | must be | cut out for

UNIT 76

lose track of time + -ing [부사절]
~하느라 시간 가는 줄 모른다

재미있는 드라마나 영화를 볼 때 시간 가는 줄 모르고 몰입해서 볼 때가 있죠? 시계를 봤는데 자신도 모르게 시간이 엄청 흘렀을 때 "어머! 벌써 7시네요. 진짜 시간 가는 줄 몰랐어!"라고 말을 한 적 있나요? 이럴 때 이 패턴을 사용하여 Oh my gosh, it's already 7 PM. I totally lost track of time!으로 말하면 돼요. lose track of time만으로도 '시간 가는 줄 모른다'라는 의미가 가능하지만 뒤에 [동사 + -ing]를 붙이면 '~하느라 시간 가는 줄 모른다'라는 표현이 돼요. 그리고 when, while 등으로 시작하는 부사절이 뒤에 올 수도 있어요.

lose의 과거형은 **lost**라는 것을 기억해 두세요.

 I always **lose track of time** hanging out there.
거기서 놀다 보면 항상 시간 가는 줄 몰라.

실생활 대화

A What should we do this weekend?
이번 주말에 뭐 할까?

B How about going to the amusement park?
I always lose track of time hanging out there!
놀이공원 가는 건 어때? 거기서 놀다 보면 항상 시간 가는 줄 몰라!

A Oh right, I heard the Halloween festival kicks off this Sunday.
I'll double-check to make sure.
아 맞다, 이번 주 일요일부터 핼러윈 축제 시작한대. 확실히 한 번 더 확인해 볼게.

B Wow, that sounds like so much fun! Just walking around the park in Halloween costumes will totally make us lose track of time!
우와, 진짜 재밌겠다! 핼러윈 복장 입고 공원 돌아다니기만 해도 시간 금방 가겠다!

---

amusement park 놀이공원   hang out 놀다, 어울리다   kick off 시작하다, (행사를) 개막하다
double-check 다시 확인하다   walk around 주변을 돌아다니다   Halloween costume 핼러윈 복장

PRACTICE 패턴 활용

문장을 써 보고 음원을 들으며 소리 내어 말하세요. 제시어 중 기본형 동사는 패턴에 맞게 바꾸고, 제시어의 // 앞까지만이라도 완성해 말하세요.

▶ 정답 322쪽

- 도서관에 있으면 항상 시간 가는 줄 몰라. I / always / when I'm at the library.
  I always lose track of time when I'm at the library.

1 우리는 전화 통화하다 보면 항상 시간 가는 줄 몰라. we / always / when we're on the phone

2 음악 들으면서 산책하면 시간 가는 줄 몰라. I / when I listen to music / and go for a walk

3 재밌게 놀다 보면 시간 가는 줄 모르기 쉬워. it's easy to / when you're having fun

4 오랜 친구랑 커피 마시며 이야기하다 보니 시간 가는 줄 몰랐어.
   I / completely / while catching up with an old friend / over coffee

5 그는 보고서 마무리에 너무 집중해서 시간 가는 줄 몰랐다고 했어. 응용
   he said / he / because he was so focused on finishing the report

6 나는 가끔 SNS 둘러보다 보면 시간 가는 줄 몰라. I / sometimes / just scroll through social media

7 그녀는 점심시간에 웃긴 영상 보다가 시간 가는 줄 몰랐어. 응용
   she / watch funny videos / online / during lunch break

8 그는 피아노 치느라 시간 가는 줄도 모르고 해 지는 것도 못 느꼈대. 응용
   he / play the piano / and didn't even notice it was getting dark

---

have fun 재미있게 놀다   catch up with ~와 오랜만에 이야기를 나누다   be focused on ~에 집중하다
scroll through 스크롤하면서 보다   get dark 어두워지다

거기서 놀다 보면 항상 시간 가는 줄 몰라.

주어 + lose track of time + 동명사
  I   always   hanging out there

UNIT 77

It's not that + 절A, it's just (that) + 절B

[절A]라서가 아니라, [절B]라서 그런 것이다

이 패턴은 상대방이 생각하는 이유를 부정하면서 자신의 진짜 이유를 설명할 때 사용해요. It's not that 뒤에는 절(주어+동사)로 자신이 부정하거나 설명하려는 내용을 쓰고, 그 뒤에 자신의 진짜 이유를 [it's just (that) + 절] 형태로 이어서 쓰면 됩니다. 예를 들어, 친구가 영화를 보자고 하는데 거절할 때 이 패턴을 사용할 수 있어요. 그 영화를 이미 봤기 때문에 다른 걸 하고 싶다고 말하고 싶을 때 It's not that I don't like the movie, it's just that I've seen it before. (그 영화가 싫은 게 아니라, 그냥 전에 봤던 거야.)라고 하면 돼요.

It's not that의 that은 필수적이고, It's just (that)의 (that)은 선택적으로 생략 가능합니다.

 It's not that I'm scared, **it's just that** I don't really enjoy horror stuff.
무서워서 그런 건 아니고, 그냥 공포물을 별로 안 좋아해.

실생활 대화

A Do you want to watch that horror movie tonight?
오늘 밤에 그 공포 영화 볼래?

B I'll pass on it, if that's okay. It's not that I'm scared, it's just that I don't really enjoy horror stuff.
괜찮으면 난 패스할게. 무서워서 그런 건 아니고, 그냥 공포물을 별로 안 좋아해.

A Oh, got it! Then how about a comedy instead?
아하, 그럼 코미디는 어때?

B That sounds perfect.
딱 좋지.

---

horror movie 공포 영화   scared 무서운   horror stuff 공포물

PRACTICE 패턴 활용

문장을 써 보고 음원을 들으며 소리 내어 말하세요. 제시어 중 기본형 동사는 패턴에 맞게 바꾸고, 제시어의 // 앞까지만이라도 완성해 말하세요. ▶ 정답 322쪽

- 그녀가 무례한 게 아니라, 단지 굉장히 솔직할 뿐이야.   she's rude / she's very honest
  It's not that she's rude, it's just that she's very honest.

1. 일찍 못 일어나는 게 아니라, 그냥 안 일어나고 싶어.   I can't wake up early / I don't want to

2. 영화가 지루했던 건 아니고, 그냥 내 취향은 아니었어.   the movie was boring / it wasn't really my thing

3. 네 요리가 싫은 건 아니야. 그냥 배가 안 고팠을 뿐이야.   I don't like your cooking / I wasn't hungry

4. 그 드레스가 예쁘지 않다는 게 아니라, 그냥 내 스타일이 아니야.
   the dress is ugly / it doesn't suit my style

5. 너에게 화가 난 게 아니라, 그냥 상황이 답답한 거야.
   I'm angry with you / I'm frustrated with the situation

6. 운동하기 싫은 게 아니라, 그냥 시간을 내기 어려운 거야.   I don't want to exercise / I can't find the time

7. 그 책이 나빴다는 게 아니라, 기대에 미치지 못한 거야.
   the book was bad / it didn't meet my expectations

8. 샐러드가 싫은 건 아니고, 지금은 그냥 피자가 더 당겨.
   I don't want salad / pizza sounds way better right now

---

not my thing 내 취향이 아닌   suit ~에게 잘 어울리나   frustrated 답답한   find the time 시간을 내다
meet one's expectations 기대에 부응하다   sound ~하게 들리다

무서워서 그런 건 아니고, 그냥 공포물을 별로 안 좋아해.

It's not that + 절A, it's just (that) + 절B

I'm scared   I don't really enjoy horror stuff

UNIT 78

주절 + to the point that + 절
~할 정도로 [주절]하다

우리가 너무 웃긴 영화를 보게 되면 "배꼽이 빠질 정도로 웃었어."라는 표현을 하죠? 이때 사용하는 패턴이 '~할 정도로, ~할 때까지'라는 의미를 가진 to the point that이에요. 즉 어떤 상황이 특정 지점이나 상태에 이를 정도라며 자신의 말을 덧붙여서 강조하거나 행동에 대한 이유를 설명할 때 사용해요. 예를 들어, "나는 네게 전화하는 것도 잊을 정도로 열심히 일했어."는 I worked to the point that I forgot to call you.라고 할 수 있지요.

to the point that 뒤에는 절(주어+동사)이 옵니다.

 We played **to the point that** our legs were sore.
다리가 아플 정도로 놀았어.

실생활 대화

A Did you have fun at the amusement park yesterday?
어제 놀이공원 재미있었어?

B Yeah, it was great. We played to the point that our legs were sore.
응, 정말 좋았어. 다리가 아플 정도로 놀았어.

A Wow, you really went all out! What rides did you go on?
와, 그렇게 열심히 놀았구나! 어떤 놀이기구 탔어?

B Almost everything. The roller coaster was scary to the point that I thought my heart might stop.
거의 다 탔어. 롤러코스터는 너무 무서워서 심장이 멎는 줄 알았어.

---

sore 아픈   go all out 전력을 다하다   ride 놀이기구   roller coaster 롤러코스터
heart might stop 심장이 멎을 것 같다

PRACTICE 패턴 활용

문장을 써 보고 음원을 들으며 소리 내어 말하세요. 제시어 중 기본형 동사는 패턴에 맞게 바꾸고, 제시어의 // 앞까지만이라도 완성해 말하세요.

▶ 정답 323쪽

- 그녀는 목이 쉴 정도로 노래했어. she sang / she lost her voice
  She sang to the point that she lost her voice.

1. 그는 밥 먹는 것도 잊을 정도로 일했어요. he worked / he forgot to eat

2. 나는 배가 아플 정도로 먹었어. I ate / my stomach actually started to hurt

3. 나는 숨이 찰 정도로 운동했어. I exercised / I was completely out of breath

4. 그들은 기록을 깰 정도로 열심히 훈련했어. they trained / they broke records

5. 그들은 똑바로 걷지도 못할 정도로 술을 마셨어. they drank / they couldn't even walk straight

6. 그들은 지갑이 텅 빌 정도로 쇼핑했어. they shopped / their wallets were completely empty

7. 그는 피아노를 너무 오래 연습해서 손가락에 물집이 잡힐 정도였어.
   he practiced the piano / blisters started forming on his fingers

8. 그녀는 너무 웃어서 배가 아플 정도였고 눈에는 눈물까지 맺혔어.
   she laughed so hard / her stomach hurt // and she started tearing up

lose one's voice 목이 쉬다   completely 완전히   out of breath 숨이 찬   break records 기록을 깨다
walk straight 똑바로 걷다   blister 물집   form 생기다   stomach 배   tear up 눈물이 맺히다

다리가 아플 정도로 놀았어.

주절 + to the point that + 절
We played / our legs were sore

UNIT 79

What's the secret to + 명사[동명사]?
~의 비결이 뭐야?

이 패턴은 어떤 일의 비결이나 성공의 비밀을 물어볼 때 사용해요. 예를 들어, "그녀의 성공 비결은 뭐야?"라고 물어보고 싶다면 What's the secret to her success?, "그렇게 행복하게 지내는 비결이 뭐야?"라고 물어보고 싶다면 What's the secret to staying so happy? 등으로 말이죠. 이렇게 긍정적이거나 칭찬할 만한 요소, 부럽기까지 한 요소에 대해 그 비결이 뭔지 알고 싶을 때 이 패턴을 사용하면 돼요. 그리고 그에 대한 대답은 [The secret is to + 동사원형] 형태로 해요. 행복하게 지내는 비결이 남을 돕는 것이라면, The secret is to help others.라고 답할 수 있겠지요.

What's the secret to 다음에는 명사나 동명사(-ing)를 써야 합니다.

 What's the secret to your mom's kimchi?
너희 어머니 김치 비결이 뭐야?

실생활 대화

A **What's the secret to your mom's kimchi?** It's always so delicious!
너희 어머니 김치 비결이 뭐야? 항상 너무 맛있던데!

B She says it's all about using the freshest ingredients and letting it ferment just right.
엄마 말씀으로는 가장 신선한 재료를 쓰고, 발효를 딱 맞게 하는 거래.

A I've tried making it, but it never turns out the same. Any other tips?
나도 만들어 봤는데, 똑같이 안 되더라. 다른 팁은 없어?

B Actually, she adds a bit of apple for sweetness.
Maybe we can ask her to teach us sometime!
사실 달콤함을 위해 사과를 조금 넣으신대. 나중에 한번 가르쳐 달라고 해 볼까?

ingredient 재료   ferment 발효시키다   turn out ~하게 되다   sweetness 단맛

PRACTICE 패턴 활용

문장을 써 보고 음원을 들으며 소리 내어 말하세요. 제시어 중 기본형 동사는 패턴에 맞게 바꾸고, 제시어의 // 앞까지만이라도 완성해 말하세요.

▶ 정답 323쪽

- 네 파스타 비밀이 뭐야?   your pasta
  What's the secret to your pasta?

1 티끌 하나 없는 네 피부 비결은 뭐야?   your flawless skin

2 네 초콜릿 케이크가 맛있는 비결이 뭐야? 진짜 빵집보다 맛있어.
   your delicious chocolate cake // it's better than the ones at bakeries

3 너희 부부가 그렇게 행복할 수 있는 비결이 뭐야? 그렇게 오래됐는데도 여전히 잘 맞아 보여.
   your happy marriage // you two seem so in sync / even after all these years

4 발표할 때 자신감이 넘치는 비결이 뭐야? 난 생각만 해도 긴장돼.
   your confidence / when speaking in public // I get so nervous even thinking about it

5 항상 바쁜데도 여유 있어 보이네. 비결이 뭐야? 응용   look so calm / even when you're super busy

6 발표를 항상 인상 깊게 잘하던데, 그 비결이 뭐야? 응용
   give such impressive presentations / every time

7 일찍 일어나서 하루 종일 에너지가 넘치는 이유가 뭐야? 응용
   wake up early // and staying energetic / all day long

8 처음 보는 사람과도 편하게 대화하는 비결이 뭐야? 응용
   talk so comfortably with people / you've just met

---

flawless 완벽한   be in sync 호흡이 척척 맞다   speak in public 대중 앞에서 말하다   energetic 활기찬
talk comfortably 편하게 이야기하다

너희 어머니 김치 비결이 뭐야?

What's the secret to + 명사?
                    └ your mom's kimchi

UNIT 80

While you're at it, could[can] you ~?
하는 김에, ~해 줄래요?

이 패턴은 어떤 일을 하는 김에 추가로 일을 부탁하거나 제안할 때 사용해요. 예를 들어, 누군가가 커피를 만들고 있을 때 "만드는 김에 제 것도 만들어 줄래요?"와 같이 추가적인 요청을 할 때 유용해요. 이 말은 While you're at it, could you make me a cup of coffee, too?라고 할 수 있어요. While you're at it은 보통 전에 어떤 일을 하고 있는지 굳이 언급할 필요가 없을 때 사용하고, 언급하고 싶으면 [While you're + -ing] 형태로 말하면 더 구체적으로 표현할 수 있어요.

While you're at it, 뒤에 추가적으로 요청하는 행동을 나타내는 절을 씁니다.

> **While you're at it, could you** ask if they can move my appointment up?
> 하는 김에 제 예약 좀 앞당길 수 있는지 물어봐 줄래요?

실생활 대화

A I'm going to call the dentist to schedule my check-up.
치과에 검진 예약하려고 전화할 거예요.

B Oh, while you're at it, could you ask if they can move my appointment up?
아, 전화하는 김에 제 예약 좀 앞당길 수 있는지 물어봐 줄래요?

A Sure. When was your original appointment again?
그럴게요. 원래 예약이 언제라고요?

B It's next month, but I'd love to get in sooner if possible.
다음 달인데, 가능하면 좀 더 빨리 하고 싶어요.

schedule 일정을 잡다 check-up 건강 검진 move up 앞당기다

PRACTICE 패턴 활용

문장을 써 보고 음원을 들으며 소리 내어 말하세요. 제시어 중 기본형 동사는 패턴에 맞게 바꾸고, 제시어의 // 앞까지만이라도 완성해 말하세요.

▶ 정답 323쪽

- **도와주는 김에 이것도 좀 도와줄래요?**   help me with this / too

  While you're at it, could you help me with this, too?

1. **만드는 김에 저도 한잔 만들어 줄래요?**   make me a cup of coffee / too

2. **확인하는 김에 제 우편물도 확인해 줄래요?**   check my mail / too

3. **가져오는 김에 옷장에서 제 재킷도 가져다 줄래요?**   grab my jacket / from the closet

4. **장 보러 가는 김에 우유도 좀 사다 줄래요?**   pick up some milk / from the store

5. **마트 가는 김에 바나나도 좀 사다 줄래요? 애들이 요즘 그거 좋아하거든요.**
   grab some bananas / too // the kids love them these days

6. **요리하는 김에 반찬 하나만 더 만들어 줄래요? 내일 도시락 싸야 해요.**
   make one more side dish // I need it for tomorrow's lunchbox

7. **꺼내는 김에 제 요가 매트도 꺼내 줄래요? 같이 하려고요.**
   grab my yoga mat / too // I'm planning to join in

8. **확인하는 김에 프린터 연결도 확인해 줄래요? 고장 난 것 같아요.** 응용
   check the printer connection / too // I thought it was broken

grab 집어 오다   pick up 사다, 집어 들다   side dish 반찬   lunchbox 도시락   join in 함께 하다
connection 연결   broken 고장 난

> 하는 김에 제 예약 좀 앞당길 수 있는지 물어봐 줄래요?
>
> **While you're at it, could you ~?**
>
> ask if they can move my appointment up

REMINDER 패턴 강화

이제 내 이야기를 해 봐요! 나에게 있음 직한 일들을 적고, 소리 내어 말해 보는 거예요. 주어가 별도로 제시되지 않으면, 주어는 항상 I(나)예요.

▶ 정답 323쪽

UNIT 76 I always **lose track of time** hanging out there!

> lose track of time + -ing[부사절]
> ~하느라 시간 가는 줄 모른다

1 해변에서 노을 보다가 시간 가는 줄 몰랐어.   watching the sunset by the beach

2 동생 숙제 도와주다 보니 시간 가는 줄 몰랐어.
   helping my little brother with his homework

3 재밌는 책 읽다가 시간 가는 줄 몰랐어.   reading a good book

UNIT 77 **It's not that** I'm scared, **it's just that** I don't really enjoy horror stuff.

> It's not that + 절A, it's just (that) + 절B
> [절A]라서가 아니라, [절B]라서 그런 것이다

4 배부른 게 아니야. 그냥 입맛이 없을 뿐이야.   I'm full / I don't feel like eating

5 달리기를 싫어하는 게 아니라 그냥 걷는 게 더 좋아.   I hate running / I prefer walking

6 지루한 게 아니라 그냥 뭘 해야 할지 모르겠어.
   I'm bored / I don't know what to do

UNIT 78 We played **to the point that** our legs were sore.

> 주절 + to the point that + 절
> ~할 정도로 [주절]하다

7 서서 잠들 정도로 너무 피곤했어.   I was so tired / I fell asleep standing

8 다음 날 몸을 못 움직일 정도로 그는 운동을 했어.
   he worked out / he couldn't move the next day

9 바닥이 흔들릴 정도로 그들은 춤을 췄어. they danced / the floor was shaking

UNIT 79 **What's the secret to** your mom's kimchi?

> **What's the secret to + 명사[동명사]?**
> ~의 비결이 뭐야?

10 완벽한 커피를 만드는 비결이 뭐야? making perfect coffee

11 재밌는 사람이 되는 비결이 뭐야? being funny

12 식물을 잘 키우는 비결이 뭐야? keeping a plant alive

UNIT 80 **While you're at it**, **could you** ask if they can move my appointment up?

> **While you're at it, could[can] you ~?**
> 하는 김에, ~해 줄래요?

13 하는 김에 쓰레기도 버려 줄래요? take out the trash

14 하는 김에 우편함도 확인해 줄래요? check the mailbox

15 하는 김에 제 음료도 하나 가져다줄래요? grab me a drink, too

REMINDER 맥락 적용

이제 앞에서 연습한 패턴을 실생활 대화 맥락에 적용해 보세요. 패턴을 일상적인 대화에 넣어서 직접 소리 내어 말해 보는 거예요. 빈칸에 들어갈 말이 기억이 나지 않는다면 다시 앞으로 가서 확인해 보세요.

UNIT 76

A Wasn't last night's concert amazing?
어젯밤 콘서트 정말 재밌지 않았어?

B It was incredible! 🐱 _____ singing along to all the songs.
대단했어! 난 노래 따라 부르느라 시간 가는 줄 몰랐어.

A Me, too! The energy in the venue was so intense, I really let loose and had fun!
나도! 공연장 열기가 너무 뜨거워서, 진짜 마음껏 즐길 수 있었어!

B Absolutely, I screamed so much that my voice is hoarse now.
맞아. 너무 소리질러서 지금 목소리가 쉬었어.

UNIT 77

A You haven't been active on social media lately?
요즘 SNS 활동을 안 하네?

B 🐱 _____ I've lost interest, 🐱 _____ I'm taking a break for my mental health.
흥미를 잃은 건 아니고, 정신 건강을 위해 잠깐 쉬고 있어.

A That makes sense; sometimes you need a break.
그래, 이해해. 때로 쉬는 것도 필요하지.

B Yes, I'll start again later.
나중에 다시 시작할 거야.

UNIT 78

A You're working out hard. Did you go today, too?
운동 열심히 하네. 오늘도 다녀왔어?

B Yes, I exercised 🐱 _____ that I was out of breath.
응. 숨이 찰 정도로 운동했어.

A That's impressive. If you keep it up, you'll get in shape quickly.
대단하다. 그렇게 계속하면 금방 몸이 좋아질 거야.

B Thanks. But now my muscles are sore 🐱 _____ that it's hard to move.
고마워. 근데 지금 근육통이 심해서 움직이기 힘들 정도야.

UNIT 79

A 🐱 _____ learning a new language quickly?
새로운 언어를 빨리 배우는 비결이 뭐야?

B Immersion is key. I try to surround myself with the language as much as possible.
몰입이 핵심이야. 난 최대한 그 언어에 둘러싸이려고 노력해.

A How do you do that if you can't travel to a country where it's spoken?
그 언어를 쓰는 나라에 갈 수 없다면?

B I watch movies, listen to podcasts, and even change my phone's language settings.
영화도 보고, 팟캐스트도 듣고, 심지어 휴대폰 언어 설정도 바꿔.

UNIT 80

A I'm about to do the laundry. Do you have any clothes you want washed?
빨래하려고 하는데. 빨래 돌릴 거 있어?

B Yes, please. And 🐱 _____, could you wash my gym bag too?
응, 부탁해. 그리고 하는 김에, 내 운동 가방도 좀 빨아 줄 수 있어?

A Your gym bag? Isn't it too bulky for the washing machine?
운동 가방이라고? 세탁기에 넣기엔 너무 크지 않아?

B You're right, maybe I'll just wash it by hand later.
맞네. 그냥 나중에 내가 손빨래할게.

어휘 venue (콘서트) 장소   intense 강렬한, 열렬한   let loose 마음대로 하다[놀다]   scream 비명을 지르다
　　　hoarse (목소리가) 쉰   keep it up 계속해 나아가다   immersion 몰입   surround 둘러싸다
　　　bulky 부피가 큰

정답 I lost track of time | It's not that, it's just that | to the point, to the point |
　　　What's the secret to | while you're at it

REMINDER 패턴 정착

앞에서 배운 20개 패턴을 머릿속에 새기는 시간이에요.
문장을 보고 패턴을 이용해 영어로 소리 내어 말해 보세요.

61 처방약 받으러 왔어요.

62 신선한 딸기가 있는지 보러 마트에 갈 거야.

63 시간 날 때 한번 가 봐.

64 너도 같이 갔으면 좋았을 텐데.

65 지하철을 타서 교통 체증을 다 피할 수 있었을 텐데.

66 미리 말했으면, 뭐 먹을 거라도 해 놨을 텐데.

67 이사하자마자 벌써 집처럼 느껴지더라.

68 우리가 결정했을 땐, 이미 다른 사람이 계약했더라고.

69 더 오래 있지 못해서 아쉬워요.

70 모두가 무사하다니 진짜 다행이야.

71 명상을 많이 할수록, 마음이 더 차분해져요.

72 요즘 수영에 푹 빠져 있어.

73 청소할 기분이 아니야.

74 회사에서 오늘 기분이 좋으셨나 봐.

75 걔는 그 일에 소질이 있는 것 같아.

76 거기서 놀다 보면 항상 시간 가는 줄 몰라!

77 무서워서 그런 건 아니고, 그냥 공포물을 별로 안 좋아해.

78 다리가 아플 정도로 놀았어.

79 너희 어머니 김치 비결이 뭐야?

80 하는 김에 제 예약 좀 앞당길 수 있는지 물어봐 줄래요?

UNIT 81

Don't be too married to + 명사[동명사]

~에 너무 얽매이지 마

이 패턴은 어떤 아이디어나 계획, 방식 등에 너무 집착하지 말라는 의미로 사용해요. be married to는 '~와 결혼하다'라는 의미 이외에 '~에 얽매이다, ~에 몰두하다, ~에 집착하다'라는 느낌을 주는 표현이에요. 상대방이 어떤 일에 집착하거나 얽매어 있는 걸 봤을 때 Don't be married to를 사용해서 충고할 수 있어요. 예를 들어, 동영상 조회 수에 너무 신경 쓰는 친구에게 이 패턴을 사용하여 Don't be too married to the numbers. I believe authenticity matters more and we are on the right path.(숫자에 너무 얽매이지 마. 진정성이 더 중요하고 나는 우리가 올바른 방향으로 가고 있다고 확신해.)라고 말할 수 있어요.

Don't be too married to 뒤에는 명사나 동명사를 써서 집착하지 말아야 할 것을 나타냅니다.

 Don't be too married to the schedule.
일정에 너무 얽매이지 마.

실생활 대화

A I really want to stick to our original itinerary for Paris. We planned everything so carefully.
파리 여행은 원래 일정대로 꼭 하고 싶어. 진짜 꼼꼼하게 다 짰잖아.

B I get that, but don't be too married to the schedule. Sometimes the best moments come from unplanned stuff.
이해는 가는데, 일정에 너무 얽매이지 마. 가끔은 계획에 없던 게 제일 재밌기도 해.

A True… Maybe we can skip one museum and just explore the streets a bit.
맞아… 박물관 하나쯤은 빼고 그냥 거리도 좀 돌아다녀 볼까?

B Exactly! That's how you discover the real charm of a city.
바로 그거지! 그런 식으로 도시의 진짜 매력을 발견하는 거야.

---

stick to ~를 고수[고집]하다   itinerary 여행 일정표   I get that, but… 이해는 하지만…   unplanned 계획되지 않은   skip 생략하다, 건너뛰다   discover the real charm of ~의 진짜 매력을 발견하다

PRACTICE 패턴 활용

문장을 써 보고 음원을 들으며 소리 내어 말하세요. 제시어 중 기본형 동사는 패턴에 맞게 바꾸고, 제시어의 // 앞까지만이라도 완성해 말하세요.

▶ 정답 324쪽

- 너의 아이디어에 **너무 얽매이지 마**. 다른 사람 의견도 들어 봐.   your idea // be open to feedback

  Don't be too married to your idea. Be open to feedback.

1. 그 방식에 너무 집착하지 마. 더 좋은 방법이 있을 수도 있어.
   that method // there might be a better way

2. 첫인상에 너무 집착하지 마. 시간이 지나면 생각이 달라질 수도 있어.
   your first impression // it can change over time

3. 완벽한 계획에 너무 얽매이지 마. 가끔은 즉흥적인 게 더 좋아.
   your perfect plan // sometimes spontaneity is better

4. 완벽한 셀카 찍으려고 너무 집착하지 마. 벌써 50장 찍었어.
   the perfect selfie // you've taken like 50 already

5. 숫자에 너무 얽매이지 마. 양보다 질이 더 중요해.   the numbers // quality matters more than quantity

6. 결과에만 너무 집착하지 마. 과정도 그만큼 중요해.   the outcome // the journey is just as important

7. 뭐든 다 혼자 하려는 거에 너무 얽매이지 마. 도움을 요청해도 돼. 응용
   do everything on your own // it's okay to ask for help

8. 같은 식당에서 먹는 거에 너무 얽매이지 말자. 새로운 데도 가 보자. 응용
   eat at the same restaurant // let's try somewhere new

---

feedback 피드백   method 방식   first impression 첫인상   over time 시간이 흐르면
spontaneity 자발[즉흥]적임   selfie 셀카   quality 질   quantity 양   outcome 결과   journey 과정

일정에 너무 얽매이지 마.

Don't be too married to + 명사
the schedule

UNIT 82

It bothers me (that) + 절

~가 신경 쓰이다[마음에 걸리다]

이 패턴은 어떤 일이 마음에 걸리거나 신경 쓰일 때 사용해요. 외출을 한 후 집에 가스 불을 끄고 나왔는지 잘 기억이 안 나서 신경이 쓰이거나 마음에 걸릴 때 있죠? 이렇게 무엇인가가 자꾸 머릿속에서 신경이 쓰일 때 쓸 수 있는 표현이 바로 It bothers me that~이에요. 또는 누군가의 말이 마음에 걸리거나 불편할 때도 사용할 수 있어요.

It bothers me (that) 뒤에는 신경이 쓰이는 내용을 담은 절(주어+동사)이 옵니다.

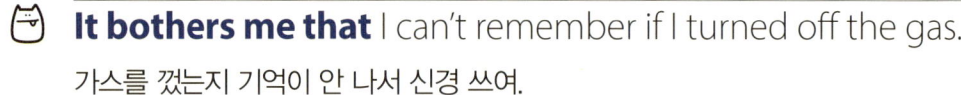

It bothers me that I can't remember if I turned off the gas.
가스를 껐는지 기억이 안 나서 신경 쓰여.

추가로, '~할 때 신경이 쓰인다'라는 표현은 It bothers me when~의 형태를 써서 나타내요. 예를 들어, "충전기를 못 찾을 때 짜증이 나."라고 말하고 싶다면 It bothers me when I can't find my charger.라고 할 수 있겠죠.

실생활 대화

A **It bothers me that I can't remember if I turned off the gas.**
가스를 껐는지 기억이 안 나서 신경 쓰여.

B **Don't worry. I clearly remember turning it off before we left.**
걱정하지 마. 나가기 전에 내가 확실히 끈 거 기억나.

A **You're the best. I honestly don't know what I'd do without you.**
넌 정말 최고야. 너 없었으면 어쩔 뻔했는지 몰라.

B **Anytime. So what do you want to do now?**
별말씀을. 자, 이제 뭐할까?

---

turn off the gas 가스를 끄다   clearly 확실히

PRACTICE 패턴 활용

문장을 써 보고 음원을 들으며 소리 내어 말하세요. 제시어 중 기본형 동사는 패턴에 맞게 바꾸고, 제시어의 // 앞까지만이라도 완성해 말하세요.

▶ 정답 324쪽

- 계속 할 일을 미루고 있다는 게 신경 쓰여. I keep putting things off

  It bothers me that I keep putting things off.

1. 걔가 내 메시지에 전혀 답장을 안 하는 게 신경 쓰여. he never replies to my messages

2. 중요한 결정을 할 때 네가 내 의견을 묻지 않는 게 신경 쓰여.
   you never ask for my opinion // when making big decisions

3. 걔가 책임지는 대신 변명만 늘어놓는 게 신경 쓰여. he keeps making excuses // instead of owning up

4. 집에 오면 방이 항상 지저분한 상태인 게 스트레스야. my room is always messy // when I get home

5. 내가 말하는데 아무도 눈을 안 마주치는 게 좀 신경 쓰여. no one makes eye contact // when I'm talking

6. 내가 도와 달라고 했을 때 사람들이 모르는 척할 때 마음 상해.
   people pretend not to hear me // when I ask for help

7. 네가 싱크대에 더러운 접시를 그대로 두면 신경 쓰여. [응용] when you leave dirty dishes in the sink

8. 버스 안에서 헤드폰 없이 동영상 보는 사람들 정말 신경 쓰여. [응용]
   when people watch videos without headphones on the bus

---

put things off 일을 미루다   reply 답장하다   ask for one's opinion 의견을 묻다   make excuses 변명하다
own up 책임지다   messy 지저분한   make eye contact 눈을 마주치다   sink 싱크대

가스를 껐는지 기억이 안 나서 신경 쓰여.

It bothers me (that) + 절

I can't remember if I turned off the gas

UNIT 83
be on the tip of my tongue
~가 생각이 날 듯 말 듯하다

이 패턴은 '~에 대해서 기억이 날 듯 말 듯 하다, 입에서 맴돈다'라는 뜻으로 일상생활에서 무언가 머릿속에서 생각이 날 듯 말 듯 한데 도저히 입 밖으로 나오지 않을 때 사용해요. 예를 들어, 차에서 노래를 듣다가 노래 제목이 기억이 날 듯 말 듯 할 때 Uhmm… it's on the tip of my tongue!이라고 말할 수 있어요.

이 패턴은 주어 it을 써서 말하거나 it 대신 다른 명사를 넣어 말할 수 있습니다.

 It**'s on the tip of my tongue**.
기억이 날 듯 말 듯해.

실생활 대화

A What's the name of that actor from the movie we watched last week?
지난주에 봤던 영화에 나온 그 배우 이름이 뭐였지?

B It's on the tip of my tongue! I'm pretty sure it starts with a "C."
기억이 날 듯 말 듯해! C로 시작하는 건 확실해.

A Oh! Was it Chris Hemsworth?
오! 크리스 헴스워스였나?

B Yes, that's it! He's also famous for playing Thor.
응, 맞아! 토르로도 유명하잖아.

pretty sure 꽤 확신하는   start with ~로 시작하다

PRACTICE 패턴 활용

문장을 써 보고 음원을 들으며 소리 내어 말하세요. 제시어 중 기본형 동사는 패턴에 맞게 바꾸고, 제시어의 // 앞까지만이라도 완성해 말하세요.   ▶ 정답 324쪽

- 그 여자 이름이 뭐였더라? 입안에서 맴도는데 생각이 안 나.   what was her name again? / it

   What was her name again? It's on the tip of my tongue.

1. 그 사람 이름이 기억이 날 듯 말 듯한데, 생각이 안 나.   his name // but I just can't place it

2. 그 브랜드 이름을 알고 있는데, 지금 머릿속에서 맴도는 중이야.
   I know that brand name / it / right now

3. 이 노래 가사를 알고 있는데, 막 생각이 날 듯 말 듯해.   I know the lyrics to this song / they / right

4. 네가 누구를 말하는지 알 것 같아. 생각이 날 듯 말 듯해.
   I think I know who you're talking about / it / right

5. 그 나라의 수도가 가물가물해. 'B'로 시작한다는 건 기억나는데.
   the capital of that country // I remember it starts with a B

6. 그 배우 이름이 생각이 날 듯 말 듯한데, 입에서 맴돌기만 해.
   the name of that actor // but I just can't get it out

7. 그 표현 영어로 뭐였지? 입에서 맴도는데 떠오르질 않네.
   what was that expression in English again / it // but I can't think of it

8. 내 초등학교 선생님 이름이 입에서 맴돌아. 기억이 날 듯 말 듯해.
   the name of my elementary school teacher // I just can't quite remember it

place (보통 부정문에서) 생각해 내다, 놓다   lyrics 가사   capital 수도   get it out 말하다, 털어놓다
expression 표현

기억이 날 듯 말 듯해.

주어 + be on the tip of my tongue.
   It's

UNIT 84

be going to go to + 장소 + to + 동사원형

[장소]에 ~하러 갈 것이다

이 패턴은 어떤 장소에 가는 것뿐만 아니라 그 장소에서 무엇을 할 예정인지 표현할 때 사용해요. 예를 들어, 카페에 친구를 만나러 가거나, 서점에 책을 사러 가는 것처럼 말이죠. 친구를 만나러 카페에 갈 예정이라면 I'm going to go to the café to meet my friend.라고 말하고, 책을 사러 서점에 갈 예정이라면 I'm going to go to the bookstore to buy some books.라고 말해요. 회화에서 going to는 줄여서 gonna로도 많이 말해요.

be going to go to 뒤에는 장소를 쓰고 그 다음에는 [to + 동사원형]으로 목적을 나타냅니다.

 I**'m going to go to** the park **to** jog.
조깅하러 공원 갈 거야.

[be going to go to + 장소] 뒤에 [to + 동사원형]이 아닌 [for + 명사]가 오기도 해요. 예를 들어, 휴가 계획을 묻는 말에 제주도에 갈 거라는 대답을 한다면, I'm going to go to Jeju for a trip.이라고 말할 수 있어요.

실생활 대화

A Where are you going so early tomorrow morning?
You're usually still asleep at that time.
내일 아침 일찍 어디 가? 평소엔 한참 자고 있을 시간이잖아.

B I'm going to go to the park to jog. I'm trying to lose some weight. Do you want to join me?
조깅하러 공원 갈 거야. 살 좀 빼 보려고. 같이 갈래?

A Sounds good! Exercise is always a good idea. What time should we meet? I'll need a little time to get ready, too.
좋아! 운동은 언제나 좋지. 몇 시에 만날까? 나도 준비 좀 해야 하니까.

B Let's meet at the park entrance at 6 AM.
Don't forget to wear workout clothes and bring a water bottle!
아침 6시에 공원 입구에서 보자. 운동복 입고 물병 챙기는 거 잊지 마!

lose weight 살을 빼다   get ready 준비하다

PRACTICE 패턴 활용

문장을 써 보고 음원을 들으며 소리 내어 말하세요. 제시어 중 기본형 동사는 패턴에 맞게 바꾸고, 제시어의 // 앞까지만이라도 완성해 말하세요.

▶ 정답 324쪽

- 오늘 저녁에 <u>운동 좀 하러 헬스장 갈 거야.</u>   I / the gym / get a workout in / this evening
  I'm going to go to the gym to get a workout in this evening.

1 곧 <u>마트에 장보러 갈 거야.</u>   I / the store / get some groceries / soon

2 오늘 오후에 <u>도서관에 공부하러 갈 거야.</u>   I / the library / this afternoon / study

3 점심 먹고 <u>우체국에 택배 부치러 갈 거야.</u>   I / the post office / after lunch / send a package

4 그녀의 남편은 <u>자동차 수리하러 정비소에 갈 거야.</u>   her husband / the repair shop / fix the car

5 그들은 <u>새 가구를 보러 이케아에 갈 거야.</u>   they / IKEA / look at some new furniture

6 다음 주에 <u>병원에 정기 검진 받으러 갈 거야.</u> 응용   I / the hospital / next week / a check-up

7 내 친구는 <u>머리 스타일 바꾸러 미용실에 갈 거야.</u> 응용   my friend / the hair salon / a new style

8 내 사촌은 <u>이번 주말에 면접 보러 서울에 갈 거야.</u> 응용
   my cousin / Seoul / this weekend / a job interview

groceries 장보기 물품   package 택배   hair salon 미용실   repair shop 정비소

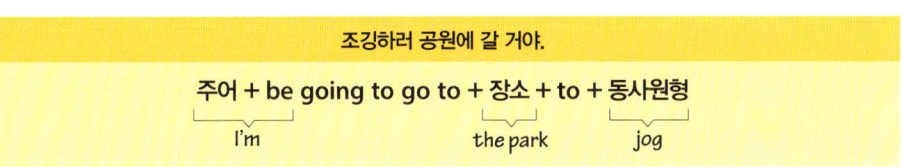

조깅하러 공원에 갈 거야.

주어 + be going to go to + 장소 + to + 동사원형
  I'm   the park   jog

UNIT 85

be free to + 동사원형

자유롭게 ~해도 된다, ~할 시간이 있다

이 패턴은 어떤 행동을 자유롭게 할 수 있다고 허락할 때 사용해요. 예를 들어, "내 전화기를 써도 돼."는 You're free to use my phone.이라고 말할 수 있어요. 그리고 본인이 시간이 있을 때, 또는 상대방에게 시간을 물어볼 때 사용해요. 예를 들어, "쇼핑몰에 갈 시간 있어요."는 I'm free to go to the mall.이라고 할 수 있어요. 친구에게 저녁 식사할 수 있는 시간이 있는지 묻고 싶다면 Are you free to have dinner tonight?, 잠시 대화할 시간이 있는지 묻고 싶다면 Are you free to have a quick conversation?이라고 말할 수 있어요.

be free to 뒤에는 동사원형을 써야 합니다.

 You're **free to** pick another place if you'd prefer.
네가 원하면 다른 데도 좋아.

be free 뒤에 [to + 동사원형]이 아닌 [for + 명사]를 쓸 수도 있어요. 예를 들어, "저녁 먹을 시간이 있다."는 I'm free for dinner.라고 간단하게 말할 수 있어요.

실생활 대화

A **Are you free for a quick chat later?**
나중에 잠깐 이야기할 시간 있어?

B **I'm free after 5 PM. Does that work for you?**
오후 5시 이후엔 시간 괜찮아. 그때 어때?

A Perfect. I was thinking we could grab a coffee.
Would you be free for that?
좋아. 커피 한잔하면서 얘기하면 어떨까 해서. 시간 괜찮아?

B Sounds great! I know a nice café within walking distance, but **you're free to pick another place if you'd prefer.**
좋지! 여기서 걸어서 갈 수 있는 괜찮은 카페 하나 알아.
근데 네가 원하면 다른 데도 좋아.

---

quick chat 짧은 대화   grab a coffee 커피 한잔하다   within walking distance 도보 거리 내에   pick 선택하다

PRACTICE 패턴 활용

문장을 써 보고 음원을 들으며 소리 내어 말하세요. 제시어 중 기본형 동사는 패턴에 맞게 바꾸고, 제시어의 // 앞까지만이라도 완성해 말하세요.

▶ 정답 324쪽

- 오늘 오후에 커피 한잔할 시간 돼.   I / grab some coffee / this afternoon

  I'm free to grab some coffee this afternoon.

1. 내일 오전에는 만날 시간 돼.   I / meet / tomorrow morning

2. 필요하면 내가 도와줄 시간 돼.   I / help you / if you need

3. 너 필요하면 내 노트북 써도 돼.   you / use my laptop / if you need it

4. 학생들은 언제든 질문할 수 있어.   students / ask questions / at any time

5. 직원들은 점심시간에 자유롭게 외출할 수 있어.   employees / leave / during lunch breaks

6. 회의실은 오후 3시부터 사용할 수 있어.   the meeting room / use / after 3 PM

7. 그들은 내일 아침 인터뷰 가능해. 응용   they / interviews / tomorrow morning

8. 우리는 7시 이후에 저녁 먹을 시간 돼. 너한테 가장 괜찮은 시간 알려 줘. 응용
   we / dinner / after 7 // so just let us know what works best for you

at any time 언제든지   employee 직원

네가 원하면 다른 데도 좋아.

주어 + be free to + 동사원형

You're   pick another place if you'd prefer

REMINDER 패턴 강화

이제 내 이야기를 해 봐요! 나에게 있음 직한 일들을 적고, 소리 내어 말해 보는 거예요.
주어가 별도로 제시되지 않으면, 주어는 항상 I(나)예요.

▶ 정답 325쪽

UNIT 81 Don't be too married to the schedule.

> Don't be too married to + 명사[동명사]
> ~에 너무 얽매이지 마

1 규율에 너무 얽매이지 마.   the rules

2 한 가지 방식에만 너무 몰두하지 마.   one way of thinking

3 원래 계획에 너무 얽매이지 마.   your original plan

UNIT 82 It bothers me that I can't remember if I turned off the gas.

> It bothers me (that) + 절
> ~가 신경 쓰이다[마음에 걸리다]

4 계획이 갑자기 바뀌는 게 짜증나.   plans suddenly change

5 사람들이 소리 내서 씹을 때 거슬려. 응용   people chew loudly

6 누군가 문자에 답장을 안 할 때 신경 쓰여. 응용   someone doesn't text back

UNIT 83 It's on the tip of my tongue!

> be on the tip of my tongue
> ~가 생각이 날 듯 말 듯하다

7 그거 영어로 뭐였는지 생각날 듯 말 듯해.   the word for it in English

8   그 사람 전화번호가 기억날 듯 말 듯해.   his phone number

9   그 영화 제목이 입에서 맴돌아.   the title of that movie

UNIT 84 I'm going to go to the park to jog.

> be going to go to + 장소
> [장소]에 (~하러) 갈 것이다

10   가게에 간식 사러 갈 거야.   the store / for some snacks

11   공원에 바람 쐬러 갈 거야.   the park / to get some fresh air

12   도서관에 조용히 책 읽으러 갈 거야.   the library / for a quiet place to read

UNIT 85 You're free to pick another place if you'd prefer.

> be free to + 동사원형
> 자유롭게 ~해도 된다, ~할 시간이 있다

13   나 잠깐 수다 떨 시간 있어.   chat for a bit

14   내 충전기 써도 돼.   you / use my charger

15   네 숙제 도와줄 수 있어.   help with your homework

257

REMINDER 맥락 적용

이제 앞에서 연습한 패턴을 실생활 대화 맥락에 적용해 보세요. 패턴을 일상적인 대화에 넣어서 직접 소리 내어 말해 보는 거예요. 빈칸에 들어갈 말이 기억이 나지 않는다면 다시 앞으로 가서 확인해 보세요.

UNIT 81

A How about going for a picnic at the beach this weekend?
주말에 바닷가로 소풍 어때?

B Sounds good. But the weather seems a bit uncertain.
좋은데. 근데 날씨가 좀 불확실해.

A Right, let's not _____ the plan. If it rains, we can switch to an indoor activity.
그래, 계획에 너무 얽매이지 말자. 비가 오면 실내 활동으로 바꾸지 뭐.

B Yeah, it's good to be flexible.
그래, 유연한 게 좋아.

UNIT 82

A Why do you always keep your shoes on when you visit my house?
왜 너는 우리 집에 올 때마다 항상 신발을 벗지 않는 거야?

B Oh, I'm sorry. It's just become a habit.
미안해. 습관이라.

A Honestly, _____ that you don't take off your shoes in my house.
솔직히, 네가 우리 집에서 신발을 벗지 않는 거 신경 쓰여.

B I didn't realize it was important to you. I'll remember next time.
너한테 이게 중요한 문제인지 몰랐어. 다음부턴 꼭 기억할게.

UNIT 83

A What's that dish we had at the Italian restaurant?
우리가 이탈리아 레스토랑에서 먹었던 그 요리 이름이 뭐였지?

B _____ ! I think it starts with an "L."
기억이 날 듯 말 듯 한데! L로 시작하는 것 같은데.

A Was it lasagna?
라자냐였나?

B Yes! That was so delicious!
응! 그거 정말 맛있었어!

UNIT 84

A   What are you doing this weekend? Do you have any fun plans?
주말에 뭐 할 거야? 재미있는 일 있어?

B   🐱 _____ the cinema to watch a new movie. I'm excited because it's been a while since I've seen a movie. Do you want to come?
신작 영화 보러 영화관에 갈 거야. 오랜만에 영화 보려고 하니까 신난다. 같이 갈래?

A   Sure! I love watching movies. What movie are you going to see? What's the genre?
좋아! 나 영화 보는 거 진짜 좋아해. 어떤 영화 볼 거야? 장르가 뭐야?

B   It's the new action movie. I heard it has good reviews and it's really entertaining. How about the 7 PM showing on Saturday? Does that work for you?
새로 나온 액션 영화야. 평점도 좋고 재밌대. 토요일 저녁 7시 상영 어때? 시간 괜찮아?

UNIT 85

A   🐱 _____ a workout tomorrow morning?
내일 아침에 운동할 시간 돼?

B   I'm free before 9 AM. What kind of workout were you thinking?
오전 9시 전에 시간 괜찮아. 어떤 운동 할 건데?

A   I was planning on a jog in the park, but you're 🐱 _____ suggest something else.
공원에서 조깅할 생각이었는데, 다른 거 하고 싶으면 편하게 말해.

B   A jog sounds perfect. I will bring some post-workout smoothies then.
조깅 좋아. 내가 운동 후에 마실 스무디를 가져갈게.

어휘   uncertain 불확실한   switch to ~로 바꾸다   indoor activity 실내 활동   flexible 유연한
entertaining 재미있는   post- (접사) ~ 다음[뒤]

정답   be too married to | it bothers me | It's on the tip of my tongue | I'm going to go to |
Are you free for, free to

UNIT 86

can't help + 동명사[명사]
~하지 않을 수 없다, ~하는 것은 어쩔 수 없다

이 패턴은 어떤 행동을 하지 않을 수 없는 상황이나 그 행동을 멈추기 힘든 상황에서 사용해요. 많은 사람들 앞에서 발표를 할 때 기대감도 있겠지만 긴장돼서 떨리지 않을 수 없겠죠? 이렇게 어쩔 수 없이 그 행동을 할 때 can't help 패턴을 사용하면 돼요. 예를 들어, 코미디 영화를 보면서 웃음을 참을 수 없다면 I can't help laughing.이라고 말할 수 있어요.

can't help 뒤에는 동명사(-ing) 또는 명사가 옵니다.

 I can't help feeling excited and nervous at the same time.
설레면서 동시에 긴장하지 않을 수 없네요.

[can't help + 동명사]는 [can't help but + 동사원형]으로 바꿔 쓸 수 있어요. 이 두 패턴은 같은 의미이지만 뒤에 오는 형태가 다르니까 구분해서 꼭 익혀 두세요. 예를 들어, 아빠가 사랑하는 딸을 보고 웃지 않을 수 없었다면 He couldn't help but smile when he saw his daughter.라고 말할 수 있겠지요.

실생활 대화

A Why do you keep checking your phone?
왜 계속 휴대폰을 확인해요?

B I can't help it. I'm waiting for an important email.
어쩔 수 없어요. 중요한 이메일을 기다리고 있거든요.

A Oh, got it. Is it about that job you applied for?
아, 그렇군요. 그 지원했던 직장이랑 관련된 거예요?

B Yeah, it is. **I can't help feeling excited and nervous at the same time.**
네. 설레면서 동시에 긴장하지 않을 수 없네요.

---

keep -ing 계속 ~하다　apply for ~에 지원하다　feel excited and nervous 설레고 긴장되다

PRACTICE 패턴 활용

문장을 써 보고 음원을 들으며 소리 내어 말하세요. 제시어 중 기본형 동사는 패턴에 맞게 바꾸고,
제시어의 // 앞까지만이라도 완성해 말하세요.

▶ 정답 325쪽

- 자기 전에 자꾸 휴대폰 보게 돼요.　　　　　　　　　　I / check my phone / before bed
  ### I can't help checking my phone before bed.

1. 귀여운 강아지를 보면 자동으로 사진 찍게 돼요.　　　I / take pictures // when I see a cute dog

2. 맛있는 냄새를 맡으면 저절로 군침이 돌아요.　　　　I / drool // when I smell good food

3. 좋아하는 노래가 나오면 저절로 따라 부르게 돼요.　I / sing along // when my favorite song comes on

4. 퇴근 시간이 다가오면 시계를 안 볼 수가 없어요.　　I / check the time // when it's almost time to leave work

5. 그녀는 감동적인 영화를 보면 울음을 참지 못해요.　she / cry / during emotional movies

6. 내 동생은 한번 게임을 시작하면 밤새 멈추지 않고 해요.
   my brother / play games / all night // once he starts

7. 그는 중요한 발표 전에 자꾸 떨어요. [응용]　　　　　he / shake / before big presentations

8. 그는 진지한 얘기를 할 때 자꾸 말을 반복해요. [응용]
   he / repeat himself // when he talks about something serious

---

drool 군침이 돌다　　smell good food 맛있는 냄새를 맡다　　sing along 따라 부르다　　emotional 감동적인
all night 밤새　　shake 떨다　　big presentation 중요한 발표　　repeat oneself 말을 반복하다

설레면서 동시에 긴장하지 않을 수 없네요.

주어 + can't help + 동명사

I　　feeling excited and nervous at the same time

UNIT 87

couldn't care less about + 명사(절)
~에 전혀 관심 없다, ~에 신경 쓰지 않다

어떤 일에 전혀 신경 쓰지 않는다는 마음을 전달하고 싶을 때, "1도 신경 안 써."라고 하죠? 이 패턴은 어떤 일이나 상황에 대해 전혀 신경 쓰지 않거나 관심이 없다는 것을 표현할 때 사용해요. 예를 들어, "나는 그 일에 대해 전혀 신경 쓰지 않아."라고 말하고 싶다면 I couldn't care less about that, "나는 네가 뭐라고 말하든 전혀 신경 쓰지 않아."라고 말하고 싶다면 I couldn't care less about what you say. 등으로 말이죠. 긍정적인 의미라면 상대방의 자율성을 존중한다는 뉘앙스일테고, 싸늘한 어조로 말한다면 상대방에게 무관심하거나 짜증을 표현하는 방식이 될 수 있겠지요.

couldn't care less about 다음에는 주로 명사나 명사절이 오지만 명사절이 오면 종종 **about**이 생략됩니다.

 I **couldn't care less about** fancy cars.
난 그런 화려한 차엔 전혀 관심 없어.

실생활 대화

A Did you hear that Sophia got a new luxury car?
   소피아가 고급 차를 새로 뽑았다는 얘기 들었어?

B Yeah, but I couldn't care less about fancy cars.
   응, 근데 난 그런 화려한 차엔 전혀 관심 없어.

A Really? Most people would be jealous.
   정말? 다들 부러워할 거 같은데.

B Not me. As long as my car runs, I'm good.
   난 아냐. 내 차가 잘만 굴러가면 난 그걸로 됐어.

---

luxury[fancy] car 고급 차   as long as ~하기만 하면   run (자동차 등이) 잘 굴러가다, 작동하다
I'm good. 난 괜찮아, 그걸로 충분해.

PRACTICE 패턴 활용

문장을 써 보고 음원을 들으며 소리 내어 말하세요. 제시어 중 기본형 동사는 패턴에 맞게 바꾸고, 제시어의 // 앞까지만이라도 완성해 말하세요.

▶ 정답 325쪽

- 난 그 가격은 전혀 신경 안 써.   I / the price

  I couldn't care less about the price.

1. 난 정치엔 진짜 관심 없어.   I / politics

2. 난 프로젝트 지연에 대해 전혀 신경 쓰지 않아.   I / the delayed project

3. 내일 비가 오든 말든 전혀 신경 쓰지 않아.   I / if it rains tomorrow

4. 그들이 이기든 지든 나는 전혀 신경 쓰지 않아.   I / whether they win or lose

5. 그녀는 유행이 뭔지 전혀 관심이 없어.   she / what's trending

6. 그는 사람들이 자기를 어떻게 생각하든 전혀 신경 안 써.   he / what people think of him

7. 난 네가 행복하다면 다른 사람들의 시선 따위는 신경 쓰지 않아.
   I / what others think // as long as you're happy

8. 그들은 여행할 때 숙소가 얼마나 좋은지는 신경 안 써.
   they / how fancy the hotel is // when they travel

---

win or lose 이기든 지든   what's trending 요즘 유행하는 것   as long as ~하는 한
how fancy 얼마나 고급스러운지

난 그런 화려한 차엔 전혀 관심 없어.

주어 + couldn't care less about + 명사
     ↓   ↓
     I   fancy cars

UNIT 88

have a hard time + 동명사
~하는 게 어렵다

이 패턴은 어떤 일을 하는 데 어려움을 겪고 있을 때 사용해요. 예를 들어, "나는 일찍 일어나는 게 어려워."라고 말하고 싶다면 I have a hard time waking up early, "나는 문제를 이해하는 게 어려워."라고 말하고 싶다면 I have a hard time understanding the problem. 등으로 말이죠.

have a hard time 뒤에는 어려움을 겪는 행동을 나타내는 동명사(-ing)를 써야 합니다.

 I **have a hard time** waking up early.
일찍 일어나는 게 너무 힘들어.

[have a hard time with + 명사] 패턴으로도 같은 의미를 나타낼 수 있어요. 예를 들어, 아들이 학교에서 수학 문제 푸는 것을 어려워하고 있다면, My son has a hard time with math problems.이라고 말할 수 있어요.

실생활 대화

A **I have a hard time waking up early.** Do you have any tips?
일찍 일어나는 게 너무 힘들어. 조언 좀 해 줄래?

B Try setting multiple alarms and leaving your phone across the room.
알람을 여러 개 맞춰 두고, 전화기를 방 반대편에 두는 걸 해 봐.

A I've tried that, but I still end up hitting snooze.
Maybe I'm just not a morning person.
그렇게 해 봤는데도 결국엔 계속 스누즈를 누르게 돼. 그냥 난 아침형 인간이 아닌가 봐.

B How about changing your bedtime routine?
Going to bed earlier might make it easier to wake up.
취침 루틴을 바꿔 보는 건 어때? 좀 더 일찍 자면 아침에 일어나기 쉬울지도 몰라.

set multiple alarms 알람을 여러 개 맞추다   hit snooze 스누즈(알람을 잠깐 미루는 기능) 버튼을 누르다
bedtime routine 취침 루틴

PRACTICE 패턴 활용

문장을 써 보고 음원을 들으며 소리 내어 말하세요. 제시어 중 기본형 동사는 패턴에 맞게 바꾸고, 제시어의 // 앞까지만이라도 완성해 말하세요.

▶ 정답 325쪽

- 밤에 잠드는 게 힘들어.   fall asleep / at night
  I have a hard time falling asleep at night.

1. 낯선 사람들과 대화하는 게 어색해.   I / talk to strangers

2. 감정을 표현하는 것이 어려워.   I / express my feelings

3. 아침에 일어나는 게 힘들어.   I / get up / in the morning

4. 친구들이 부탁할 때 거절하는 게 어려워.   I / say no // when my friends ask for favors

5. 그는 실수를 인정하는 걸 힘들어 해.   he / admit his mistakes

6. 부모님은 스마트폰 사용하는 걸 어려워하셔.   my parents / use smartphones

7. 그녀는 긴 회의에서 집중하는 걸 어려워해.   she / concentrate / during long meetings

8. 우리는 해외 여행할 때 언어 장벽 때문에 어려워. `응용`   we / the language barrier / when we travel

fall asleep 잠들다   stranger 낯선 사람   say no 거절하다   ask for a favor 부탁하다   admit 인정하다
concentrate 집중하다   language barrier 언어 장벽

일찍 일어나는 게 너무 힘들어.

주어 + have a hard time + 동명사
   I   waking up early

UNIT 89

It just occurred to me (that) + 절
~가 갑자기 생각났다, ~가 문득 떠올랐다

이 패턴은 이야기를 하다가 갑자기 어떤 생각이 딱 떠올랐을 때 사용해요. 예를 들어, "집에 가스 안 끄고 나온 게 갑자기 생각났어!"는 It just occurred to me that we left the stove on at home!이라고 말하면 돼요. 또는 주어 it 대신 다른 내용으로 바꿔서 쓸 수도 있어요. "샤워하는 동안 많은 아이디어가 떠올랐어."는 Many ideas occurred to me while I was showering.라고 할 수 있어요.

It just occurred to me (that) 뒤에 갑자기 떠오른 생각이나 아이디어를 담은 절(주어 + 동사)이 옵니다

 It just occurred to me that today's the due date for returning the library books.
방금 생각났는데, 오늘이 도서관 책 반납일이야.

뒤에 절이 아닌 [to + 동사원형]으로도 말할 수 있어요. 예를 들어, 아무 생각 없이 외출을 하려다가 왠지 비가 올 것 같아 나가기 전에 날씨를 확인해야겠다는 생각이 문득 들었다면 It occurred to me to check the weather before leaving.이라고 말할 수 있어요.

실생활 대화

A Shall we go watch a movie?
영화 보러 갈까?

B Wait, it just occurred to me that today's the due date for returning the library books.
잠깐, 방금 생각났는데 오늘이 도서관 책 반납일이야.

A Then shall we stop by the library first and go to the movies after?
그럼 먼저 도서관 들렀다가 영화관에 갈까?

B Sounds good. I'll check the movie times, too.
좋아, 영화 시간도 확인해 볼게.

---

due date 반납일   return books 책을 반납하다   stop by 잠깐 들르다

PRACTICE 패턴 활용

문장을 써 보고 음원을 들으며 소리 내어 말하세요. 제시어 중 기본형 동사는 패턴에 맞게 바꾸고, 제시어의 // 앞까지만이라도 완성해 말하세요.

▶ 정답 325쪽

- 방금 떠올랐는데, 내일이 마감일이야. the deadline is tomorrow
  It just occurred to me that the deadline is tomorrow.

1 방금 생각났는데, 우리 내일 회의가 있어. we have a meeting / tomorrow

2 방금 생각났는데, 차 보험료를 아직 안 냈어. I haven't paid the car insurance / yet

3 방금 생각났는데, 이번 주 장을 봐야겠어. I need to buy groceries / for the week

4 방금 생각났는데, 오늘 저녁에 친구랑 약속이 있었어. I made plans with a friend / for dinner / tonight

5 방금 생각났는데, 오늘이 엄마 생신이야. 퇴근하고 잊지 말고 꽃을 사야 돼.
today is my mom's birthday // I need to remember to buy flowers / after work

6 지하철 타고 가다가 갑자기 생각났어. 어제 세탁기에서 빨래 꺼내는 걸 까먹었어.
on the subway / I forgot to take the laundry out / yesterday

7 방금 생각났어. 주말에 친구 결혼식인데, 선물을 아직 준비 안 했네.
my friend's wedding is this weekend // and I haven't bought a gift / yet

8 갑자기 생각났는데, 냉장고에 있는 음식 유통기한이 오늘일 수도 있어. 집에 가면 확인해야지. **응용**
check the food in the fridge // to make sure nothing is expired

---

car insurance 자동차 보험   buy groceries 장을 보다   make plans 약속을 잡다
[remember to + 동사원형] ~할 것을 기억하다   take ~ out ~를 꺼내다   fridge 냉장고
expire 유통기한이 끝나다

방금 생각났는데, 오늘이 도서관 책 반납일이야.

It just occurred to me that + 절

today's the due date for returning the library books

UNIT 90

be handy to + 동사원형

~하기에 유용하다, ~하면 편리하다

이 패턴은 어떤 것이 유용하거나 편리하다는 것을 표현할 때 사용해요. 예를 들어, 다른 나라로 여행을 갔을 때 간단한 현지어를 알고 있으면 참 유용하겠죠? "현지 언어로 몇 가지 기본 표현을 알면 유용해."는 It's handy to know some basic phrases in the local language.라고 말할 수 있어요. 주어 자리에 it이 아닌 일반 명사가 올 수도 있어요.

be handy to 뒤에는 동사원형을 써야 합니다.

 A blanket would **be handy to** sit on.
돗자리가 앉기 편리해.

[to + 동사원형] 말고 [for + 명사/동명사] 패턴도 쓸 수 있어요. 예를 들어, "이 도구는 수리를 하는 데 유용해."라고 말하고 싶다면 This tool is handy for repairs, "이 앱은 길을 찾는 데 유용해."라고 말하고 싶다면 This app is handy for finding directions.라고 말이죠.

실생활 대화

A How about going on a picnic this weekend?
이번 주말에 소풍 가는 거 어때?

B Sounds great! We should definitely bring a picnic blanket.
좋지! 꼭 돗자리를 챙기자.

A Yeah, a blanket would be handy to sit on. What about food? Should we make some sandwiches?
맞아, 돗자리가 앉기 편리해. 음식은 어때? 샌드위치 만들까?

B Good idea! Let's also pack some fruit and drinks. Oh, and don't forget the sunscreen!
좋은 생각이야! 과일이랑 음료수도 챙기자. 아, 그리고 선크림 잊지 마!

pack 싸다   sunscreen 선크림

PRACTICE 패턴 활용

문장을 써 보고 음원을 들으며 소리 내어 말하세요. 제시어 중 기본형 동사는 패턴에 맞게 바꾸고, 제시어의 // 앞까지만이라도 완성해 말하세요.

▶ 정답 326쪽

- 이 앱은 일일 지출을 추적하는 데 <u>유용해</u>. 　　　　this app / track daily expenses
  This app is handy to track daily expenses.

1 　정전일 때 손전등이 있으면 <u>유용해</u>.　　　　a flashlight / have / during a power outage

2 　재사용 가능한 물병은 하루 종일 들고 다니기 <u>편리해</u>.　a reusable water bottle / carry around / all day

3 　여행할 때 보조 배터리를 들고 다니면 <u>유용해</u>.　　　it / carry a power bank / when traveling

4 　아이와 외출할 때는 물티슈를 챙기는 게 정말 <u>유용해</u>.　wet wipes / bring / when going out with kids

5 　요리할 때 계량컵이 있으면 정확한 재료 측정에 <u>도움이 돼</u>.
　　a measuring cup / use / when cooking / for accurate measurements

6 　멀티탭은 집 안 어디서든 많은 전자기기를 사용할 수 있게 해 줘서 있으면 <u>유용해</u>.
　　a power strip / have around the house / for using multiple devices

7 　접이식 테이블은 캠핑이나 피크닉 할 때 사용하기에 정말 좋아. `응용`
　　a folding table / set things up / during camping / or picnics

8 　메모장을 가까이 두면 아이디어를 빠르게 적어 두기 <u>편리해</u>. `응용`
　　keeping a notepad nearby / jot down ideas

---

track expenses 지출을 추적하다　　**flashlight** 손전등　　**power outage** 정전　　**carry around** 들고 다니다
power bank 보조 배터리　　**wet wipe** 물티슈　　**measuring cup** 계량컵　　**accurate measurement** 정확한 측정
power strip 멀티탭　　**multiple** 많은, 다수의　　**device** 기기　　**folding table** 접이식 테이블
set up (물건을) 설치하다, 차리다　　**jot down** 빠르게 적다

돗자리가 앉기 편리해.

주어 + be handy to + 동사원형
　A blanket would be　　　sit on

REMINDER 패턴 강화

이제 내 이야기를 해 봐요! 나에게 있음 직한 일들을 적고, 소리 내어 말해 보는 거예요.
주어가 별도로 제시되지 않으면, 주어는 항상 I(나)예요.

▶ 정답 326쪽

UNIT 86 I **can't help** feeling excited and nervous at the same time.

> can't help + 동명사[명사]
> ~하지 않을 수 없다, ~하는 것은 어쩔 수 없다

1 강아지를 보면 저절로 웃게 돼.   smiling when I see puppies

2 그의 농담에 웃음을 참을 수가 없어.   laughing at his jokes

3 그녀가 한 말이 자꾸 생각나. 응용   but think about what she said

UNIT 87 I **couldn't care less about** fancy cars.

> couldn't care less about + 명사(절)
> ~에 전혀 관심 없다, ~에 신경 쓰지 않다

4 연예인 소문에는 1도 관심 없어.   celebrity gossip

5 그들이 어떻게 생각하든 전혀 상관없어.   what they think

6 누가 누구랑 사귀는지 전혀 궁금하지도 않아.   who's dating who

UNIT 88 I **have a hard time** walking up early.

> have a hard time + 동명사
> ~하는 게 어렵다

7 아이들에게 작별 인사하는 게 힘들어.   saying goodbye to my kids

8 절친 앞에서는 웃음 참는 게 너무 어려워.
   keeping a straight face around my best friend

9 부모님께 기술 관련 설명하는 게 진짜 힘들어.   explaining tech stuff to my parents

UNIT 89 **It just occurred to me that** today's the due date for returning the library books.

> It just occurred to me (that) + 절
> ~가 갑자기 생각났다, ~가 문득 떠올랐다

10 전자레인지에 커피 놓고 나온 게 지금 생각났어.   I left my coffee in the microwave

11 방금 생각났는데, 화장지 사는 거 깜빡했어.   we forgot to buy toilet paper

12 방금 생각났는데, 저 배우 어디서 본 적 있어.
    I've seen that actor somewhere before

UNIT 90 A blanket would **be handy to** sit on.

> be handy to + 동사원형
> ~하기에 유용하다, ~하기 편리하다

13 이 앱은 더치페이 할 때 유용해.   this app / split the bill

14 물병은 여름에 들고 다니기 유용해.   a water bottle / carry in summer

15 지도 앱은 근처 카페 찾을 때 유용해.   the map app / find nearby cafés

REMINDER 맥락 적용

이제 앞에서 연습한 패턴을 실생활 대화 맥락에 적용해 보세요. 패턴을 일상적인 대화에 넣어서 직접 소리 내어 말해 보는 거예요. 빈칸에 들어갈 말이 기억이 나지 않는다면 다시 앞으로 가서 확인해 보세요.

UNIT 86

A I heard you broke up with that person. Why are you still checking her social media?
그 사람이랑 헤어졌다면서? 왜 아직도 그 사람 SNS를 보고 있어?

B I know, but _____ checking because I'm curious about her updates.
그러니까. 그런데 그 사람 소식이 궁금해서 보지 않을 수 없어.

A I understand, but don't you think it might be better to distance yourself for a while?
이해해. 그래도 잠시 거리를 두는 게 더 좋지 않을까?

B You're right. It's just hard to let go completely. I'll try to focus on other things.
네 말이 맞아. 그냥 완전히 잊기가 힘들어서. 다른 데 집중하도록 노력해야지.

UNIT 87

A What should we do for our anniversary this year?
올해 우리 기념일에 뭐 할까?

B Honestly, _____ what we do. I'm just pleased to spend time with you.
솔직히 뭘 하든 상관없어. 나는 그냥 너랑 시간 보낼 수 있어서 기뻐.

A That's sweet, but I'd still like to plan something special. Any preferences?
감동이야. 그래도 뭔가 특별한 걸 하고 싶은데. 뭐 하고 싶은 거 있어?

B How about going to our go-to restaurant for a nice dinner? We used to go there a lot when we were dating. _____ fancy places.
우리 자주 가는 식당 가서 저녁 먹는 건 어때? 우리 데이트할 때 자주 갔었잖아. 고급 식당 같은 건 중요하지 않아.

UNIT 88

A We _____ finding a babysitter for Friday nights.
금요일 밤에 아이 볼 사람 구하는 거 너무 힘들어.

B Have you tried using a babysitting app? They're pretty reliable these days.
베이비시터 앱을 써 봤어? 요즘은 꽤 믿을 만해.

A I'm a bit hesitant about leaving our kids with strangers. Is it really safe?
낯선 사람에게 아이를 맡기는 게 좀... 정말 안전할까?

B I've been using one for two years, and the reviews are great. I can recommend it to you. It's been great!
나는 2년째 사용하고 있는데, 리뷰도 좋은 데 내가 추천해 줄 수 있어. 진짜 좋았어!

UNIT 89

A Why are you in such a hurry?
왜 그렇게 서두르는 거야?

B _____ that I had a doctor's appointment at 3.
3시에 병원 예약이 있는 게 방금 생각났어.

A What time is it now? Should we take a taxi?
지금 몇 시지? 택시 탈까?

B Yeah, I think that's a good idea. Can you help me catch a taxi?
응. 그래야 할 것 같아. 택시 좀 잡아줄 수 있어?

UNIT 90

A What should we pack for our trip?
여행에 뭘 챙겨 가야 할까?

B Make sure to pack a portable charger! _____ when you're out.
보조 배터리는 꼭 챙겨! 외출할 때 정말 유용해.

A Good idea! We won't have to worry about battery life. Should we also bring a map or guidebook?
좋은 생각이야! 배터리 걱정 없이 다니겠네. 지도나 가이드북도 가져갈까?

B Actually, I think we can just use our phones for that. But let's make sure to download offline maps.
그건 그냥 핸드폰으로 볼 수 있을 것 같아. 대신 오프라인 지도를 미리 다운받아 두자.

어휘 distance 떼어놓다   preference 선호(되는 것)   go-to 자주 찾는   reliable 믿을 만한   hesitant 주저하는
Why are you in such a hurry? 왜 그렇게 서두르니?   portable charger 보조 배터리

정답 I can't help | I couldn't care less about, I couldn't care less about | have a hard time |
It just occurred to me | It's really handy

UNIT 91

be dying to + 동사원형
~하고 싶어 죽겠다

이 패턴은 무언가를 매우 간절히 원하거나 하고 싶다는 강한 욕구를 표현할 때 사용해요. 예를 들어, "나는 정말 휴가를 가고 싶어."라고 말하고 싶다면 I'm dying to go on vacation.이라고 말하면 돼요.

be dying to 뒤에는 동사원형을 써야 합니다.

 I'm dying to go back already.
벌써 다시 가고 싶어 죽겠어.

[be dying to + 동사원형]과 같은 의미로 [be dying for + 명사] 패턴을 쓰기도 해요. "나는 정말 커피를 마시고 싶어."라고 말하고 싶다면 I'm dying for a cup of coffee.라고 하면 돼요.

실생활 대화

A How was your weekend trip?
주말 여행 어땠어?

B It was amazing! I'm dying to go back already.
정말 멋졌어! 벌써 다시 가고 싶어 죽겠어.

A What did you like most about it?
가장 좋았던 점은 뭐였어?

B The beautiful scenery and the friendly locals.
It was all just unforgettable.
아름다운 경치랑 친절한 현지인들. 모든 게 정말 잊을 수 없었어.

---

go back 다시 가다   scenery 경치   local 현지인   unforgettable 잊을 수 없는

PRACTICE 패턴 활용

문장을 써 보고 음원을 들으며 소리 내어 말하세요. 제시어 중 기본형 동사는 패턴에 맞게 바꾸고, 제시어의 // 앞까지만이라도 완성해 말하세요.

▶ 정답 326쪽

- 이번 휴가 때 여행 가고 싶어 죽겠어.　　　　　　　　　　　　I / travel / during this vacation

  I'm dying to travel during this vacation.

1 새 차를 사고 싶어 죽겠어.　　　　　　　　　　　　　　　　　I / buy a new car

2 아이들은 놀이공원에 가고 싶어 안달이야.　　　　　the kids / go to the amusement park

3 부모님이 손주들이 보고 싶어 죽겠대.　　　　　　　my parents / see their grandkids

4 막 오픈한 레스토랑을 꼭 가보고 싶어.　　　I / try the new restaurant // that just opened

5 그는 이자율이 많이 떨어져서 집을 너무 사고 싶대. 지금은 매수자 시장이래.
   he / buy a house / since interest rates have dropped so much // he said it's a buyer's market now

6 특히 오늘처럼 더운 날에는 시원한 맥주가 정말 마시고 싶어. 정말 상쾌할 것 같아! 응용
   I / a cold beer / especially on a hot day / like today // it would be so refreshing

7 그녀는 오랜만에 푹 자고 싶대. 요즘 너무 바빠서 제대로 못 쉬었거든. 응용
   she / a good night's sleep // she's been so busy lately // and hasn't been able to rest properly

8 맛있는 피자가 먹고 싶어 죽겠어. 특히 페퍼로니 피자가 당겨. 내가 제일 좋아하는 피자거든. 응용
   I / a delicious pizza / especially pepperoni // it's my favorite

---

amusement park 놀이공원　　grandkid 손주　　buyer's market 매수자 시장　　refreshing 상쾌한
properly 제대로

벌써 다시 가고 싶어 죽겠어.

주어 + be dying to + 동사원형

I'm　　　　go back already

UNIT 92

There's no way (that) + 절

~일 리가 없다, ~하는 것은 불가능하다

이 패턴은 어떤 일이 불가능하다고 생각할 때나 믿기 힘들 때, 그리고 상대방에게 어떠한 가능성도 열어 주지 않으며 단호하게 말할 때 사용해요. 예를 들어, 반에서 꼴지를 하던 친구 잭이 갑자기 전교 1등을 하게 된다면 불가능하다고 느끼겠죠? 이때 이 패턴을 사용하여 There's no way Jack could go from last to first in one test.라고 말할 수 있어요. 또는 돈을 빌려 가면 항상 갚지 않는 친구가 이번에 또 돈을 빌려 달라고 한다면 거절하면서 There's no way I'm lending you money again.라고 말할 수 있어요. There's no way 뒤에 that은 써도 되지만 생략하는 것이 원어민에게 자연스럽게 들려요.

There's no way (that) 뒤에는 불가능한 내용을 담은 절(주어+동사)이 옵니다.

 There's no way I'm believing that unless I see it myself.
내가 직접 보기 전까진 난 못 믿겠어.

실생활 대화

A John says he can eat 50 hot dogs in one sitting.
존이 앉은 자리에서 핫도그를 한 번에 50개 먹을 수 있다고 하더라고.

B **There's no way he can do that.** It's physically impossible.
그건 말도 안 돼. 그건 물리적으로 불가능해.

A He claims he's been practicing for weeks.
몇 주째 연습 중이라나 봐.

B **There's no way I'm believing that unless I see it myself.**
내가 직접 보기 전까진 난 못 믿겠어.

---

physically 물리적으로   impossible 불가능한   unless ~하지 않는 한

PRACTICE 패턴 활용

문장을 써 보고 음원을 들으며 소리 내어 말하세요. 제시어 중 기본형 동사는 패턴에 맞게 바꾸고, 제시어의 // 앞까지만이라도 완성해 말하세요.

▶ 정답 326쪽

- 그가 또 내 생일을 잊었을 리 없어.   he forgot my birthday / again

  There's no way he forgot my birthday again.

1. 그들이 우리의 제안을 거절할 리가 없어.   they'll turn down our offer

2. 그녀가 혼자서 그렇게 많은 음식을 먹을 수는 없어.   she can eat that much food / by herself

3. 그가 이런 날씨에 등산을 갈 수는 없어.   he's going hiking / in this weather

4. 티켓 없이 그 콘서트에 들어갈 수는 없어.   we're getting into the concert / without tickets

5. 우리가 시간 내에 도착할 리가 없어. 벌써 늦었어.   we'll get there on time // we're already late

6. 우리가 저기까지 걸어서 갈 수 있을 리가 없어. 너무 멀어.
   we can walk / all the way there // it's way too far

7. 그들이 이 가격에 집을 팔 리가 없어. 너무 싸잖아.
   they're selling the house / at that price // it's way too cheap

8. 그가 시험에서 만점을 받았을 리가 없어. 어제 밤새 게임만 했잖아.
   he got a perfect score / on the test // he was up all night playing games

---

turn down 거절하다   offer 제안   way too far 너무 먼   at that price 그 가격에
get a perfect score 만점을 받다

내가 직접 보기 전까진 난 못 믿겠어.

There's no way (that) + 절

I'm believing that unless I see it myself

UNIT 93

forgot to + 동사원형
~하는 것을 깜빡했다

바쁘다 보면 어떤 일을 잊어버릴 때가 자주 있죠? 그때 forget의 과거형인 forgot을 써서 표현하면 돼요. 예를 들어, "지갑 가져오는 걸 깜빡해서 지금 아무것도 살 수 없어."라고 말하고 싶다면 I forgot to bring my wallet, so now I can't buy anything.이라고 하면 돼요. forgot 다음에는 명사가 올 수도 있어요. 예를 들어, 약속을 잊었다면 I forgot the appointment, 급하게 나오느라 키를 깜빡했다면 I forgot my keys.라고 말하면 돼요.

forgot 뒤에는 명사나 to 부정사 외에도 that절이나 의문사로 시작하는 절 형태도 쓸 수 있습니다.

 I completely **forgot to** pay it.
결제하는 걸 완전 깜빡했네.

실생활 대화

A Did you pay the electricity bill?
전기요금 냈어?

B Oh no, I completely forgot to pay it. I'll do it right now.
아, 결제하는 걸 완전 깜빡했네. 지금 바로 할게.

A Hurry up, it's due today. Do you need the account number?
서둘러, 오늘까지야. 계좌번호 필요해?

B Yes, please. I can't believe I forgot something this important.
응, 알려 줘. 이렇게 중요한 걸 깜빡하다니.

electricity bill 전기요금   due 마감인   account number 계좌번호

PRACTICE 패턴 활용

문장을 써 보고 음원을 들으며 소리 내어 말하세요. 제시어 중 기본형 동사는 패턴에 맞게 바꾸고, 제시어의 // 앞까지만이라도 완성해 말하세요.

▶ 정답 326쪽

- 어디에 주차했는지 확인하는 걸 깜빡했어.   I / check / where I parked
  I forgot to check where I parked.

1. 나가기 전에 문 잠그는 걸 깜빡했어.   I / lock the door / before leaving

2. 오늘 아침에 강아지 밥 주는 걸 깜빡했어.   I / feed the dog / this morning

3. 그들이 없는 동안 식물에 물 주는 걸 깜빡했어.   I / water the plants // while they were away

4. 폭풍 오기 전에 창문 닫는 걸 깜빡했어.   I / close the windows / before the storm

5. 그는 지갑을 가져오는 걸 깜빡해서 나한테 현금을 빌려야 했어.
   he / bring his wallet // so he had to borrow some cash from me

6. 내 동생은 이메일 비밀번호를 메모하는 걸 깜빡해서 이제 중요한 메시지를 확인할 수 없어.
   my brother / write down his email password // and now he can't access his important messages

7. 그녀는 집을 나서기 전에 가스레인지를 끄는 걸 깜빡해서 아직 켜져 있을까 봐 걱정해.
   she / turn off the stove / before leaving // and now she's worried it might still be on

8. 네가 망고 알레르기가 있는지 확인하는 걸 깜빡해서 과일 샐러드에 실수로 망고를 넣었어.
   I / check if you're allergic to mangoes // and I accidentally added some to the fruit salad

---

lock the door 문을 잠그다   feed the dog 개 밥을 주다   write down 적어두다   password 비밀번호
turn off the stove 가스레인지를 끄다   check if ~인지 확인하다   be allergic to ~에 알레르기가 있다
accidentally 실수로

결제하는 걸 완전 깜빡했네.

주어 + forgot to + 동사원형
     I   completely   pay it

UNIT 94 · can't imagine + 동명사[명사/절]
~는 상상할 수 없다

이 패턴으로 다양한 감정을 나타낼 수 있어요. 놀라운 소식에 믿기지 않다는 마음을 표현할 때, 어떤 경험이나 상황에 대해 감탄하거나 놀라움을 표현할 때, 상대방의 업적이나 성과를 축하할 때, 상대방에게 공감하거나 위로를 전할 때 사용해요. 예를 들어, "그 일이 얼마나 힘들었을지 상상이 안 돼."라고 놀라움과 함께 위로의 말을 하고 싶다면 I can't imagine how hard that was, "네가 얼마나 기뻤을지 상상도 안 돼."라고 축하와 공감의 표현을 하고 싶다면 I can't imagine how happy you were.라고 말할 수 있어요.

can't imagine 다음에는 동명사, 명사, that절, wh절, how절 등 다양한 형태가 올 수 있어요.

 I **can't imagine** waking up that early.
그렇게 일찍 일어나는 건 상상할 수 없어.

실생활 대화

A I started waking up at 5 AM every day.
나 요즘 매일 아침 5시에 일어나.

B Seriously? I can't imagine waking up that early.
진짜로? 그렇게 일찍 일어나는 건 상상할 수 없어.

A It was hard at first, but now I love the quiet mornings.
처음엔 힘들었는데, 지금은 조용한 아침이 너무 좋아.

B Still, I can't imagine myself doing that.
그래도 나는 상상할 수도 없는 일이야.

---

that early 그렇게 일찍   quiet morning 조용한 아침

PRACTICE 패턴 활용

문장을 써 보고 음원을 들으며 소리 내어 말하세요. 제시어 중 기본형 동사는 패턴에 맞게 바꾸고, 제시어의 // 앞까지만이라도 완성해 말하세요.

▶ 정답 327쪽

- 우주 여행을 하는 건 상상할 수 없어. 너무 비현실적으로 느껴져! I / travel to space // it seems so surreal
  I can't imagine traveling to space. It seems so surreal!

1. 요즘 전기 없이 사는 것은 상상할 수 없어. 그건 우리가 자주 당연하게 받아드려.
   I / live without electricity / these days // it's something we often take for granted

2. 그녀의 아이들은 아침에 만화를 안 보는 삶은 상상도 못 해.
   her kids / life without cartoons / in the morning

3. 아침 커피 없이 하루를 시작하는 것은 상상할 수 없어.
   I / not / have my morning coffee / to start the day

4. 직접 라스베이거스 스피어를 보면 얼마나 감동적일지 상상이 안 돼.
   I / how amazing it must be / to see the Las Vegas Sphere in person

5. 새로 태어난 아기를 안았을 때 그 기분이 얼마나 놀라웠을지 상상이 안 돼.
   I / how incredible it must feel / to hold your newborn baby

6. 그녀는 일 끝나고 넷플릭스를 안 보는 저녁은 상상할 수 없대. 하루를 마무리하는 힐링 시간이지.
   she / an evening after work without watching Netflix // it's her way of winding down

7. 우리 고양이는 간식 없는 아침을 상상조차 못 해. 안 주면 계속 따라다녀.
   our cat / a morning / without her treats // she literally follows us around until she gets them

8. 그들은 여름에 에어컨 없이 사는 걸 상상도 못 해. 특히 요즘 같이 더운 날씨에는 말이야.
   they / live without air conditioning in summer // especially with how hot it gets / these days

surreal 비현실적인   electricity 전기   take for granted 당연하게 여기다   incredible 믿을 수 없는
newborn baby 신생아   wind down 마무리 짓다   treat (반려동물에게 주는) 간식   literally 문자 그대로
air conditioning 에어컨

그렇게 일찍 일어나는 건 상상할 수 없어.

주어 + can't imagine + 동명사
  I   waking up that early

UNIT 95

be debating + 전치사구[명사구/명사절/명사]

~를 고민하고 있다

이 패턴은 어떤 결정을 내리기 전에 두 가지 이상의 선택지 사이에서 고민하고 있을 때 사용해요. I'm still debating.은 "아직 고민 중이야."라는 뜻으로 일상에서 자주 쓰는 표현이에요. debate 뒤에는 다양한 형태가 올 수 있는데, '~할지 말지' 고민 중이라는 의미로 [whether to + 동사원형]이 있어요. 예를 들어, 물건을 살지 말지 고민 중이라고 할 때, I'm debating whether to buy it.이라고 말할 수 있어요. 여기에 or not을 덧붙여 I'm debating whether to buy it or not.이라고 말해서 안 살 가능성까지 언급할 수도 있어요.

be debating 뒤에는 고민하고 있는 사항을 나타내는 전치사구, 명사구, 명사, 동명사, 명사절 등 다양하게 올 수 있습니다.

 I'm still **debating** between Max and Charlie.
맥스랑 찰리 중에서 아직 고민 중이야.

실생활 대화

A   Did you decide on a name for your new pet?
    새로 데려온 반려동물 이름 정했어?

B   No, I'm still debating between Max and Charlie.
    아니, 맥스랑 찰리 중에서 아직 고민 중이야.

A   Both are great names. Which one do you prefer?
    둘 다 좋은 이름인데. 넌 어떤 게 좋아?

B   Max sounds strong, while Charlie feels friendly.
    I can't decide which suits him better.
    맥스는 듣기에 강해 보이고, 찰리는 친근한 느낌이라. 어떤 게 더 어울릴지 모르겠어.

decide on ~를 결정하다

PRACTICE 패턴 활용

문장을 써 보고 음원을 들으며 소리 내어 말하세요. 제시어 중 기본형 동사는 패턴에 맞게 바꾸고, 제시어의 // 앞까지만이라도 완성해 말하세요.   ▶ 정답 327쪽

- 빨간 드레스와 파란 드레스 사이에서 아직 고민 중이야.
  I / still / between the red dress and the blue one

  I'm still debating between the red dress and the blue one.

1. 여름 휴가를 바다로 갈지, 산으로 갈지 아직도 결정 못 하고 있어.
   I / still / between the beach or the mountains / for summer vacation

2. 반려동물을 키우는 것의 장단점을 고민 중이야.   I / the pros and cons of getting a pet

3. 그 일자리 제안을 받아들일지 고민 중이야.   I / if I should take the job offer

4. 더 나은 기회를 위해 직장을 옮길지 고민 중이야.   I / whether to switch jobs / for better opportunities

5. 새 차를 살지, 아니면 기존 차를 계속 탈지 고민 중이야.
   I / whether to buy a new car / or keep the old one

6. 우리 부모님은 새 도시로 이사 갈지 말지 고민 중이셔. 응용
   my parents / whether to move to a new city / or stay where they are

7. 그녀는 해외 유학을 갈지 아니면 국내 대학을 다닐지를 고민 중이야. 응용
   she / whether to study abroad / or attend a local university

8. (그 당시에) 친구들은 졸업 후 취직할지 대학원에 갈지 한참 고민하고 있었지. 응용
   my friends / whether to get a job / right after graduation / or go to graduate school
   * [had been -ing] 사용

   pros and cons 장단점   switch jobs 직장을 옮기다   attend a local university 국내 대학에 다니다
   go to graduate school 대학원에 가다

맥스랑 찰리 중에서 아직 고민 중이야.

주어 + be debating + 전치사구

I'm / still   between Max and Charlie

REMINDER 패턴 강화

이제 내 이야기를 해 봐요! 나에게 있음 직한 일들을 적고, 소리 내어 말해 보는 거예요.
주어가 별도로 제시되지 않으면, 주어는 항상 I(나)예요.

▶ 정답 327쪽

UNIT 91 I'm dying to go back already.

be dying to + 동사원형
~하고 싶어 죽겠다

1 하루 푹 제대로 쉬고 싶어. take a proper day off

2 따뜻한 바나나 빵 한 조각이 간절해. a warm slice of banana bread

3 고양이 카페 가고 싶어 죽겠어. visit a cat café

UNIT 92 There's no way I'm believing that unless I see it myself.

There's no way (that) + 절
~일 리가 없다, ~하는 것은 불가능하다

4 네가 벌써 방 청소를 다 했을 리가 없어. you cleaned your whole room already

5 내가 그 계획에 동의했을 리가 없어. I agreed to that plan

6 그녀가 저 피자를 혼자 다 먹었을 리가 없어. she finished all that pizza alone

UNIT 93 I completely forgot to pay it.

forgot to + 동사원형
~하는 것을 깜빡했다

7 네 문자에 답장하는 걸 깜빡했어. reply to your text

8   어젯밤에 폰 충전하는 걸 깜빡했어.   charge my phone last night

9   예약하는 걸 깜빡했어.   make a reservation

UNIT 94 I **can't imagine** waking up that early.

> can't imagine + 동명사[명사/절]
> ~는 상상할 수 없다

10   와이파이 없이 사는 건 상상도 안 돼.   living without Wi-Fi

11   그가 진짜 그렇게 말했다니 상상이 안 돼.   that he actually said that

12   이 날씨에 뜨거운 커피 마시는 건 상상도 못 해.
     drinking hot coffee in this weather

UNIT 95 I'm still **debating** between Max and Charlie.

> be debating + 전치사구[명사구/명사절/명사]
> ~를 고민하고 있다

13   라면과 피자 사이에서 뭘 먹을지 고민하고 있어.
     between getting ramen or pizza

14   말할지 말지 고민하고 있어.   whether to speak up or stay quiet

15   외출할지 집에 있을지 고민 중이야.   whether to go out or stay in

REMINDER 맥락 적용

이제 앞에서 연습한 패턴을 실생활 대화 맥락에 적용해 보세요. 패턴을 일상적인 대화에 넣어서 직접 소리 내어 말해 보는 거예요. 빈칸에 들어갈 말이 기억이 나지 않는다면 다시 앞으로 가서 확인해 보세요.

UNIT 91

A Have you tried the new coffee shop that opened nearby?
이 근처에 새로 생긴 커피숍 가 봤어?

B Not yet, but _____ try their pumpkin lattes.
아직. 근데 호박 라떼는 꼭 마셔보고 싶어.

A I heard they also offer delicious brunch!
거기 맛있는 브런치도 판대.

B Let's go there tomorrow morning for breakfast.
내일 아침에 거기 가서 아침 먹자.

UNIT 92

A Are you going to try out for the basketball team?
농구 팀에 지원할 거야?

B _____ I'll make the team with my current skills.
지금 내 실력으로는 팀에 뽑힐 리가 없어.

A Come on, you can improve with practice! Believe in yourself.
괜찮아. 연습하면 더 나아질 수 있어! 너 자신을 믿어!

B I appreciate your support! You're right; I won't know until I give it a try.
응원 고마워! 맞아, 시도해 보기 전엔 모르는 거니까.

UNIT 93

A Weren't we supposed to meet at 3 PM?
우리 3시에 만나기로 하지 않았어?

B I'm so sorry, I completely _____ come!
정말 미안. 약속을 완전 까먹은 거 있지.

A Hurry up! I've been waiting for an hour! Since you forgot, dinner is on you!
빨리 와! 지금 한 시간째 기다리고 있어! 약속 까먹었으니까 저녁은 네가 사.

B Of course, I will treat you to dinner tonight. I'm on my way. I feel terrible about this. I'll be there as fast as possible.
물론 오늘 저녁은 내가 살게. 지금 가는 중이야. 정말 미안해. 최대한 빨리 갈게.

UNIT 94

A My parents are selling the house and going on a world tour.
부모님이 집을 팔고 세계 여행을 가신대.

B Wow, that's amazing! **I can't imagine** taking such an adventure at their age.
대단하시다! 그 연세에 그런 모험을 하시다니, 난 상상도 할 수 없어.

A I was surprised, too. They say they're fulfilling their retirement dream.
나도 놀랐어. 은퇴 후의 꿈을 이루는 중이시래.

B That's really cool. But **I can't imagine** not having your family home anymore.
정말 멋지다. 근데 이제 너희 집이 없어지는 건 상상이 안 되네.

UNIT 95

A Are you going to buy the new smartphone model?
신상 스마트폰 살 거야?

B **I'm debating** if it's really necessary or if I should wait for the next version.
진짜 필요한 건지, 아니면 다음 버전을 기다릴지 고민 중이야.

A Which features matter most to you?
어떤 기능에 제일 중요한데?

B The camera is great, but I heard rumors about a major upgrade coming next year. It's a tough decision.
카메라는 좋긴 한데, 내년에 주요 업그레이드가 있을 거란 소문이 있어. 결정하기 쉽지 않네.

어휘　make the team 팀에 들어가다　treat ~ to ~에게 …를 대접하다　fulfill 실현하다　retirement 은퇴
　　　tough decision 어려운 결정

정답　I'm dying to ｜ There is no way ｜ forgot to ｜ I can't imagine, I can't imagine ｜ I'm debating

UNIT 96

end up + 동명사

결국 ~하게 되다, 끝내 ~하고 말다

이 패턴은 결과를 강조하거나 최종적으로 상황이 어떻게 마무리되었는지 설명할 때 사용해요. 예를 들어, "외식으로 무엇을 먹을지 1시간 동안 이야기하다가, 결국 한식을 먹었어."는 We talked for an hour about what to eat out, and we ended up eating Korean food, "일찍 일어나기 싫었지만, 결국 알람 때문에 일찍 일어났어."는 I didn't want to wake up early, but I ended up waking up early because of the alarm.이라고 말할 수 있어요.

end up 뒤에는 보통 동명사(-ing)를 씁니다.

 We **ended up** spending way more money than we planned.
계획보다 돈을 훨씬 더 쓰게 됐어.

[end up + 동명사] 패턴 뒤에는 instead of 구문이 자연스럽게 연결되기도 해요. 아침에 늦잠을 자고 싶은데 결국 일찍 일어나야 했다는 말은 I ended up getting up early instead of staying in bed longer.라고 말할 수 있겠지요.

실생활 대화

A How was your weekend trip?
주말 여행 어땠어?

B It was fun, but we ended up spending way more money than we planned.
재밌었는데, 계획보다 돈을 훨씬 더 쓰게 됐어.

A Oh no, what happened? Did you have any unexpected expenses?
어머, 무슨 일 있었어? 예상 못 한 지출이라도 있었어?

B Yeah, our hotel canceled last minute, so we had to book a more expensive one. And we also ate out more than we expected.
응, 호텔이 갑자기 취소돼서 더 비싼 곳으로 예약해야 했어. 그리고 예상보다 외식도 더 많이 했고.

unexpected 예상치 못한

PRACTICE 패턴 활용

문장을 써 보고 음원을 들으며 소리 내어 말하세요. 제시어 중 기본형 동사는 패턴에 맞게 바꾸고, 제시어의 // 앞까지만이라도 완성해 말하세요.

▶ 정답 327쪽

- 그냥 온라인 쇼핑 구경만 하고 있었는데, 결국 뭔가 사 버렸어.
  I was just browsing online / but / I / buy something

  I was just browsing online, but I ended up buying something.

1. 버스 타려고 했는데 결국 걸어갔어.   I was going to take the bus / but / walk

2. 운동하러 나갔는데 결국 카페에 앉아 있었어.   I went out for a workout / but / sit in a café

3. 잠깐 눈 붙이려고 했는데 결국 2시간이나 자 버렸어.
   I meant to take a quick nap / but / sleep / for two hours

4. 옷 한 벌만 사려고 갔는데 결국 다섯 벌을 샀어.   I went to buy one piece of clothing / but / buy five

5. 내 동생은 결국 밤새 비디오 게임을 했어.   my brother / play video games / all night

6. 그들은 유럽 여행을 가려다가 결국 제주도로 갔어. 응용   they / go to Jeju / instead of Europe

7. 우리는 간단하게 산책하려다가 결국 두 시간 걸었어. 응용
   we / walk / for two hours / instead of a short stroll

8. 선생님은 간단히 설명만 하려다 결국 한 시간을 강의하셨어. 응용
   the teacher / give a full lecture / instead of a brief explanation

go out for a workout 운동하러 나가다   take a quick nap 잠깐 낮잠 자다   instead of ~ 대신에
give a full lecture 한 시간 강의하다   brief explanation 간단한 설명

계획보다 돈을 훨씬 더 쓰게 됐어.

주어 + end up + 동명사
We   ended   spending way more money than we planned

UNIT 97　It's beyond me[myself] + 의문사절
~가 도무지 이해가 안 가다

이 패턴은 어떤 것을 이해할 수 없거나 받아들이기 어려운 상황을 표현할 때 사용해요. 여기서는 It's beyond me 뒤에 how절이 왔지만 why절도 많이 써요. 예를 들어, "그가 왜 그렇게 행동하는지 이해할 수 없어."라고 말하고 싶다면 It's beyond me why he acts like that, "그들이 왜 그 결정을 내렸는지 이해할 수 없어."라고 말하고 싶다면 It's beyond me why they made that decision.으로 표현할 수 있어요. me 대신 myself도 쓸 수 있으니, 한번 앞의 두 문장을 myself로 바꿔 말해 보세요.

It's beyond me[myself] 뒤에는 놀랍거나, 이해하기 어려운 상황을 나타내는 의문사절이 옵니다.

 It's beyond me how I pulled it off.
어떻게 해냈는지 나도 모르겠어.

이 패턴은 무언가가 상상을 뛰어넘을 정도로 놀라울 때도 사용해요. 예를 들어, "맛있다."는 말 정도로는 표현이 안 된다는 걸 강조하고 싶을 때 [It's beyond + 형용사] 형태를 사용해서 It's beyond delicious! (정말 맛있어서 설명할 수 없을 정도야!)라고 말할 수 있어요. 이 패턴은 상황에 따라 긍정적으로도, 부정적으로도 표현이 가능해요.

실생활 대화

A　I heard you got a perfect score on the final exam!
　　기말시험 만점 받았다며!

B　Yeah, but honestly, it's beyond me how I pulled it off.
　　응, 근데 진짜 어떻게 해냈는지 나도 모르겠어.

A　Well, you studied like crazy for weeks. You earned it.
　　너 몇 주 동안 미친 듯이 공부했잖아. 자격 있어.

B　Still, I was sure I messed up at least one question!
　　그래도 적어도 하나는 틀렸다고 생각했는데 말이야!

pull it off 해내다　You earned it. 넌 그럴 만한 자격이 있어.　mess up 망치다

PRACTICE 패턴 활용

문장을 써 보고 음원을 들으며 소리 내어 말하세요. 제시어 중 기본형 동사는 패턴에 맞게 바꾸고, 제시어의 // 앞까지만이라도 완성해 말하세요.   ▶ 정답 327쪽

- 어떻게 이런 일이 계속 벌어지는지 모르겠어.   how this keeps happening
  It's beyond me how this keeps happening.

1. 왜 그가 그 말을 농담이라고 생각했는지 이해할 수 없어.   how he thought that was a joke

2. 왜 사람들이 줄을 서서 20달러짜리 커피를 사는지 도무지 이해가 안 돼.
   why people line up / to buy a $20 cup of coffee

3. 그가 왜 그런 좋은 기회를 거절했는지 정말 이해할 수 없어.
   why he turned down such a great opportunity

4. 왜 사람들이 여전히 그 가게에 가는지 이해가 안 돼. 항상 서비스가 별로인데.
   why people still go to that store // the service is always terrible

5. 이 도시의 야경은 상상 이상으로 아름다워. `응용`   the night view of this city / beautiful

6. 그녀의 친절함은 말로 다 표현할 수 없을 정도야. `응용`   her kindness / indescribable

7. 이 식당의 서비스는 정말 만족스러워. `응용`   the service at this restaurant / satisfying

8. 그 영화의 반전은 정말 충격적이야. `응용`   the twist in that movie / shocking

line up 줄을 서다   turn down 거절하다   night view 야경   indescribable 형언할 수 없는   twist 반전, 전개

어떻게 해냈는지 나도 모르겠어.

It's beyond me[myself] + 의문사절
how I pulled it off

UNIT 98
will let you know (+ 명사절/명사)
(~를) 네게 알려 줄 것이다

이 패턴은 '네게 알려 줄 것이다'라는 뜻으로, 어떤 정보를 상대방에게 전달하거나 알려주겠다고 할 때 사용해요. let you know는 I 등의 주어와 함께 단독으로 쓰이는 경우가 많지만, 뒤에 명사절이나 명사를 써서 상대방에게 알려 줄 정보나 자세하게 말하고 싶은 내용을 전달할 수도 있습니다. 예를 들어, "회의 일정 알려 줄게."라고 말하고 싶다면 I'll let you know the meeting schedule, 또는 "내가 영화가 언제 시작하는지 알려 줄게."라고 말하고 싶다면 I'll let you know when the movie starts.라고 표현할 수 있어요.

will let you know 뒤에 전달할 정보를 나타내는 명사절이 온다면 if절 또는 when, where, what 등의 의문사절이 오며, that 또한 올 수 있는데 이 that은 종종 생략됩니다.

 I'll let you know right away if everything works out!
계약이 잘 성사되면 바로 알려 줄게!

실생활 대화

A How did the contract for the new apartment go?
Did you get a good deal?
새 아파트 계약은 어떻게 됐어? 좋은 조건으로 계약했어?

B I haven't signed the final contract yet.
I'm negotiating a few conditions with the landlord.
아직 최종 계약은 안 했어. 집주인과 몇 가지 조건을 조율 중이야.

A I hope everything goes smoothly!
모든 일이 잘 되길 바라!

B **I'll let you know right away if everything works out!**
Dinner's on me that night!
계약이 잘 성사되면 바로 알려 줄게! 그날 저녁은 내가 쏜다!

---

contract 계약　a good deal (가성비) 좋은 거래　sign 서명하다　negotiate 협상하다　landlord 집주인
smoothly 원만하게

PRACTICE 패턴 활용

문장을 써 보고 음원을 들으며 소리 내어 말하세요. 제시어 중 기본형 동사는 패턴에 맞게 바꾸고,
제시어의 // 앞까지만이라도 완성해 말하세요.   ▶ 정답 328쪽

- 회의 일정이 다시 잡히는 대로 바로 알려 줄게.   I / as soon as the meeting is rescheduled

  I'll let you know as soon as the meeting is rescheduled.

1 수프에 간이 부족하면 알려 줄게.   I / if the soup lacks seasoning

2 다른 준비해야 할 것이 있으면 알려 줄게.   I / if there's anything else you need to prepare

3 결혼 날짜를 정하면 알려 줄게.   I / when I decide on a date / for my wedding

4 걱정 안 해도 되게 집 도착하면 알려 줄게.   I / when I get home // so you don't have to worry

5 결과 받으면 바로 알려 줄게. 그래야 같이 다음 단계를 결정할 수 있으니까.
   I / as soon as I get the results // so we can figure out the next steps together

6 제인과 이야기한 후에 우리가 몇 시에 만나야 할지 알려 줄게.
   I / what time we should meet / after talking to Jane

7 그녀가 파티가 취소되면 알려 줄 거야.   she / if the party is canceled

8 고객센터에서 배송 상황을 알려 줄 거야.   customer service / the delivery status

reschedule 일정을 변경하다   lack seasoning 간이 부족하다   decide on a date 날짜를 정하다
figure out 생각해 내다, 이해하다   delivery status 배송 상황

계약이 잘 성사되면 바로 알려 줄게!

주어 + will let you know + 절
   I   right away   if everything works out

293

UNIT 99
It's hard to tell + 의문사절[if절]
~인지 알기 어렵다

이 패턴은 어떤 것을 판단하거나 구분하기 어려운 상황일 때 사용해요. 여기서 tell은 '말하다'라는 뜻이 아니라 '구별하다, 판단하다, 알아차리다'라는 의미예요. tell 뒤에는 주로 [if + 주어 + 동사] 형태로 판단하기 어려운 상태를 나타내요. 무언가가 확실하지 않고 아리송할 때가 있죠? 예를 들어, 어떤 결정을 내렸는데 이 결정이 맞는지 아닌지 확실하지 않을 때 "이게 좋은 결정인지 알기 어려워요."라고 말하고 싶다면 It's hard to tell if this is a good decision.이라고 하면 돼요. 그리고 누가(who), 언제(when), 왜(why) 등의 정보를 모를 때는 tell 뒤에 [의문사 + 주어 + 동사] 형태를 써서 나타내요. 예를 들어, 친구가 왜 일찍 떠났는지 알지 못하겠다면, It's hard to tell why he left early. (그가 왜 일찍 떠났는지 알기 어려워요.)라고 말할 수 있는 거예요.

It's hard to tell 뒤에는 보통 어떤 상황인지 판단하기 어려운 내용을 나타내는 의문사절이나 if절이 옵니다.

 It's hard to tell how old it is without looking at the label.
라벨을 보지 않고는 몇 년 산인지 알기 어려워요.

실생활 대화

A How old do you think this wine is?
이 와인이 얼마나 오래됐을 것 같아요?

B It's hard to tell how old it is without looking at the label.
라벨을 보지 않고는 몇 년 산인지 알기 어려워요.

A True. I wonder if it'll go well with dinner.
맞아요. 저녁이랑 잘 어울릴지 궁금하네요.

B Why don't we open it and find out?
열어 보고 확인해 볼까요?

go well with ~와 잘 어울리다, 궁합이 잘 맞다

PRACTICE 패턴 활용

문장을 써 보고 음원을 들으며 소리 내어 말하세요. 제시어 중 기본형 동사는 패턴에 맞게 바꾸고, 제시어의 // 앞까지만이라도 완성해 말하세요.   ▶ 정답 328쪽

- 여기서는 물이 얼마나 깊은지 알기 어려워요.   how deep the water is / from here

  It's hard to tell how deep the water is from here.

1. 내일 날씨가 어떨지 알기 어려워요.   what the weather will be like / tomorrow

2. 그가 진지한 건지 농담하는 건지 구분하기 어려워요.   if he's being serious / or just joking

3. 그녀의 나이를 가늠하기 어려워요. 나이에 비해 젊어 보여요.
   how old she is // she looks young for her age

4. 어느 팀이 이길지 알기 어려워요. 막상막하에 둘 다 잘하고 있거든요.
   which team is going to win // it's a neck-and-neck game // and they're both playing really well

5. 그는 워낙 말을 잘해서 진심인지 아닌지 파악하기 어려워요.
   if he is sincere // because he's such a smooth talker

6. 첫인상만 보고는 그 사람이 어떤 사람인지 판단하기 어렵잖아요.
   what kind of person someone is / just from a first impression

7. 그는 늘 웃고 있어서 정말 기분이 좋은 건지 아닌지 잘 모르겠어요.
   if he's actually happy / or just pretending // because he always smiles

8. 날씨가 계속 변해서 오늘 비가 올지 아닐지 예측하기가 어렵네요.
   whether it's going to rain today // because the weather keeps changing

joke 농담하다   for her age 그녀 나이에 비해   neck-and-neck 막상막하인   sincere 진심의
smooth talker 말 잘하는 사람

라벨을 보지 않고는 몇 년 산인지 알기 어려워요.

It's hard to tell + 의문사절

how old it is without looking at the label

UNIT 100

주어A + thought ~, but + 주어B + turned out to + 동사원형
~인 줄 알았는데, 알고 보니 [주어B]는 ~였다

이 패턴은 어떤 것을 예상하거나 기대했지만 실제로는 그 예상과 기대를 벗어났을 때 사용할 수 있는 유용한 표현이에요. 여기서 turn out은 '(예상치 못한 결과로) ~인 것으로 드러나다'라는 뜻이에요. 예를 들어, 유명한 맛집에 음식을 먹으러 가서 맛있을 줄 알았는데, 맛이 없었거나(but it turned out to be not good), 영화가 재밌을 줄 알았는데, 알고 보니 따분했던 경우(but it turned out to be boring) 등 예상 밖의 결과를 설명할 때 이 패턴을 사용해요.

turned out to 뒤에는 동사원형을 써야 합니다.

 I **thought** so, too, **but** it **turned out to** be surprisingly affordable.
저도 그렇게 생각했는데, 알고 보니 의외로 저렴했어요.

[but + 주어 + turned out to + 동사원형]은 [but it turned out (that) + 절]의 형태로도 바꿀 수 있어요. 예를 들어, but it turned out to be not good은 but it turned out that the food was not good으로 바꿀 수 있어요. 여기서 that은 생략해도 괜찮아요.

실생활 대화

A I thought the restaurant would be expensive.
그 레스토랑이 비쌀 거라고 생각했어요.

B I thought so too, but it turned out to be surprisingly affordable.
저도 그렇게 생각했는데, 알고 보니 의외로 저렴했어요.

A How was the food?
I was worried it might not taste good if it was cheap.
음식은 어땠어요? 너무 싸면 맛이 없을까 봐 걱정했거든요.

B Don't worry. The food was actually really good.
It's a great bang for your buck kind of place.
걱정 마세요. 음식이 진짜 맛있었어요. 가성비 최고인 그런 곳이에요.

---

surprisingly 의외로   **affordable** 감당할 수 있는, 저렴한   **bang for your buck** 가격 대비 최고의 효과, 가성비

PRACTICE 패턴 활용

문장을 써 보고 음원을 들으며 소리 내어 말하세요. 제시어 중 기본형 동사는 패턴에 맞게 바꾸고, 제시어의 // 앞까지만이라도 완성해 말하세요.

▶ 정답 328쪽

- 그가 나를 도와줄 수 없을 거라고 생각했는데, 알고 보니 매우 도움이 되었어요.
  I / he couldn't help me / he / be very helpful
  I thought he couldn't help me, but he turned out to be very helpful.

1. 그가 친절한 사람일 거라고 생각했는데, 알고 보니 무례한 사람이었어요.
   I / he was a kind person / he / be rude

2. 그가 외국인일 거라고 생각했는데, 알고 보니 한국 사람이었어요.
   I / he was a foreigner / he / be Korean

3. 이 문제가 쉬울 거라고 생각했는데, 알고 보니 매우 어려웠어요.
   I / this problem would be easy / it / be very difficult

4. 온라인으로 주문한 드레스가 우아하고 세련될 줄 알았는데, 알고 보니 촌스러웠어요.
   I / the dress I ordered online would be elegant and chic / it / look frumpy

5. 우리는 그 식당이 비쌀 줄 알았는데, 알고 보니 꽤 저렴했어요.
   we / the restaurant would be expensive / it / be quite affordable

6. 그녀는 새로 산 신발이 편할 줄 알았는데, 알고 보니 하루 종일 아팠대요.
   she / the new shoes would be comfortable / they / hurt her feet / all day

7. 내 친구는 그 사람이 독신일 거라고 생각했는데, 알고 보니 결혼했대요. 응용
   my friend / he was single / he was married

8. 팀장은 그 고객이 까다로울 줄 알았는데, 알고 보니 아주 친절했어요. 응용
   the manager / the client would be difficult / she was very kind

elegant 우아한   chic 세련된   frumpy 촌스러운   hurt one's feet 발이 아프다

저도 그렇게 생각했는데, 알고 보니 의외로 저렴했어요.

주어A + thought ~, but + 주어B + turned out to + 동사원형
  I   so, too   it   be surprisingly affordable

REMINDER 패턴 강화

이제 내 이야기를 해 봐요! 나에게 있음 직한 일들을 적고, 소리 내어 말해 보는 거예요.
주어가 별도로 제시되지 않으면, 주어는 항상 I(나)예요.

▶ 정답 328쪽

UNIT 96 We **ended up** spending way more money than we planned.

> end up + 동명사
> 결국 ~하게 되다, 끝내 ~하고 말다

1 결국 시즌 전체를 정주행 했어.   binge-watching the whole season

2 결국 간식에 돈을 다 써 버렸어.   spending all my money on snacks

3 결국 소파에서 잠들어 버렸어.   falling asleep on the couch

UNIT 97 **It's beyond me** how I pulled it off.

> It's beyond me[myself] + 의문사절
> ~가 도무지 이해가 안 가다

4 왜 난 자꾸 열쇠를 잃어버리는지 모르겠어.   why I keep losing my keys

5 그가 어떻게 항상 그렇게 침착해 보이는지 모르겠어.   how he always looks so calm

6 그 고양이가 어떻게 그렇게 유명해졌는지 정말 모르겠어.   how that cat got so famous

UNIT 98 **I'll let you know** right away if everything works out!

> will let you know (+ 명사절/명사)
> (~를) 네게 알려 줄 것이다

7 오늘 밤에 갈 수 있을지 알려 줄게.   if I can make it tonight

8 이번 주말에 내가 언제 시간이 되는지 알려 줄게.　when I'm free this weekend

9 회의 시간 알려 줄게.　the meeting time

UNIT 99 **It's hard to tell** how old it is without looking at the label.

> It's hard to tell + 의문사절[if절]
> ~인지 알기 어렵다

10 이 우유가 아직 괜찮은지 알기 어려워요.　if this milk is still good

11 그가 실제로 몇 시에 올지 판단하기 어려워요.　what time he'll actually show up

12 우리에게 시간이 얼마나 남았는지 알기 어려워요.　how much time we have left

UNIT 100 I **thought** so, too, **but** it **turned out to** be surprisingly affordable.

> 주어A + thought ~, but + 주어B + turned out to + 동사원형
> ~인 줄 알았는데, 알고 보니 [주어B]는 ~였다

13 우리가 일찍 온 줄 알았는데 오히려 늦은 거였어요.
we were early / we / be actually late

14 영화가 지루할 줄 알았는데 엄청 재밌었어요.
the movie would be boring / it / be super fun

15 그가 처음 보는 사람인 줄 알았는데 예전에 만난 적 있더라고요. `응용`
he was a stranger / we'd actually met before

REMINDER 맥락 적용

이제 앞에서 연습한 패턴을 실생활 대화 맥락에 적용해 보세요. 패턴을 일상적인 대화에 넣어서 직접 소리 내어 말해 보는 거예요. 빈칸에 들어갈 말이 기억이 나지 않는다면 다시 앞으로 가서 확인해 보세요.

UNIT 96

A Did you buy the shoes you wanted?
원하던 신발은 샀어?

B No, they were sold out, so I 😺_____ buying a different pair.
아니, 품절이어서 결국 다른 걸로 샀어.

A That's disappointing. Are you satisfied with the ones you got instead?
아쉽겠다. 대신 산 신발은 괜찮아?

B Actually, yes. I 😺_____ finding a style I like even better.
응, 마음에 들어. 오히려 더 마음에 드는 스타일을 찾게 됐어.

UNIT 97

A Jessica ran a marathon after being awake for 24 hours.
제시카가 24시간을 안 자고 마라톤을 했어.

B Unbelievable. 😺_____ how she can push herself to that limit.
대박. 어떻게 그렇게 극한까지 몰아붙이는지 난 도무지 알 수 없다.

A They say her mental strength is incredible.
걔 정신력이 장난이 아니라더라.

B That's really amazing. I'm tired even after sleeping for 8 hours.
진짜 대단하다. 난 8시간 자고도 피곤한데.

UNIT 98

A Are you coming to the party on Saturday?
토요일 파티에 올 거야?

B I'm not sure yet. Depends on whether my boss lets me leave early.
아직 확실하지 않아. 직장 상사가 날 일찍 보내주냐, 아니냐에 달렸지 뭐.

A Haha, I'll send your boss an invite, too.
하, 그러면 너네 상사도 초대할까?

B Please do! 😺_____ by Friday.
제발 좀 그래라! 금요일까지 알려줄게!

UNIT 99

A Do you think Kevin likes me?
케빈이 나를 좋아하나?

B 🐱 I'll let you know. He's nice to everyone.
모르겠네. 그 앤 모두에게 친절하거든.

A But he seems to pay extra attention to me. Isn't that a sign?
나한테 특별히 신경 쓰는 것 같은데. 그게 신호 아닐까?

B Could be, but it's still 🐱 hard to tell. Why don't you just ask him directly? That's the fastest way!
그럴 수도. 근데 아직도 모르겠어. 그냥 직접 물어보는 게 어때? 제일 빠른 방법이야!

UNIT 100

A I thought the online course would be easy.
그 온라인 수업이 쉬울 거라고 생각했는데.

B I thought so, too, 🐱 but it turned out to be quite challenging.
나도 그렇게 생각했는데. 알고 보니 꽤 어렵더라.

A But you must have learned a lot, right?
그래도 배운 게 많았지?

B Yes, it was difficult but I learned a lot. It was worth the challenge.
응. 어려웠지만 그만큼 많이 배웠어. 도전해 볼 만해.

어휘   mental strength 정신력   depend on ~에 달려 있다   pay extra attention 더 주의를 기울이다
정답   ended up, ended up | It's beyond me | I'll let you know | It's hard to tell, hard to tell |
       but it turned out

REMINDER 패턴 정착

앞에서 배운 20개 패턴을 머릿속에 새기는 시간이에요.
문장을 보고 패턴을 이용해 영어로 소리 내어 말해 보세요.

81 일정에 너무 얽매이지 마.

82 가스를 껐는지 기억이 안 나서 신경 쓰여.

83 기억이 날 듯 말 듯해!

84 조깅하러 공원 갈 거야.

85 네가 원하면 다른 데도 좋아.

86 설레면서 동시에 긴장하지 않을 수 없네요.

87 난 그런 화려한 차엔 전혀 관심 없어.

88 일찍 일어나는 게 너무 힘들어.

89 방금 생각났는데, 오늘이 도서관 책 반납일이야.

90 돗자리가 앉기 편리해.

91 벌써 다시 가고 싶어 죽겠어.

92 내가 직접 보기 전까진 난 못 믿겠어.

93 결제하는 걸 완전 깜빡했네.

94 그렇게 일찍 일어나는 건 상상할 수 없어.

95 맥스랑 찰리 중에서 아직 고민 중이야.

96 계획보다 돈을 훨씬 더 쓰게 됐어.

97 어떻게 해냈는지 나도 모르겠어.

98 계약이 잘 성사되면 바로 알려 줄게!

99 라벨을 보지 않고는 몇 년 산인지 알기 어려워요.

100 저도 그렇게 생각했는데, 알고 보니 의외로 저렴했어요.

패턴 활용 & 패턴 강화
정답

UNIT 1   PRACTICE

1 I want you to go hiking with me.
2 I want my dog to stop barking at strangers.
3 I want my father to quit smoking for his health.
4 I want you to clean your room before the guests arrive.
5 He wants you to text him later.
6 He wants his kids to eat more vegetables.
7 We want you to stay for the whole meeting.
8 They want their boss to be more understanding.

UNIT 2   PRACTICE

1 I'm craving coffee, but I'm trying to cut down on caffeine.
2 I'm craving a vacation somewhere far away.
3 I'm seriously craving chocolate right now.
4 I'm craving a hot bowl of soup on this chilly day.
5 They're craving bubble tea again.
6 She's craving anything spicy right now.
7 He's craving something cold, like ice cream or a smoothie.
8 He's craving a good night's sleep after working late all week.

UNIT 3   PRACTICE

1 I'm okay at cooking.
2 I'm bad at drawing.
3 I'm good at singing.
4 I'm good at playing the guitar.
5 She's good at remembering names.
6 She's bad at keeping secrets.
7 He's really good at cooking Italian food.
8 Jane is okay at speaking English, but still makes mistakes.

UNIT 4   PRACTICE

1 It's time to clean the house.
2 It's time to take a shower.
3 It's time to eat breakfast.
4 It's time to stop procrastinating.
5 It's time to renew your driver's license.
6 It's time to leave, or we might get stuck in traffic on the way.
7 It's time for everyone to sit down.
8 It's time for my son to start school.

UNIT 5   PRACTICE

1 I can't wait to see the fireworks tonight.
2 I can't wait to travel to Canada this fall.
3 I can't wait to try the new Italian restaurant.
4 I can't wait to move into my new apartment next week.
5 He can't wait to get his driver's license.
6 He can't wait to go skiing this winter.
7 We can't wait to try out the new café that just opened.
8 We can't wait to welcome our guests to the housewarming party.

UNIT 1~5   REMINDER

1 I want you to be honest with me.
2 I want you to try this cake.
3 I want him to apologize to her.
4 I'm craving something sweet like ice cream.
5 I'm craving some alone time.
6 I'm craving anything spicy for dinner.
7 I'm okay at speaking in front of others.
8 I'm bad at saving money.
9 I'm good at cooking without a recipe.

10 It's time to send the email.
11 It's time to start the day.
12 It's time for the kids to have some snacks.
13 I can't wait to tell him the good news.
14 I can't wait to graduate from high school.
15 I can't wait to go on summer vacation to Jeju.

UNIT 6   PRACTICE

1 I have something to tell you.
2 I have something to ask you.
3 I have something to do this weekend.
4 I have something to read this week.
5 They have something interesting to show you.
6 She has something important to submit by this week.
7 He has something urgent to finish before noon.
8 We have something fun to do with the kids next weekend.

UNIT 7   PRACTICE

1 I have nothing to do with that gossip.
2 I have nothing to do with the mess in the kitchen.
3 I have nothing to do with mom's missing wallet.
4 You have nothing to do with this problem, so don't worry.
5 We have nothing to do with the fight. We just got there after it happened.
6 They have nothing to do with this issue! They didn't cause it.
7 I have nothing to do with why she's mad.
8 She has nothing to do with the decision! She wasn't even in the meeting.

UNIT 8   PRACTICE

1 It doesn't hurt to save a little money each month.
2 It doesn't hurt to get a second opinion from another doctor.
3 It doesn't hurt to double-check important documents before submitting.
4 It doesn't hurt to learn a new language if you want to expand your horizons.
5 It doesn't hurt to bring a jacket in case it gets cold.
6 It probably doesn't hurt to be honest about how you feel.
7 It doesn't hurt to leave early, just in case there's traffic.
8 It doesn't hurt to bring some cash, just in case your card doesn't work.

UNIT 9   PRACTICE

1 I used to read books every night.
2 I used to eat a lot of junk food.
3 I used to jump rope but not anymore.
4 I used to hate vegetables, but now I love them.
5 That restaurant used to be a bookstore.
6 The bus used to come every 10 minutes, but now it's less frequent.
7 She used to be very shy and introverted but now she is extroverted.
8 She used to be a know-it-all when we were growing up, but now she's more open to listening to others.

UNIT 10   PRACTICE

1 I'm used to speaking in front of people.
2 I'm used to commuting for over an hour every day.
3 I'm used to taking the subway.
4 I'm used to wearing a mask.
5 He's used to staying calm in emergencies because he's a firefighter.
6 She's used to walking long distances because she doesn't have a car.
7 We're used to working on weekends because we run a family business.
8 He's used to waking up early because he has morning classes every day.

UNIT 6~10 REMINDER

1. I have something to apologize for.
2. We have something important to announce.
3. She has something difficult to deal with.
4. I have nothing to do with the broken phone.
5. I have nothing to do with the spilled coffee.
6. I have nothing to do with the argument.
7. It doesn't hurt to read the instructions.
8. It doesn't hurt to practice every day.
9. It doesn't hurt to ask again.
10. I used to smoke.
11. I used to wake up late.
12. He used to play soccer.
13. I'm used to spicy food.
14. She's used to hot weather.
15. I'm used to eating alone.

UNIT 11 PRACTICE

1. I'm about to eat breakfast.
2. I'm about to do the dishes.
3. I'm about to leave. Do you need anything?
4. I'm about to propose to her. My heart feels like it's going to explode.
5. The bus is about to leave. Hurry up!
6. The show is about to begin. Please take your seats.
7. The plane is about to land. Please fasten your seatbelt.
8. We're about to head out for dinner. Do you want to come?

UNIT 12 PRACTICE

1. Do you happen to know what time the meeting starts?
2. Do you happen to speak Spanish? We need an interpreter.
3. Do you happen to have a charger I could borrow?
4. Did you happen to bring an umbrella? It looks like it might rain.
5. He happens to be free this evening.
6. I happen to have some extra tickets. Do you want one?
7. She happens to have a friend who works there.
8. He happened to find this on the street. Is it yours?

UNIT 13 PRACTICE

1. One of the cakes looks delicious.
2. One of the phones is ringing.
3. One of the members is from Korea.
4. One of the guests is allergic to peanuts.
5. One of the dogs in this neighborhood is always barking at night.
6. One of the books that I borrowed from the library is missing, and I can't seem to find it anywhere.
7. One of the plants on the balcony isn't doing well, so I need to water it more often.
8. One of the shirts I bought yesterday doesn't fit me, so I'm going to ask for a refund.

UNIT 14 PRACTICE

1. There is no such thing as an easy job.
2. There is no such thing as luck without effort.
3. There is no such thing as a magic pill for weight loss.
4. There is no such thing as overnight success.
5. There is no such thing as someone who never makes mistakes.
6. There is no such thing as a life without challenges. It's how we grow and learn.
7. There is no such thing as perfect timing. You just have to take action.
8. There is no such thing as a stupid question. Every question is a chance to learn something new.

UNIT 15 PRACTICE

1. I don't know if you know, but there's a new café near our school.
2. I don't know if you know, but it's Jacob's birthday today.

3　I don't know if you know, but Emily got engaged last weekend.
4　I don't know if you know, but Sarah is moving to New York next month.
5　I don't know if you know, but the coffee machine broke down again.
6　I'm not sure if you know, but you need to submit the form by Friday.
7　I don't know if you know, but a new art gallery recently opened downtown.
8　I'm not sure if you know, but you can get a student discount here.

UNIT 11~15　REMINDER

1　I'm about to go to bed.
2　I'm about to watch YouTube.
3　I'm about to go out.
4　Do you happen to know the answer?
5　I happen to be free this weekend.
6　I happened to see everything.
7　One of the cars has a flat tire.
8　One of the members is late.
9　One of my friends lives abroad.
10　There is no such thing as a talking cat.
11　There is no such thing as a perfect car.
12　There is no such thing as a homework-free school.
13　I don't know if you know, but you can cancel the reservation online.
14　I don't know if you know, but parking here is not free.
15　I'm not sure if you know, but you can book the meeting room in advance.

UNIT 16　PRACTICE

1　I just want to let you know (that) you did a great job today.
2　I just want to let you know (that) your package arrived.
3　I just want to let you know (that) I made a reservation for 7 PM.
4　I just want to let you know (that) I'll be a little late today.
5　I just want to let you know (that) your presentation was impressive.
6　I just want to let you know (that) we're out of coffee in the break room.
7　I just want to let you know (that) you have an ear for music.
8　By the way, I (just) want to let you know (that) the kids miss you a lot.

UNIT 17　PRACTICE

1　I'll assume (that) you're available at 3 PM.
2　I'll assume (that) you received my message.
3　I'll assume (that) you're busy and check back later.
4　I'll assume (that) we're going on a family trip this weekend.
5　I'll assume (that) you can handle spicy food.
6　I'll assume (that) you agree with my plan.
7　I'll assume (that) you'll let me know if anything changes.
8　I'll assume (that) you're free this weekend since you haven't said otherwise.

UNIT 18　PRACTICE

1　There is no need to hurry. We have plenty of time to get there.
2　There is no need to call a taxi. I can give you a ride home.
3　There is no need to get dolled up. It's just a casual get-together with friends.
4　There is no need to spend so much on a gift. It's the thought that counts.
5　I'm telling you, there is no need to spend that much money.
6　I'm telling you, there is no need to stress over it.
7　I'm telling you, there is no need to apologize. It wasn't your fault.
8　I'm telling you, there is no need to compare yourself to others.

UNIT 19　PRACTICE

1　No offense, but I see it a bit differently.
2　No offense, but I think you're overreacting.

3. No offense, but I honestly don't like this soup.
4. No offense, but I really don't like pineapple on pizza.
5. No offense, but your handwriting is really hard to read.
6. No offense, but I just think that outfit is a bit too much.
7. No offense, but your presentation was a bit boring.
8. I don't mean to offend you, but I find it hard to agree with you on this.

UNIT 20   PRACTICE

1. It's not like you to miss class.
2. It's not like you to be this quiet.
3. It's not like you to forget something important.
4. It's not like you to get angry over something small.
5. You haven't said much during the meeting. It's not like you to be quiet. Do you have any concerns?
6. We need to make a decision soon. It's not like you to be indecisive. What's holding you back?
7. It seems like you haven't been exercising lately. It's not like you to skip workouts. Is everything okay?
8. It's not like you to ignore messages for hours. Are you okay?

UNIT 16~20   REMINDER

1. I just want to let you know (that) we ran out of milk.
2. I just want to let you know (that) the meeting has been canceled.
3. I just want to let you know (that) dinner is ready.
4. I'll assume (that) everything went well.
5. I'll assume (that) you already know about it.
6. I'll assume (that) you no longer need help.
7. There's no need to explain.
8. There's no need to get upset.
9. There's no need to be nervous.
10. No offense, but you seem a bit distracted today.
11. No offense, but there is a better way to say that.
12. No offense, but this movie is kind of boring.
13. It's not like you to not reply.
14. It's not like you to act distant.
15. It's not like you to show up late.

UNIT 21   PRACTICE

1. I'm sorry for forgetting to buy milk. I'll go to the store right now.
2. I'm sorry for being late to the meeting. It won't happen again.
3. I'm sorry for missing your call. I was in a meeting and couldn't answer.
4. I'm sorry for borrowing your sweater without asking. I'll wash it and return it tomorrow.
5. We apologize for making you wait.
6. They're sorry for canceling at the last minute.
7. He's sorry for not calling you back.
8. She's sorry for missing your party last night. She wasn't feeling well and didn't want to ruin the mood.

UNIT 22   PRACTICE

1. I promise to practice the piano every day.
2. I promise to return the book I borrowed by next week.
3. I promise to try harder in my studies this semester.
4. I promise to take better care of my health from now on.
5. He promised to be more careful next time.
6. They promised to arrive on time next time.
7. She promised to study harder this semester.
8. The company promised to send a refund within 3 days.

UNIT 23   PRACTICE

1. I have no way of getting a refund without the receipt.
2. I have no way of contacting him since he changed his number.
3. I have no way of making it to that place without a car. I'm between a rock and a hard place.

4 I have no way of entering the house without my keys, unless I break a window.
5 He has no way of paying back the loan this month.
6 We have a way of knowing where he went.
7 We have no way of knowing who will win the election.
8 They have no way of predicting how customers will react to the new product.

UNIT 24 PRACTICE

1 That explains why it's so hard to find.
2 that explains why she's always running.
3 That explains why it's so crowded today.
4 That explains why he's been smiling ear to ear all day.
5 That explains why he's been avoiding solid food.
6 That explains why he's been so forgetful lately.

UNIT 25 PRACTICE

1 The first thing I'm going to do is check my emails.
2 The first thing I'm going to do is paint the living room.
3 The first thing I'm going to do after work is hit the gym for a workout.
4 The first thing I'm going to do after the rain dies down is go for a jog.
5 The first thing I'm going to do after winning the lottery is quit my job.
6 The first thing she's going to do is get a haircut because she hasn't had one in months.
7 The first thing they're going to do after the wedding is fly to Hawaii for their honeymoon.
8 The first thing we're going to do to save money is cut down on eating out.

UNIT 21~25 REMINDER

1 I'm sorry for dropping by without notice.
2 I'm sorry for hurting your feelings.
3 I'm sorry for raising my voice.

4 I promise to keep my word.
5 I promise to tell the truth.
6 I promise to do my best.
7 I have no way of contacting you.
8 I have no way of getting there without a car.
9 I have no way of fixing this.
10 That explains why the weather was so warm.
11 That explains why she is off today.
12 That explains why the Wi-Fi is slow.
13 The first thing I'm going to do is pay off my debt.
14 The first thing I'm going to do is call my mom.
15 The first thing I'm going to do is go to bed early.

UNIT 26 PRACTICE

1 I have no choice but to ask for help.
2 I have no choice but to find a new job.
3 I have no choice but to stay late at work.
4 I have no choice but to wake up early tomorrow.
5 We have no choice but to postpone our wedding due to the pandemic.
6 They have no choice but to sell their car to pay for the medical bills.
7 We have no choice but to cancel our vacation plans because we have a pile of work to do.
8 He has no choice but to postpone his trip because of the bad weather.

UNIT 27 PRACTICE

1 I never thought I would win the game.
2 I never thought I would enjoy jogging this much.
3 I never thought I would become a morning person.
4 I never thought I would be able to quit smoking.
5 She never thought she would pass the exam.
6 We never thought we would get tickets to the concert.
7 The company never thought it would grow this fast.
8 We never thought this small café would become so popular.

UNIT 28 PRACTICE

1. Don't tell me you lost your keys. That's the third time this month!
2. Don't tell me you forgot to feed the cat this morning.
3. Don't tell me you're quitting your job. You just got that promotion last month.
4. Don't tell me you ate the last piece of cake. I was saving that for later after my diet.
5. Don't tell me you didn't bring the tickets. We're already at the entrance!
6. Don't tell me it's going to rain all weekend. We planned this trip for months!
7. Don't tell me they raised the rent again. We just got used to the last increase!
8. Don't tell me we've been waiting in the wrong line for the past 30 minutes.

UNIT 29 PRACTICE

1. Feel free to bring your dog. She's always welcome here.
2. Feel free to use my car this weekend. Just fill up the tank when you're done.
3. Feel free to call me anytime, even if it's late. I'm a night owl anyway.
4. Feel free to help yourself to anything in the kitchen. Make yourself at home.
5. Feel free to use my Netflix account. Just don't mess up my watchlist.
6. If your kids get bored, feel free to use the toys in the playroom.
7. She said to feel free to email her directly with any concerns.
8. The teacher told the students to feel free to ask questions during the lecture.

UNIT 30 PRACTICE

1. I didn't mean to hurt your feelings with that joke.
2. I didn't mean to break your mug. It slipped from my hand.
3. I didn't mean to upset you. I just wanted to be honest.
4. I didn't mean to ignore your message. I was really busy at work.
5. We didn't mean to sit at your table.
6. Sarah didn't mean to cry. She just got emotional.
7. Tom didn't mean to break the window. It was an accident.
8. He didn't mean to take your pen. He thought it was his.

UNIT 26~30 REMINDER

1. I have no choice but to take the subway.
2. I have no choice but to wait in line.
3. I have no choice but to bite my tongue.
4. I never thought I would live abroad.
5. I never thought I would fall in love with someone like you.
6. I never thought I would be on TV.
7. Don't tell me you missed the bus.
8. Don't tell me you still love him.
9. Don't tell me you didn't sleep at all.
10. Feel free to call anytime.
11. Feel free to reach out.
12. Feel free to use this room.
13. I didn't mean to be rude.
14. I didn't mean to leave you out.
15. I didn't mean to cause trouble.

UNIT 31 PRACTICE

1. The price is likely to go up next month.
2. This road is likely to be busy during rush hour.
3. He's likely to be late again. He always is.
4. It's likely to rain tomorrow, so don't forget your umbrella.
5. Given her experience, it's likely to be a successful presentation.
6. That shop is likely to close early today because of the holiday, so let's go now.
7. She is likely to pass the exam because she studied hard. I hope her efforts lead to good results.
8. The team is likely to win the championship this year because they've been playing better than ever.

UNIT 32   PRACTICE

1. I'm really happy with my decision to move here.
2. I'm really happy with my new laptop. It's fast and lightweight.
3. I'm really happy with the haircut I got today. The stylist did a great job.
4. I'm really happy with the food at that new restaurant. We should go again.
5. My parents are really happy with living in the countryside.
6. Tom and Sarah are really happy with spending weekends together.
7. We're really happy with saving more money every month.
8. We're really happy with how the event turned out. Everything went smoothly.

UNIT 33   PRACTICE

1. I love it when a plan comes together smoothly.
2. I love it when someone remembers the little things I say.
3. I hate it when people talk over me.
4. I hate it when people don't get my sense of humor.
5. We hate it when the Internet connection is slow.
6. They hate it when their plans get canceled at the last minute.
7. The teacher hates it when students don't do their homework.
8. He loves it when his grandmother tells him stories from her childhood.

UNIT 34   PRACTICE

1. I'm supposed to fly to New York next Monday.
2. I'm supposed to have a dentist appointment at 2 PM tomorrow.
3. I'm supposed to be off today, but my boss just called me in.
4. I'm supposed to be on vacation right now, not working overtime.
5. You're supposed to tip waiters in restaurants here.
6. This coffee is supposed to be hot, but it's lukewarm.
7. Passengers are supposed to fasten their seatbelts during takeoff and landing.
8. You're supposed to take off your shoes before entering someone's home in Korea.

UNIT 35   PRACTICE

1. What I'm trying to say is (that) this isn't just your responsibility.
2. What I'm trying to say is (that) we can't afford to wait any longer.
3. What I'm trying to say is (that) communication is crucial in a relationship.
4. What I'm trying to say is (that) I didn't mean to hurt your feelings.
5. What they're trying to say is (that) the event might be postponed.
6. What the doctor is trying to say is (that) you should take it easy for a while.
7. What my parents are trying to say is (that) they're worried about my health.
8. What she's trying to say is (that) she needs more time to finish the project.

UNIT 31~35   REMINDER

1. It's likely to be delayed.
2. It's likely to happen again.
3. It's likely to be crowded.
4. I'm really happy with managing my time better these days.
5. I'm really happy with the final outcome of the project.
6. I'm really happy with sticking to my budget.
7. I love it when it rains and I don't have to go out.
8. I love it when I find money in my old coat.
9. I hate it when I step in water with socks on.
10. I'm supposed to finish this by tomorrow.
11. I was supposed to meet my friend tonight.
12. You're supposed to know the answer.
13. What I'm trying to say is (that) you matter to me.
14. What I'm trying to say is (that) I need some time.
15. What I'm trying to say is (that) this means a lot to me.

UNIT 36 PRACTICE

1. There's no better time to start exercising than now.
2. There's no better time to learn a new language than now, regardless of your age.
3. There's no better time to buy a house than now, especially with current interest rates being so low.
4. There's no better time to start a side hustle than now. It could become your main source of income.
5. There's no better time to call your parents than now, even if it's just to say hi and ask how they're doing.
6. There's no better time to talk to her than now, since she's in a good mood.
7. There's no better time to learn a new skill than now, when you have a bit more free time.
8. There's no better time to fix it than now, before it turns into a bigger problem.

UNIT 37 PRACTICE

1. Let's say (that) you want to start a new hobby. What hobby would you choose?
2. Let's say (that) you find a great deal on a new laptop. Will you buy it immediately?
3. Let's say (that) we move to a new place. Which city would you want to move to?
4. Let's say (that) we go on a family trip next year. Where should we go?
5. Let's say (that) you won the lottery. What would you buy first?
6. Let's say (that) you could meet any celebrity. Who would you choose?
7. Let's say (that) your car broke down in the middle of nowhere. What would you do?
8. Let's say (that) someone offered you a million dollars to leave your job. Would you do it?

UNIT 38 PRACTICE

1. That's a great way to save money.
2. That's a great way to stay healthy.
3. That's a great way to improve your listening skills.
4. That's a great way to stay focused and cut out distractions.
5. That's a great way to clear your mind and organize your thoughts.
6. It's a great way to stay connected even when we're busy.

UNIT 39 PRACTICE

1. It's no wonder (that) you're hungry. You didn't have any breakfast.
2. It's no wonder (that) the market was bustling. Thanksgiving is coming.
3. You are such a nice person. It's no wonder (that) everyone likes you.
4. It's no wonder (that) you're tired. You barely slept last night.
5. It's no wonder (that) they broke up. They were always arguing.
6. It's no wonder (that) the bed was uncomfortable. The mattress is over 20 years old.
7. It's no wonder (that) this place is popular. The food is amazing.
8. It is no wonder (that) she excels in her field because she puts in non-stop dedication.

UNIT 40 PRACTICE

1. Nothing can beat mom's home-cooked meals.
2. Nothing can beat the feeling of helping someone.
3. Nothing can beat a hot shower after a long day.
4. Nothing can beat a heartfelt conversation with an old friend.
5. Nothing can beat a walk on the beach at sunset.
6. Nothing can beat the feeling you get when you finally finish something you've been working hard on.
7. Nothing can beat spending time with family.
8. Nothing can beat having a deep conversation with someone who truly understands me.

UNIT 36~40 REMINDER

1. There's no better time to speak up than now.
2. There's no better time to invest in yourself than now.

3   There's no better time to start saving money than now.
4   Let's say (that) the Internet goes out.
5   Let's say (that) nobody comes.
6   Let's say (that) you pass the exam.
7   That's a great way to start the day.
8   That's a great way to make friends.
9   That's a great way to connect with people.
10 It's no wonder (that) she's popular.
11 It's no wonder (that) he's in a bad mood.
12 It's no wonder (that) he's exhausted.
13 Nothing can beat mom's cooking.
14 Nothing can beat listening to your favorite song.
15 Nothing can beat accomplishing a goal.

UNIT 41 PRACTICE

1   The stress of planning a wedding is no joke.
2   The cost of raising a child these days is no joke.
3   The difficulty of mastering a new language is no joke.
4   Winter in Canada is no joke. Temperatures can drop below minus 30 degrees Celsius.
5   Getting into that university is no joke.
6   Waking up early every day for work is no joke. It really drains your energy.
7   Taking care of a baby 24/7 is no joke. It's exhausting but worth it.
8   Learning English idioms is no joke. They don't always make sense literally.

UNIT 42 PRACTICE

1   I can't bring myself to tell my little sister that Santa isn't real.
2   I can't bring myself to eat anything with cilantro in it.
3   I can't bring myself to tell my boss that I'm quitting.
4   I can't bring myself to tell Mom that I broke her favorite vase.
5   We can't bring ourselves to sell the house where we raised our kids.
6   He can't bring himself to discipline the puppy. It's just too cute.
7   We can't bring ourselves to eat that. What is it even made of?
8   She can't bring herself to throw away the photos of her ex.

UNIT 43 PRACTICE

1   I feel better after the shower.
2   I feel better after the nap.
3   I feel better after crying a little.
4   I feel better after getting things off my chest.
5   The baby feels better after a diaper change.
6   Our dog feels better after going for a walk.
7   People usually feel better after expressing their feelings.
8   He always feels better after exercising, even if he's tired.

UNIT 44 PRACTICE

1   Don't get me wrong, I love kids, but I'm not ready to have one yet.
2   Don't get me wrong, I'm happy for you, but I'm also a bit jealous.
3   Don't get me wrong, online classes are convenient, but I miss seeing people in person.
4   Don't get me wrong, I enjoy spending time with you, but I need some space, too.
5   Don't get me wrong, he's a nice person, but I don't think he's right for this job.
6   Don't get me wrong, the food was delicious, but I thought it was a bit pricey for what it was.
7   Don't get me wrong, she's a good manager, but her communication style can be a bit unclear at times.
8   Don't get me wrong, your new haircut looks great, but it's just so different from your usual style.

UNIT 45 PRACTICE

1   If you happen to come across Tom today, tell him I called.
2   If you happen to come across my lost notebook, please bring it to me.

3   If you happen to come across a quiet place to study, I'd love to know.
4   If you happen to come across this snack in a store, can you buy it for me?
5   If you happen to come across my phone charger, please bring it back when you visit.
6   If you happen to come across any photos of us, send them to me. I want to change my profile picture.
7   If you happen to come across Jane at the event tonight, please tell her I'll be a bit late.
8   If you happen to come across this book in a bookstore, it's totally worth reading.

UNIT 41~45   REMINDER

1   Raising kids is no joke.
2   Working night shifts is no joke.
3   Living in a big city is no joke.
4   I can't bring myself to watch that movie again.
5   I can't bring myself to ask for help.
6   I can't bring myself to say goodbye.
7   I feel better after getting some fresh air.
8   I feel better after finishing my work.
9   I feel better after talking to a friend.
10 Don't get me wrong, I like spending time with them.
11 Don't get me wrong, this job means a lot to me.
12 Don't get me wrong, I respect your opinion.
13 If you happen to come across an old photo of us, send it to me.
14 If you happen to come across my missing keys, let me know.
15 If you happen to come across a nice little café, tell me about it.

UNIT 46   PRACTICE

1   I have a hunch that my lost phone is somewhere in the house.
2   I have a hunch that we're going to get good news soon.
3   I have a hunch that we'll win the game tomorrow.
4   I have a hunch that the stock market will improve next month.
5   We have a hunch that the meeting will be canceled.
6   He has a hunch that she likes him.
7   He has a hunch that he left his phone at the restaurant.
8   She has a hunch that someone has been using her laptop.

UNIT 47   PRACTICE

1   The bottom line is (that) you need to make a decision.
2   The bottom line is (that) we need to get this done by this Friday.
3   The bottom line is (that) laughter really is the best medicine for stress.
4   The bottom line is (that) it's important to communicate openly with each other.
5   The bottom line is (that) you have to take responsibility for your actions.
6   The bottom line is (that) if you don't practice regularly, you won't improve.
7   The bottom line is (that) we have to meet the deadline, even if it means working overtime.
8   The bottom line is (that) we don't have enough time, so we need to focus on the most important tasks.

UNIT 48   PRACTICE

1   All I'm saying is (that) you need to stop comparing yourself to others.
2   All I'm saying is (that) it's okay to say no sometimes.
3   All I'm saying is (that) communication is key in any relationship.
4   All I'm saying is (that) your efforts will definitely pay off in the end.
5   All I'm saying is (that) you deserve to be treated with respect no matter what.
6   All the doctor is saying is (that) you need more rest.
7   All he's saying is (that) you shouldn't blame yourself.
8   All she's asking is (that) you call her once in a while. She misses hearing from you.

UNIT 49 PRACTICE

1. I've always wanted to try skydiving.
2. I've always wanted to bake a cake from scratch.
3. I've always wanted to start my own business.
4. I've always wanted to visit all 50 states in the US.
5. We've always wanted to live by the beach and wake up to the sound of waves.
6. They've always wanted to take a road trip across the United States.
7. She's always wanted to visit Paris and see the Eiffel Tower in person.
8. My sister has always wanted to adopt a dog, but our parents wouldn't allow it.

UNIT 50 PRACTICE

1. All you have to do is sign this document, and we can finalize the agreement.
2. All you have to do is help me with the dishes, and I'll take care of dessert.
3. All you have to do is call him and explain the situation. I'm sure he'll understand.
4. All you have to do is text me when you get home, so I know you got home safely.
5. All you have to do is press this button and the coffee machine does the rest.
6. All the students have to do is submit the assignment by Friday.
7. All he has to do is smile like that, and everyone in the room starts laughing.
8. All my little brother has to do is say "Please" and my mom gives him whatever he wants.

UNIT 46~50 REMINDER

1. I have a hunch that she's hiding something.
2. I have a hunch that they're planning a surprise.
3. I have a hunch that something's going on.
4. The bottom line is (that) we need to cut costs.
5. The bottom line is (that) time is running out.
6. The bottom line is (that) she deserves better.
7. All I'm saying is (that) I need coffee.
8. All I'm saying is (that) this show is amazing.
9. All I'm saying is (that) I didn't eat your fries.

10. I've always wanted to try making my own pizza.
11. I've always wanted to travel alone.
12. I've always wanted to talk to that person.
13. All you have to do is believe in yourself.
14. All you have to do is show up on time.
15. All you have to do is follow the recipe.

UNIT 51 PRACTICE

1. We might as well leave early since there's no traffic.
2. We might as well eat out tonight. There's nothing in the fridge.
3. Since I'm already here, I might as well do some shopping.
4. I can't change what happened, so I might as well move on.
5. I really wanted to go out, but it's raining, so I might as well stay home and watch a movie.
6. There's nothing else to watch on TV, so I might as well watch this documentary.
7. I forgot my umbrella, and I'm already soaked, so I might as well walk home instead of waiting.
8. I already paid for the gym membership, so I might as well try to go at least a few times a week.

UNIT 52 PRACTICE

1. It was your first presentation and you did great! Don't be too hard on yourself.
2. Don't be too hard on yourself. Everyone makes mistakes sometimes.
3. Don't be too hard on the team. They've been working overtime all week.
4. She's been going through a lot lately, so don't be too hard on her.
5. Don't be too hard on yourself for not finishing the project on time. It happens.
6. Don't be too hard on yourself for taking a day off. Everyone needs a break sometimes.
7. He's just a kid. Don't be too hard on him for making one mistake.
8. Don't be too hard on your partner for forgetting small things. Nobody's perfect.

UNIT 53 PRACTICE

1. It's okay to take time for yourself every now and then.
2. It's okay to take a break when you're feeling overwhelmed.
3. It's okay to ask questions if you don't understand something.
4. It's okay to say no if you're not comfortable with something.
5. It's okay to admit you don't know something. Being honest is more valuable than pretending.
6. It's okay to binge-watch an entire season in one night. We've all been there.
7. It's okay to feel tired, confused, or even lost. You don't have to have it all together all the time.
8. It's okay to cry if you're feeling overwhelmed. It doesn't make you weak, it just means you're human.

UNIT 54 PRACTICE

1. Honesty is key in building trust.
2. Listening is key to effective communication.
3. Patience is key when learning a new skill.
4. Consistency is key if you want to get in shape.
5. Coffee is key to surviving the Monday blues.
6. Remembering people's names is key to giving a good first impression.
7. Getting enough sleep is key to staying focused throughout the day.
8. Confidence is key when giving a presentation. It helps your audience believe in what you're saying.

UNIT 55 PRACTICE

1. A: What are the odds of our flight being delayed?
2. A: What are the odds of you finishing your homework before the movie starts?
3. A: What are the odds of me finding the leftover pizza in the fridge?
   B: The odds are slim. You know how fast your brother eats.
4. A: What are the odds of passing this test without studying?
   B: The odds are close to zero but miracles happen.
5. A: What are the odds of Sarah saying yes if I ask her out?
   B: Honestly? The odds are pretty good. She's been smiling at you a lot lately.

UNIT 51~55 REMINDER

1. We might as well go get some ice cream.
2. We might as well take a nap.
3. We might as well watch another episode.
4. Don't be too hard on your first try.
5. Don't be too hard on your dance moves.
6. Don't be too hard on that barista.
7. It's okay not to have all the answers.
8. It's okay to forget what day it is. That's what calendars are for.
9. It's okay to ask for help.
10. Practice is key.
11. Being yourself is key.
12. Timing is key.
13. A: What are the odds of running into your ex?
    B: The odds are not impossible.
14. A: What are the odds of finding a parking spot?
    B: The odds are better than usual today.
15. A: What are the odds of it raining today?
    B: The odds are about fifty-fifty.

UNIT 56 PRACTICE

1. Don't even think about my snacks. I've been saving them.
2. Don't even think about dessert. Eat your dinner first.
3. Don't even think about a party this weekend. We already have a trip planned.
4. Don't even think about my laptop. I need it for work today.
5. Don't even think about turning off the alarm. We've already overslept twice this week.

6   Don't even think about quitting now. You've already come so far, and you'll regret it later.
7   Don't even think about blaming me for what happened. You were part of the decision, too.
8   Don't even think about lying to me again. I trusted you once, and I won't make that mistake twice.

UNIT 57   PRACTICE

1   I tend to forget names, but I always remember faces.
2   I tend to drink coffee in the morning to help me wake up.
3   I tend to check my phone as soon as I wake up.
4   I tend to get distracted easily when I study at home.
5   Children tend to imitate the behavior of adults around them, especially their parents.
6   People tend to believe rumors more easily when they hear them from multiple sources.
7   Older people tend to prefer face-to-face communication over texting or messaging apps.
8   My dog tends to bark loudly whenever someone walks past our house.

UNIT 58   PRACTICE

1   When I saw her smile, I thought to myself, "She's really happy today."
2   Finishing the marathon, I thought to myself, "I can't believe I did it!"
3   Looking at the test results, I thought to myself, "All that studying paid off."
4   As the rain poured down, I thought to myself, "I should have brought an umbrella."
5   After watching the movie, I thought to myself, "It was actually pretty good."
6   I thought to myself that I should start exercising more regularly.
7   I thought to myself that I needed to apologize before things got worse.
8   I thought to myself that I should really start saving more money.

UNIT 59   PRACTICE

1   It's no use worrying about the weather. We can't control it anyway.
2   It's no use trying to hide the truth. It will come out eventually.
3   It's no use trying to fix this old computer. We should just buy a new one.
4   It's no use waiting for the perfect moment. Sometimes you just need to start.
5   It's no use trying to persuade him. He's made up his mind.
6   It's no use acting cool when you're obviously super excited about your birthday party.
7   It's no use waiting for the bus. It's already 30 minutes late, so we should probably call a taxi.
8   It's no use pretending you don't love karaoke. You grabbed the mic before the first song even started!

UNIT 60   PRACTICE

1   He made every effort to get along with his new coworkers.
2   I made every effort to arrive on time, but the traffic was terrible.
3   She made every effort to improve her English before the trip.
4   We're making every effort to get this project done on time.
5   I'm making every effort to reduce plastic use at home.
6   I'm making every effort to be a loving father and support my children in everything they do.
7   I'm going to make every effort to pass that exam. = I'll make every effort to pass that exam.
8   I'll make every effort to be there on time, but I can't promise.

UNIT 56~60   REMINDER

1   Don't even think about leaving early.
2   Don't even think about wearing my hoodie.
3   Don't even think about eating my chocolates.
4   I tend to overthink things.
5   I tend to laugh at my own jokes.

6   I tend to check my phone too often.
7   I thought to myself, "I should've stayed home."
8   I thought to myself, "He's definitely lost."
9   I thought to myself, "Maybe I'm overreacting."
10 It's no use arguing with him.
11 It's no use trying to change her mind.
12 It's no use stressing over it.
13 I made every effort to stay calm.
14 I made every effort to meet the deadline.
15 I made every effort to understand his point of view.

UNIT 61   PRACTICE

1   I'm here for the job interview at 10 AM.
2   I'm here for the meeting that's happening at 2 PM.
3   I'm here to pick up my order that I got online. Can you check it for me?
4   I'm here to get my test results from last week.
5   You're here to learn and grow, so don't be afraid to make mistakes.
6   He's here to fix the Wi-Fi, so we should let him know where the router is.
7   The doctor is here to answer your questions, so feel free to ask anything.
8   She's here for her grandmother's birthday, and the whole family is getting together.

UNIT 62   PRACTICE

1   We looked outside to see if it was still raining.
2   We reached out to him to see if he was home.
3   He refreshed the page to see if the results had been posted.
4   I checked the schedule to see if there were any changes.
5   I called the restaurant to see if they had any tables available.
6   She checked her bank account to see if the payment had gone through.
7   Before buying the car, I'm going to test-drive it to see if I really like it.
8   I always check the air quality and fine dust levels to see if I need to wear a mask.

UNIT 63   PRACTICE

1   If you get a chance, just give me a call or send a message.
2   When you get a chance, can you help me with my laundry?
3   If you get a chance, let's catch up over coffee sometime.
4   If you get a chance, can you pick up some snacks on your way home?
5   When you get a chance, could you water the plants on the balcony? They're looking a little dry.
6   When you get a chance, send me the photos from last night. I forgot to take any!
7   When you get a chance, take a break and go for a short walk. You've been working for hours.
8   If you get a chance, could you help me choose a gift for Sarah? I have no idea what to get her.

UNIT 64   PRACTICE

1   I should've worn more comfortable shoes. My feet are killing me.
2   We should've made a reservation. There's a long wait.
3   I should've taken a picture of that dessert. It looked amazing.
4   I should've grabbed a coffee before the meeting. I can barely stay awake.
5   You should've told me you were at the café. I was there, too!
6   I should've brought my reusable bag. Now I have to pay for a plastic bag again.
7   I shouldn't have posted that online. Now everyone knows.
8   I shouldn't have eaten so much last night. I feel so bloated.

UNIT 65   PRACTICE

1   I could have made dinner, but you already ordered food.
2   I could have taken the earlier bus, but I wanted a few more minutes of sleep.
3   I could have bought the stock when it was at 10 dollars, but I didn't.

4 I could have gone out, but I ended up staying in and watching Netflix.
5 He could have taken the train, but he chose to drive instead.
6 They could have made it to the airport if they had left earlier.
7 We could have saved a lot of money if we had booked our tickets earlier.
8 She could have gone to the concert with us, but she decided to stay home.

UNIT 61~65   REMINDER

1 I'm here to help you out.
2 I'm here to support my friend.
3 I'm here to talk about the project.
4 I checked my phone to see if she replied.
5 I headed to the bakery to see if they had the bread I like.
6 I asked around to see if anyone had seen my wallet.
7 When you get a chance, check the group chat.
8 When you get a chance, clean the microwave.
9 If you get a chance, watch the video I sent.
10 I should have texted you back.
11 I should have listened to you.
12 I should have charged my phone.
13 You could have called me earlier.
14 I could have finished it yesterday.
15 I could have taken a better photo.

UNIT 66   PRACTICE

1 I would've worn a jacket if I had known it was going to be this cold.
2 I would've helped you move if I hadn't had plans that day.
3 I would've come earlier if I'd known the traffic was this bad.
4 If I had known it was your birthday, I would've bought you a cake.
5 If you had told me you were feeling sick, I would've made you some soup.
6 We would've made it on time if we hadn't missed the bus.
7 He wouldn't have lost his phone if he hadn't been in such a rush.
8 We would've missed the show if we hadn't booked the tickets in advance.

UNIT 67   PRACTICE

1 The minute I arrive in New York, I'll let you know.
2 The minute I tasted it, I knew something was off.
3 The minute we stepped outside, it started to rain.
4 The minute she walked into the room, everyone turned to look at her.
5 The minute she opened the box, her face lit up with excitement.
6 The minute the teacher walked in, the class went completely silent.
7 The baby started crying the minute his mother left the room.
8 He knew he'd made a mistake the minute the words left his mouth.

UNIT 68   PRACTICE

1 By the time I got to the station, the train had just left.
2 By the time we got there, the store was closed.
3 By the time he called, she had already gone to bed.
4 By the time you read this message, I will have already left.
5 By the time I finish this book, the sequel will probably be out.
6 By the time the movie started, we had already finished our popcorn.
7 By the time we get to the restaurant, it might be too crowded.
8 By the time I realized my mistake, I was already full of regret for not acting sooner.

UNIT 69   PRACTICE

1 It's a shame (that) we forgot to take a group photo.
2 It's a shame (that) the concert tickets sold out so fast.

3   It's a shame (that) my favorite café closed right after I discovered it.
4   It's a shame (that) the concert was canceled due to bad weather.
5   It's a shame (that) the ice cream melted before I even took a bite.
6   It's such a shame (that) the bakery ran out of croissants. I was really craving one.
7   It's such a shame (that) my vacation's already over. I need another one!
8   It's such a shame (that) he didn't get the promotion. He's been working so hard these past few months.

UNIT 70   PRACTICE

1   It's a relief (that) he found his wallet.
2   It's a relief (that) we didn't miss the train.
3   It's a relief (that) the test wasn't as hard as I expected.
4   It's a relief (that) the car repair didn't cost too much.
5   It's a relief (that) the storm passed without causing any damage.
6   It's a relief (that) I brought my charger with me. My phone battery was down to 3%.
7   It's (such) a relief to finally finish that report.
8   It's (such) a relief to hear that the surgery went well.

UNIT 66~70   REMINDER

1   I would have saved you a seat.
2   I would have got you your favorite drink.
3   I would have reminded you about the meeting.
4   The minute I smelled the smoke, I left the building.
5   The minute he mentioned food, I got hungry.
6   The minute the show started, my phone rang.
7   By the time she texted me, I was already asleep.
8   By the time they called us, we were on the way.
9   By the time I woke up, my alarm had stopped.
10 It's a shame (that) the weather didn't hold up.
11 It's a shame (that) we didn't try that new ramen place.
12 It's a shame (that) the concert got canceled.
13 It's a relief (that) I didn't lose my wallet.
14 It's a relief (that) the deadline was extended.
15 It's a relief (that) the bus came quickly.

UNIT 71   PRACTICE

1   The more you smile, the happier you feel.
2   The more you drink water, the better your skin looks.
3   The less I talk when I'm angry, the less I regret later.
4   The more you exercise, the more confident you become in your body.
5   The more honest you are, the more people will trust you.
6   The faster you finish, the more free time you'll have.
7   The less sugar I eat, the less tired I feel.
8   The less time I spend on social media, the less stressed I am.

UNIT 72   PRACTICE

1   I'm totally into watching cooking videos on YouTube lately.
2   I'm into walking these days. I try to get 10,000 steps a day.
3   I'm into playing soccer. I joined a local team recently, and we practice twice a week.
4   I'm into yoga. It helps me stay flexible and reduces my stress levels.
5   I'm not really into sports, but I love watching the World Cup.
6   I wasn't into jogging before, but now it's part of my routine.
7   She's really into fashion and always wears trendy clothes.
8   She's not that into sports, but instead, she is really passionate about coding.

UNIT 73   PRACTICE

1   I don't feel like a game right now.
2   I don't feel like a long conversation right now.
3   I don't feel like cooking tonight. Let's just order in.
4   I don't feel like going out tonight. I just want to relax at home.

5 We don't feel like going out in this weather. Let's just chill at home.
6 I don't feel like studying right now. I've been at it for hours and my brain needs a break.
7 She doesn't feel like dressing up today. That's why she wore sweats.
8 He doesn't feel like working today. He's totally burned out.

UNIT 74   PRACTICE

1 You must be really busy these days.
2 You must be excited for your trip tomorrow.
3 You must be John's sister. You are the spitting image of him.
4 You must be thrilled to see your family after such a long time.
5 You must have been absolutely thrilled to meet your favorite singer.
6 He must have been really disappointed when he didn't get the promotion.
7 You must have been incredibly proud when your daughter graduated from college.
8 She must have been young when she started playing the violin, probably still in elementary school.

UNIT 75   PRACTICE

1 You're cut out for learning foreign languages. Your pronunciation is really good.
2 You're really cut out for cooking! Are you sure this is your first-time cooking?
3 I'm not sure if I'm cut out for a career in finance. I don't think I'm good with numbers.
4 She's really cut out for teaching. She's patient, creative, and knows how to connect with students.
5 I don't think I'm cut out for a desk job. I get restless sitting in one place for too long.
6 You're totally cut out for public speaking. You're confident, clear, and engaging.
7 He considered the military but realized he wasn't cut out for the discipline.
8 I'm beginning to realize I'm not cut out for city life.

UNIT 71~75   REMINDER

1 The more you talk to him, the more he opens up.
2 The more you clean, the more it gets messy again.
3 The more you smile, the more people like you.
4 I'm into coffee art.
5 I'm into learning new languages.
6 I'm into editing short videos.
7 I don't feel like doing the dishes.
8 I don't feel like small talk.
9 I don't feel like going out tonight.
10 You must be exhausted. / You must have been exhausted.
11 You must be starving. / You must have been starving.
12 You must be thrilled. / You must have been thrilled.
13 I'm cut out for life in the city.
14 I'm not cut out for handling pressure.
15 I'm cut out for this kind of work.

UNIT 76   PRACTICE

1 We always lose track of time when we're on the phone.
2 I lose track of time when I listen to music and go for a walk.
3 It's easy to lose track of time when you're having fun.
4 I completely lost track of time while catching up with an old friend over coffee.
5 He said he lost track of time because he was so focused on finishing the report.
6 I sometimes lose track of time just scrolling through social media.
7 She lost track of time watching funny videos online during lunch break.
8 He lost track of time playing the piano and didn't even notice it was getting dark.

UNIT 77   PRACTICE

1 It's not that I can't wake up early, it's just (that) I don't want to.

2   It's not that the movie was boring, it's just (that) it wasn't really my thing.
3   It's not that I don't like your cooking, it's just (that) I wasn't hungry.
4   It's not that the dress is ugly, it's just (that) it doesn't suit my style.
5   It's not that I'm angry with you, it's just (that) I'm frustrated with the situation.
6   It's not that I don't want to exercise, it's just (that) I can't find the time.
7   It's not that the book was bad, it's just (that) it didn't meet my expectations.
8   It's not that I don't want salad, it's just (that) pizza sounds way better right now.

UNIT 78   PRACTICE

1   He worked to the point that he forgot to eat.
2   I ate to the point that my stomach actually started to hurt.
3   I exercised to the point that I was completely out of breath.
4   They trained to the point that they broke records.
5   They drank to the point that they couldn't even walk straight.
6   They shopped to the point that their wallets were completely empty.
7   He practiced the piano to the point that blisters started forming on his fingers.
8   She laughed so hard to the point that her stomach hurt and she started tearing up.

UNIT 79   PRACTICE

1   What's the secret to your flawless skin?
2   What's the secret to your delicious chocolate cake? It's better than the ones at bakeries.
3   What's the secret to your happy marriage? You two seem so in sync even after all these years.
4   What's the secret to your confidence when speaking in public? I get so nervous even thinking about it.
5   What's the secret to looking so calm even when you're super busy?
6   What's the secret to giving such impressive presentations every time?
7   What's the secret to waking up early and staying energetic all day long?
8   What's the secret to talking so comfortably with people you've just met?

UNIT 80   PRACTICE

1   While you're at it, could[can] you make me a cup of coffee, too?
2   While you're at it, could[can] you check my mail, too?
3   While you're at it, could[can] you grab my jacket from the closet?
4   While you're at it, could[can] you pick up some milk from the store?
5   While you're at it, could[can] you grab some bananas, too? The kids love them these days.
6   While you're at it, could[can] you make one more side dish? I need it for tomorrow's lunchbox.
7   While you're at it, could[can] you grab my yoga mat, too? I'm planning to join in.
8   While you're at it, could[can] you check the printer connection, too? I thought it was broken.

UNIT 76~80   REMINDER

1   I lost track of time watching the sunset by the beach.
2   I lost track of time helping my little brother with his homework.
3   I lost track of time reading a good book.
4   It's not that I'm full, it's just (that) I don't feel like eating.
5   It's not that I hate running, it's just (that) I prefer walking.
6   It's not that I'm bored, it's just (that) I don't know what to do.
7   I was so tired to the point that I fell asleep standing.
8   He worked out to the point that he couldn't move the next day.
9   They danced to the point that the floor was shaking.
10 What's the secret to making perfect coffee?

11 What's the secret to being funny?
12 What's the secret to keeping a plant alive?
13 While you're at it, could[can] you take out the trash?
14 While you're at it, could[can] you check the mailbox?
15 While you're at it, could[can] you grab me a drink, too?

UNIT 81   PRACTICE

1 Don't be too married to that method. There might be a better way.
2 Don't be too married to your first impression. It can change over time.
3 Don't be too married to your perfect plan. Sometimes spontaneity is better.
4 Don't be too married to the perfect selfie. You've taken like 50 already.
5 Don't be too married to the numbers. Quality matters more than quantity.
6 Don't be too married to the outcome. The journey is just as important.
7 Don't be too married to doing everything on your own. It's okay to ask for help.
8 Don't be too married to eating at the same restaurant. Let's try somewhere new.

UNIT 82   PRACTICE

1 It bothers me (that) he never replies to my messages.
2 It bothers me (that) you never ask for my opinion when making big decisions.
3 It bothers me (that) he keeps making excuses instead of owning up.
4 It bothers me (that) my room is always messy when I get home.
5 It bothers me (that) no one makes eye contact when I'm talking.
6 It bothers me (that) people pretend not to hear me when I ask for help.
7 It bothers me when you leave dirty dishes in the sink.
8 It bothers me when people watch videos without headphones on the bus.

UNIT 83   PRACTICE

1 His name is on the tip of my tongue, but I just can't place it.
2 I know that brand name. It's on the tip of my tongue right now.
3 I know the lyrics to this song. They're right on the tip of my tongue.
4 I think I know who you're talking about. It's right on the tip of my tongue.
5 The capital of that country is on the tip of my tongue. I remember it starts with a B.
6 The name of that actor is on the tip of my tongue, but I just can't get it out.
7 What was that expression in English again? It's on the tip of my tongue, but I can't think of it.
8 The name of my elementary school teacher is on the tip of my tongue. I just can't quite remember it.

UNIT 84   PRACTICE

1 I'm going to go to the store to get some groceries soon.
2 I'm going to go to the library this afternoon to study.
3 I'm going to go to the post office after lunch to send a package.
4 Her husband is going to go to the repair shop to fix the car.
5 They're going to go to IKEA to look at some new furniture.
6 I'm going to go to the hospital next week for a check-up.
7 My friend is going to go to the hair salon for a new style.
8 My cousin is going to go to Seoul this weekend for a job interview.

UNIT 85   PRACTICE

1 I'm free to meet tomorrow morning.
2 I'm free to help you if you need.
3 You're free to use my laptop if you need it.
4 Students are free to ask questions at any time.
5 Employees are free to leave during lunch breaks.

6 The meeting room is free to use after 3 PM.
7 They're free for interviews tomorrow morning.
8 We're free for dinner after 7, so just let us know what works best for you.

UNIT 81~85   REMINDER

1 Don't be too married to the rules.
2 Don't be too married to one way of thinking.
3 Don't be too married to your original plan.
4 It bothers me (that) plans suddenly change.
5 It bothers me when people chew loudly.
6 It bothers me when someone doesn't text back.
7 The word for it in English is on the tip of my tongue.
8 His phone number is on the tip of my tongue.
9 The title of that movie is on the tip of my tongue.
10 I'm going to go to the store for some snacks.
11 I'm going to go to the park to get some fresh air.
12 I'm going to go to the library for a quiet place to read.
13 I'm free to chat for a bit.
14 You're free to use my charger.
15 I'm free to help with your homework.

UNIT 86   PRACTICE

1 I can't help taking pictures when I see a cute dog.
2 I can't help drooling when I smell good food.
3 I can't help singing along when my favorite song comes on.
4 I can't help checking the time when it's almost time to leave work.
5 She can't help crying during emotional movies.
6 My brother can't help playing games all night once he starts.
7 He can't help but shake before big presentations.
   = He can't help shaking before big presentations.
8 He can't help but repeat himself when he talks about something serious.
   = He can't help repeating himself when he talks about something serious.

UNIT 87   PRACTICE

1 I couldn't care less about politics.
2 I couldn't care less about the delayed project.
3 I couldn't care less if it rains tomorrow.
4 I couldn't care less whether they win or lose.
5 She couldn't care less (about) what's trending.
6 He couldn't care less (about) what people think of him.
7 I couldn't care less (about) what others think, as long as you're happy.
8 They couldn't care less (about) how fancy the hotel is when they travel.

UNIT 88   PRACTICE

1 I have a hard time talking to strangers.
2 I have a hard time expressing my feelings.
3 I have a hard time getting up in the morning.
4 I have a hard time saying no when my friends ask for favors.
5 He has a hard time admitting his mistakes.
6 My parents have a hard time using smartphones.
7 She has a hard time concentrating during long meetings.
8 We have a hard time with the language barrier when we travel.

UNIT 89   PRACTICE

1 It just occurred to me (that) we have a meeting tomorrow.
2 It just occurred to me (that) I haven't paid the car insurance yet.
3 It just occurred to me (that) I need to buy groceries for the week.
4 It just occurred to me (that) I made plans with a friend for dinner tonight.
5 It just occurred to me (that) today is my mom's birthday. I need to remember to buy flowers after work.
6 It just occurred to me on the subway (that) I forgot to take the laundry out yesterday.
7 It just occurred to me (that) my friend's wedding is this weekend, and I haven't bought a gift yet.

8   It just occurred to me to check the food in the fridge to make sure nothing is expired.

UNIT 90   PRACTICE

1   A flashlight is handy to have during a power outage.
2   A reusable water bottle is handy to carry around all day.
3   It's handy to carry a power bank when traveling.
4   Wet wipes are handy to bring when going out with kids.
5   A measuring cup is handy to use when cooking for accurate measurements.
6   A power strip is handy to have around the house for using multiple devices.
7   A folding table is handy for setting things up during camping or picnics.
    = A folding table is handy to set things up during camping or picnics.
8   Keeping a notepad nearby is handy for jotting down ideas.
    = Keeping a notepad nearby is handy to jot down ideas.

UNIT 86~90   REMINDER

1   I can't help smiling when I see puppies.
2   I can't help laughing at his jokes.
3   I can't help but think about what she said.
4   I couldn't care less about celebrity gossip.
5   I couldn't care less about what they think.
6   I couldn't care less about who's dating who.
7   I have a hard time saying goodbye to my kids.
8   I have a hard time keeping a straight face around my best friend.
9   I have a hard time explaining tech stuff to my parents.
10 It just occurred to me (that) I left my coffee in the microwave.
11 It just occurred to me (that) we forgot to buy toilet paper.
12 It just occurred to me (that) I've seen that actor somewhere before.
13 This app is handy to split the bill.
14 A water bottle is handy to carry in summer.
15 The map app is handy to find nearby cafés.

UNIT 91   PRACTICE

1   I'm dying to buy a new car.
2   The kids are dying to go to the amusement park.
3   My parents are dying to see their grandkids.
4   I'm dying to try the new restaurant that just opened.
5   He's dying to buy a house since interest rates have dropped so much. He said it's a buyer's market now.
6   I'm dying for a cold beer, especially on a hot day like today. It would be so refreshing!
7   She's dying for a good night's sleep. She's been so busy lately and hasn't been able to rest properly.
8   I'm dying for a delicious pizza, especially pepperoni. It's my favorite.

UNIT 92   PRACTICE

1   There's no way (that) they'll turn down our offer.
2   There's no way (that) she can eat that much food by herself.
3   There's no way (that) he's going hiking in this weather.
4   There's no way (that) we're getting into the concert without tickets.
5   There's no way (that) we'll get there on time. We're already late.
6   There's no way (that) we can walk all the way there. It's way too far.
7   There's no way (that) they're selling the house at that price. It's way too cheap.
8   There's no way (that) he got a perfect score on the test. He was up all night playing games.

UNIT 93   PRACTICE

1   I forgot to lock the door before leaving.
2   I forgot to feed the dog this morning.
3   I forgot to water the plants while they were away.
4   I forgot to close the windows before the storm.
5   He forgot to bring his wallet, so he had to borrow some cash from me.

6   My brother forgot to write down his email password, and now he can't access his important messages.
7   She forgot to turn off the stove before leaving, and now she's worried it might still be on.
8   I forgot to check if you're allergic to mangoes, and I accidentally added some to the fruit salad.

UNIT 94   PRACTICE

1   I can't imagine living without electricity these days. It's something we often take for granted.
2   Her kids can't imagine life without cartoons in the morning.
3   I can't imagine not having my morning coffee to start the day.
4   I can't imagine how amazing it must be to see the Las Vegas Sphere in person.
5   I can't imagine how incredible it must feel to hold your newborn baby.
6   She can't imagine an evening after work without watching Netflix. It's her way of winding down.
7   Our cat can't imagine a morning without her treats. She literally follows us around until she gets them.
8   They can't imagine living without air conditioning in summer, especially with how hot it gets these days.

UNIT 95   PRACTICE

1   I'm still debating between the beach or the mountains for summer vacation.
2   I'm debating the pros and cons of getting a pet.
3   I'm debating if I should take the job offer.
4   I'm debating whether to switch jobs for better opportunities.
5   I'm debating whether to buy a new car or keep the old one.
6   My parents are debating whether to move to a new city or stay where they are.
7   She's debating whether to study abroad or attend a local university.
8   My friends had been debating whether to get a job right after graduation or go to graduate school.

UNIT 91~95   REMINDER

1   I'm dying to take a proper day off.
2   I'm dying for a warm slice of banana bread.
3   I'm dying to visit a cat café.
4   There's no way (that) you cleaned your whole room already.
5   There's no way (that) I agreed to that plan.
6   There's no way (that) she finished all that pizza alone.
7   I forgot to reply to your text.
8   I forgot to charge my phone last night.
9   I forgot to make a reservation.
10 I can't imagine living without Wi-Fi.
11 I can't imagine that he actually said that.
12 I can't imagine drinking hot coffee in this weather.
13 I'm debating between getting ramen or pizza.
14 I'm debating whether to speak up or stay quiet.
15 I'm debating whether to go out or stay in.

UNIT 96   PRACTICE

1   I was going to take the bus but ended up walking.
2   I went out for a workout but ended up sitting in a café.
3   I meant to take a quick nap but ended up sleeping for two hours.
4   I went to buy one piece of clothing but ended up buying five.
5   My brother ended up playing video games all night.
6   They ended up going to Jeju instead of Europe.
7   We ended up walking for two hours instead of a short stroll.
8   The teacher ended up giving a full lecture instead of a brief explanation.

UNIT 97   PRACTICE

1   It's beyond me how he thought that was a joke.
2   It's beyond me why people line up to buy a $20 cup of coffee.

3. It's beyond me why he turned down such a great opportunity.
4. It's beyond me why people still go to that store. The service is always terrible.
5. The night view of this city is beyond beautiful.
6. Her kindness is beyond indescribable.
7. The service at this restaurant is beyond satisfying.
8. The twist in that movie is beyond shocking.

UNIT 98 PRACTICE

1. I'll let you know if the soup lacks seasoning.
2. I'll let you know if there's anything else you need to prepare.
3. I'll let you know when I decide on a date for my wedding.
4. I'll let you know when I get home, so you don't have to worry.
5. I'll let you know as soon as I get the results, so we can figure out the next steps together.
6. I'll let you know what time we should meet after talking to Jane.
7. She'll let you know if the party is canceled.
8. Customer service will let you know the delivery status.

UNIT 99 PRACTICE

1. It's hard to tell what the weather will be like tomorrow.
2. It's hard to tell if he's being serious or just joking.
3. It's hard to tell how old she is. She looks so young for her age.
4. It's hard to tell which team is going to win. It's a neck-and-neck game, and they're both playing really well.
5. It's hard to tell if he's sincere because he's such a smooth talker.
6. It's hard to tell what kind of person someone is just from a first impression.
7. It's hard to tell if he's actually happy or just pretending, because he always smiles.
8. It's hard to tell whether it's going to rain today because the weather keeps changing.

UNIT 100 PRACTICE

1. I thought he was a kind person, but he turned out to be rude.
2. I thought he was a foreigner, but he turned out to be Korean.
3. I thought this problem would be easy, but it turned out to be very difficult.
4. I thought the dress I ordered online would be elegant and chic, but it turned out to look frumpy.
5. We thought the restaurant would be expensive, but it turned out to be quite affordable.
6. She thought the new shoes would be comfortable, but they turned out to hurt her feet all day.
7. My friend thought he was single, but it turned out (that) he was married.
8. The manager thought the client would be difficult, but it turned out (that) she was very kind.

UNIT 96~100 REMINDER

1. I ended up binge-watching the whole season.
2. I ended up spending all my money on snacks.
3. I ended up falling asleep on the couch.
4. It's beyond me why I keep losing my keys.
5. It's beyond me how he always looks so calm.
6. It's beyond me how that cat got so famous.
7. I'll let you know if I can make it tonight.
8. I'll let you know when I'm free this weekend.
9. I'll let you know the meeting time.
10. It's hard to tell if this milk is still good.
11. It's hard to tell what time he'll actually show up.
12. It's hard to tell how much time we have left.
13. I thought we were early, but we turned out to be actually late.
14. I thought the movie would be boring, but it turned out to be super fun.
15. I thought he was a stranger, but it turned out (that) we'd actually met before.